THE IMPACT OF EDUCATIONAL TELEVISION

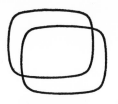

THE
IMPACT
OF
EDUCATIONAL
TELEVISION

Selected Studies from the Research
Sponsored by the National Educational
Television and Radio Center

Edited for the Center
by Wilbur Schramm, Director
Institute for Communication Research
Stanford University

GREENWOOD PRESS, PUBLISHERS
WESTPORT, CONNECTICUT

Library of Congress Cataloging in Publication Data

National Educational Television and Radio Center.
The impact of educational television.

Reprint of the ed. published by the University of
Illinois Press, Urbana.
Includes bibliographies.
1. Television in education. I. Schramm, Wilbur
Lang, 1907–   II. Title.
[LB1044.7.N359 1977]   371.33'58   77–606
ISBN 0–8371–9495–4

Originally published in 1960 by the University of Illinois Press,
Urbana

Reprinted with the permission of The University of Illinois Press

Reprinted in 1977 by Greenwood Press, Inc.

Library of Congress catalog card number 77-606

ISBN 0-8371-9495-4

Printed in the United States of America

FOREWORD

Educational television came on the American scene in 1953, and with it rode the hopes of millions that in the wedding of this wondrous medium with the intellectual and cultural resources of the nation a veritable renaissance would take place. Seven years and nearly fifty educational television stations later no one can claim a "renaissance," but perhaps more importantly and by every applicable measure educational television has shown a remarkable capacity to reach, to interest, to teach, to enlighten.

A latecomer on the scene, after television program patterns and viewing habits were well established, educational television promised substantive programing at optimum hours. How well it has succeeded in these early years is the subject of a considerable body of research. The subject has been attractive to researchers throughout the country who sensed the turbulent joining of the disciplined attitudes and goals of learning with the powerful undisciplined interests of television.

Two or three generations of Americans had been brought up under the influence of the electronic mass media—radio, motion pictures, television—and had been taught on the whole to regard them as devices of entertainment and *divertissement*. Substantive presentations were both novel and noteworthy. Ideas were a drag both on "box office" and on ratings. "Cultural democracy" held sway and the popular level of expectancy from these media was not high.

While expectancy traditionally was low, once the dream and the image of "what might be" caught the imagination of community after community, both large and small, the demand for education's own channels could not be denied. It is with these channels and the television stations that operate on them that this report is concerned. What programing, when, where, for whom, and with what effect?

The chapters in this book are based on studies supported by research grants-in-aid made by the National Educational Television and Radio Center. The Center—the national program service agency for educational television—made fifty research grants-in-aid to educational research bodies during the four-year period of 1956–59, for scientific inquiries into attitudes, motivations, audience composition, audience size, viewing habits, presentational patterns, attitude change, and learning—all relating to educational television.

In any report drawn from this program of research the work of Ryland W. Crary must be acknowledged. As a member of the Center's staff, Dr. Crary was administratively responsible for research during the time when most of the studies were in progress on which the several chapters are based. Much of the data recorded in these pages reflect his influence in stimulating and criticizing the research designs.

Appreciation must be expressed also to Wilbur Schramm, the Chairman of the Center's Research Committee, for the wisdom and energy he has brought to this editorial assignment and for his past and continuing service to research in educational television and his perception and skill in drawing fruitful applications from it.

ROBERT B. HUDSON

Vice President National Educational
Television and Radio Center

New York
January 1, 1960

CONTENTS

EDUCATIONAL TELEVISION IN THE COMMUNITY

Educational stations are now putting more than 1,800 hours of programs on the air each week. Whereas a typical commercial station spends three-quarters of its air time on entertainment or advertising, the educational station reverses that proportion and spends three-fourths of its time on information and teaching. Roughly 40 per cent of educational station program hours are used for broadcasting courses into the schools, or credit courses to students at home. The "curriculum" is divided fairly evenly among the four great disciplinary areas of knowledge—social science and public affairs, humanities, natural science, and fine arts. The present content of educational television is described in detail in this report, which was prepared for NETRC in the Institute for Communication Research at Stanford University.

THE CONTENT OF
EDUCATIONAL TELEVISION

*Compiled for the National Eductional Television
and Radio Center*

This report is concerned with the amount and kind of educational television the educational stations are putting on the air. The statements we shall be able to make about this subject are based on the program logs of 30 of the 45 educational television stations that were active in the autumn of 1959. These stations furnished their logs for a composite week in October and November of that year. The first day of this random week was Friday, October 2; the last was Sunday, November 8. In addition to their logs, the stations provided program descriptions, sources, and classifications. The stations which supplied this information are:

Thirteen community-owned stations—WMVS (Milwaukee), WTTW (Chicago), WHYY (Philadelphia), WGBH (Boston), KVIE (Sacramento), KQED (San Francisco), WQED and WQEX (Pittsburgh), WNED (Buffalo), WKNO (Memphis), KTCA (Minneapolis), WCET (Cincinnati), WTVS (Detroit).

Nine university-owned stations—KUHT (Houston), KNME (New Mexico at Albuquerque), KUED (Utah at Salt Lake City), KUON (Nebraska at Lincoln), WMSB (Michigan State at East Lansing), WUNC (North Carolina at Chapel Hill), WUFT (Florida at

Gainesville), WOSU (Ohio State at Columbus), KUAT (Arizona at Tucson).

Three school-system stations—KRMA (Denver), WTHS (Miami), KDPS (Des Moines).

Two network groups—WAIQ, WBIQ, and WCIQ (Alabama), KOED and KETA (Oklahoma).

Several other stations submitted logs, but the material either came too late or was incomplete.

The material was double-coded for reliability. Results are presented in the following pages.

HOW LONG ARE EDUCATIONAL STATIONS ON THE AIR?

The average educational station is on the air five days a week, and about 8 hours and 41 minutes a day. For individual stations, however, this varies from two broadcasting days a week (WNED) to seven days (WUNC and WMSB), and from WTHS's average of over 15 hours a day to KUAT's average of less than 4. This is the distribution by broadcast days:

Two days a week   1 station (WNED)
Five days a week   21 stations
Six days a week   6 stations [1]
Seven days a week 2 stations (WUNC and WMSB)

Table 1 shows the time patterns by type of station.

TABLE 1

Type of Station	Total Hours per Week for All Stations	Average Hours per Station per Day	Range in Daily Average
13 community stations	571:55	8:31	13:03– 4:49
9 university stations	341:40	6:50	10:51– 3:52
5 network stations	322:40	12:55	13:30–12:01
3 school-system stations	127:46	8:31	15:16– 4:53
Total	1364:01	8:41	

Projecting this total figure to the total number of educational stations, with allowance for the nature of stations not represented

[1] WTTW, WGBH, WTVS, WQED, and WQEX broadcast Monday through Friday, and Sunday; KUAT broadcasts Monday through Saturday.

in this sample, we can be reasonably confident that at least 1,800 hours of educational television per week were on the American airways in the autumn of 1959.

Six of these stations are in the UHF band. These are WCET, WHYY, WTVS, WQEX, WNED, and WOSU. Contrary to what we might expect, the daily average air time for these stations was 9:31, nearly an hour above the general average.

THE SOURCE OF PROGRAMS

About one-fourth of all educational television hours are filled by NET. This varies, however, by kind of station, as Table 2 shows.

TABLE 2

Percentage of Program Time from	13 Community Stations	9 University Stations	3 School Stations	5 Network Stations	Mean: 30 Educational Stations
NET	32.8%	32.4%	30.4%	10.3%	26.1%
Local and other non-NET sources	67.2	67.6	69.6	89.7	73.9

It will be seen that there is very little difference in the amount of use made of NET by community, university, and school-system stations, but that the state networks seem to use a far lower proportion of NET programs. To see why this should be, we must look at the intended audiences of these different stations.

FOR WHAT AUDIENCES ARE THESE STATIONS PROGRAMING?

Insofar as possible, all programs on the educational stations were coded as to whether they were intended for (1) in-school or credit-course use, (2) chiefly children's viewing (out of school), or (3) chiefly adult viewing (but not for course credit). The first category caused no trouble, and the second one caused very little. The third one was troublesome because of the familiar fact that children view many adult programs. We tried to distinguish between categories 2 and 3, therefore, in terms of whether the programs were intended to attract any considerable adult audiences. If they were intended to attract *both* adults and children, we called them adult programs; if they were to attract mostly children, we called them children's programs.

Table 3 shows how the different kinds of stations divided their program hours among these categories.

TABLE 3

Percentage of Program Time for	13 Community Stations	9 University Stations	3 School Stations	5 Network Stations	Mean: 30 Educational Stations
Adults	51.6%	53.1%	44.8%	30.6%	46.2%
Children	16.2	16.3	16.8	4.3	12.9
In-school or credit courses	32.2	30.6	38.4	66.9	40.9

There is thus very little difference between the targeting policies of community and university stations, but school stations put somewhat more emphasis on in-school programing, and the network stations in our sample devoted more than *twice* as much of their program time to in-school courses and formal extension classes as did either university or community stations. In each case, the additional time for broadcasting formal classes is gained at the cost of adult education and children's programs, and this is why NET fills a smaller proportion of the network stations' day.

WHAT FORMS DO THE PROGRAMS TAKE?

Nothing so clearly distinguishes the educational from the commercial television station as does the form of the programs they put on the air. The commercial station takes its forms and skills from the dramatic and vaudeville theater; the educational station derives from the classroom, the lecture hall, and the forum. In 1953, 47 per cent of all New York television time for a week was drama, and another 12 per cent was variety shows. The educational stations, on the other hand, used 53 per cent of their program time for lecture and accompanying demonstration, and another 13 per cent for discussion. Table 4 will show how the different types of educational stations divided their time by program form.

The community stations distinguish themselves from the others

TABLE 4

Percentage of Program Time for	13 Community Stations	9 University Stations	3 School Stations	5 Network Stations	Mean: 30 Educational Stations
Discussion	15.1%	14.8%	14.9%	5.5%	12.8%
Talks	8.5	13.7	5.0	3.8	8.5
Documentary	7.2	5.9	13.7	7.5	7.6
Drama	17.2	3.8	5.4	.8	9.1
Lecture-demonstration	38.9	53.0	52.7	80.8	53.0
Music	13.1	8.8	8.3	1.6	9.0

by being a little more like the commercial stations in format—more drama, less lecturing. The network stations distinguish themselves from the others by being least like the commercial stations in format—indeed, by devoting a whopping 80 per cent of their time to lectures. The other two are on middle ground, and, in this respect, are very much alike.

WHAT KIND OF PROGRAM CONTENT?

Table 5 shows the differences in program content between different types of educational stations.

TABLE 5

Percentage of Program Time for	13 Community Stations	9 University Stations	3 School Stations	5 Network Stations	Mean: 30 Educational Stations
Entertainment	15.0%	12.4%	6.4%	2.0%	10.4%
Religion	.5	.8	.4	0	.5
Agriculture	0	1.6	.7	1.6	.9
News	3.3	3.3	1.2	3.6	3.2
Children's	13.1	8.0	6.7	1.0	8.3
Sports	.9	1.6	.4	0	.7
Teaching and other information	67.2	72.3	84.2	91.8	76.0

Here, again, it is the network stations principally, and the school stations to a lesser extent, that stand apart from the others by virtue of their single-minded devotion to teaching over the air.

CONTENT BY DISCIPLINES

Now let us divide the program hours of an educational station, like the program of a university or a school, in terms of the chief areas of knowledge. Over 80 per cent of the program hours can be so coded, provided that one introduces another area, "utility," to handle programs on gardening, cooking, home repairs, and the like. In Table 6, social science is defined to include public affairs; humanities to include language, literature, history, and philosophy; natural science to include engineering; and fine arts to include graphic and plastic arts, music, and design.

TABLE 6

Percentage of Program Time for	13 Community Stations	9 University Stations	5 School Stations	3 Network Stations	Mean: 30 Educational Stations
Social science	22.8%	20.6%	16.7%	21.0%	21.3%
Humanities	24.7	23.3	30.5	14.8	22.5
Natural science	17.8	28.3	19.6	39.9	25.9
Fine arts	24.0	21.3	19.2	8.2	19.1
Utility	10.7	6.5	14.0	16.1	11.2

This, then, is the "curriculum" of the educational stations—roughly equal emphasis on the four great areas of knowledge, although natural science is a bit higher than the others, and fine arts a little lower. Community stations are high in their emphasis on fine arts, reflecting these stations' use of the cultural resources around them. School stations are high in the humanities, reflecting chiefly their use to teach language. University and network stations (which, in this case, are chiefly operated by universities) are high in natural science, probably reflecting both resources and a feeling of urgency.

EXAMPLES OF PROGRAMING

Community Stations

Let us now put some flesh and bones on the dry numbers of this analysis by looking at some examples of how different kinds of stations actually use their program time.

This schedule (for Tuesday, October 20) illustrates the highly varied programs presented by community station WQED in Pittsburgh:

8:25 a.m.	High School Physics
9:05	Seventh-Grade Reading (for in-school use)
9:30	America (Encyclopaedia Britannica film, for school use, on American history, geography, and leaders)
9:45	Elementary Science (for fifth- and sixth-grade classes)
10:00	Physics (repeat)
10:32	Alice in Poetryland (literature and speech for school classes)
10:47	Cheese (film giving recipes)
10:51	Frankfurters (recipes)
11:05	Fifth-Grade Science (in-school use)
11:30	Adventures with Sculpture (art appreciation for schools)
12:00	World of Music (classical music program)
1:05 p.m.	Seventh-Grade Reading (in-school)
1:35	Talking Town (speech improvement for schools)
1:55	Pennsylvania History (for ninth-grade civics classes)
2:15	Drivers' Training (from NET)
2:50	History with Herb Hake (from NET)
3:20	Cheese again
3:24	Frankfurters again
3:30	Facts of Medicine (from NET)
3:58	Household Workers (social security rules regarding domestic servants, etc.)
4:00	Kid Bits (local)
	Number of Things (from NET—both children's programs)
4:30	Crossroads USA (oil industry film on free enterprise)
4:54	Otto Asks a Riddle (safety rules for children)
5:00	Children's Corner (puppets, songs, stories)
5:30	World of Music (classical music)
6:30	Key to City (interviews with prominent visitors)
6:45	Journey—Traveling Man (documentary film on tankers)
7:00	Shorthand (for beginners and brush-ups)
7:30	Operation Hour Glass (how diesel engines came to be)
8:00	Pitt Huddle (highlights of Pitt football games and other athletic events)
8:45	Inside Football (film on the single-wing formation)
9:00	The Atom (popular science from NET)
9:30	Legally Speaking (county bar association answers viewers' questions on law)
10:00	Art and Artists (from NET)
10:30	Briefing Session (from NET)
11:00	Sign off with national anthem

This is certainly more varied and more widely popular program fare than is offered by the average educational stations, and doubtless explains the high audience ratings which have been reported for WQED.

Station WGBH-TV, Boston, another community station, does more than most stations to build repetition into its program. Thus, on a morning when a film of President Eisenhower's press conference is available, the station is likely to program like this:

8:30 a.m. President's Press Conference
9:15   Exploring Nature (natural science for fifth grade)
10:00   President's Press Conference
10:45   Exploring Nature
11:30   President's Press Conference
7:00 p.m. Exploring Nature

During the rest of its day, WGBH makes good use of the cultural resources close at hand. Thus, on Tuesday evening, October 20, WGBH was offering, among other programs:

6:45   Elliott Norton Reviews (local dramatic critic discusses current plays with members of cast)
8:00   Bengtz on Drawing (course on advanced figure drawing from the Boston Museum of Fine Arts)
9:00   Concert by the M.I.T. Band

On Sunday, WGBH presents a program largely drawn from the commercial networks and from NET. An example (November 8, 1959):

11:55 a.m. Harry Reasoner and the News (CBS)
12:00   Johns Hopkins File (ABC)
12:30 p.m. Face the Nation (CBS)
1:00   College News Conference (ABC)
1:30   Heritage (interview with Ormandy, from NET)
2:00   Art and Artists (NET)
2:30   Max Lerner's Seminar (NET)
3:00   Open Hearing (discussion of current news, from ABC)
3:30   Metropolis (weekly program by Boston College on problems of Boston area)
4:00   Beethoven's *Fidelio* (NBC opera)
6:00   Meet the Press (from NBC)
6:29   Local roundup of news
6:36   Sign off

This kind of programing stands in relation to the rest of U.S. television much as the "Third Programme" stands in relation to the rest of British broadcasting.

University Stations

The program schedules of university stations are sometimes less likely than those of community stations to reflect the community around them. On the other hand, they are likely to demonstrate unusual resources in teaching and demonstration. The Tuesday, October 20, program of WUNC-TV, operated by the University of North Carolina, illustrates this. Notice, for example, the program called "Explorations into Creativity," which treats creative engineering and design, using a great many examples and practitioners of the art. Just before the design program, an hour is devoted to a talk and a lesson, in sign language, for the deaf. It would be a rare commercial station that would dare give an hour of prime evening time to a program exclusively for deaf persons!

Here is the October 20 offering of WUNC:

6:00 a.m.	Continental Classroom: Physics (from NBC)
6:30	Continental Classroom: Chemistry (from NBC)
6:59:30	Sign off
8:49:50	Sign on. Music until
9:00	United States History (classroom course for schools)
9:30	Physical Science (also for in-school use)
10:00	World History (in-school)
10:30	Eighth-Grade Mathematics
11:00	Face of Earth (geography program from NET)
11:30	Seminar on American Civilization (from NET)
12:00	Tales of Poindexter (children's program from NET)
12:15 p.m.	Midday News
12:30	Today on the Farm (information for the farmer presented by North Carolina State Agriculture Extension Service)
12:59:30	Sign off
5:50	Sign on. Music until
6:00	Number of Things (children's program from NET)
6:15	Uncle Wonder's Workshop (science for preschool children, from NET)
6:30	News report
6:45	Engineering Drawing (college credit course)
7:30	You the Deaf (Greensboro minister talks to the deaf through sign language, about current events and other items of interest to the deaf)
8:00	Language of the Deaf (teaches sign language for the deaf)
8:30	Explorations into Creativity (discussions of creative engineering and design)

9:00	Big Picture (documentary on mission of the Army)
9:30	Heritage (interview with a famous American, from NET)
10:00	Final edition news
10:10	Sign off, and national anthem

School-System Stations

Here for comparison is a day's schedule of KRMA-TV, which is operated by the Denver Public Schools. Notice how, like good teachers, they repeat the televised language lessons early in the evening so that the parents can take part in the process of reviewing the lesson and can practice with the child the words, phrases, and sentences that have been learned.

This may seem a little short and bare compared to some of the schedules we have just been looking at. However, there is more than an indication that the school stations, the community stations, and the university stations in cities may be growing closer together. For example, a recent program schedule of KRMA reads very much like one of the community stations, and the day is crowned with an hour concert by the Denver Symphony.

Here is KRMA for October 20:

1:00 p.m.	Parlons Français (in-school French teaching for grades four, five, and six)
1:16	Je Parle Français (in-school French teaching for level-two students in grades four, five, and six)
1:28	Smokey the Bear (brief conservation film)
1:32	Mathematics 4 (for students in fourth grade, and for home-bound students)
1:58	Do You Know? ("filler" film, demonstrating how to replace the washer on a faucet)
2:02	Geography 4 (for fourth-grade and homebound students)
2:30	Foods, Facts, and Fun (program in homemaking series on food choice, preparation, and storage)
2:59:30	Sign off for afternoon
6:00	Continental Classroom (NBC film—college credit course in physics accepted at local colleges and universities)
6:30	Friendly Giant (children's program, from NET)
6:45	Tales of Poindexter (children's program, NET)
7:00	Parlons Français (repeat of afternoon in-school film, so that students may review and families may help)
7:15	Je Parle Français (repeat of afternoon in-school program, for same purpose as above)
7:30	Heritage (interview with famous American, NET)
8:00	Young Audiences (program for children, NET)
8:58:30	Sign off

State Network Stations

Now let us look at a typical day's program on a state network.

The three stations of the Alabama state network are on the air continuously from just before 8:30 a.m. to 10:00 p.m. On Tuesday, October 20, 1959, the day began and ended with the Lord's Prayer. Except for brief identifications and announcements, the stations offered a steady succession of programs. Where marked with an asterisk (*), programs are for home rather than classroom use; they are of local origin except where the origin is indicated in parentheses (e.g., NBC, NETRC). This is the broadcast day:

8:30 a.m. High School Russian
9:00   Biology
9:30   Primary Science
9:45   Primary Physical Education
10:00   Number of Things (NET)
10:15   Uncle Wonder (NET)
10:30   Alabama History
11:00   Today's Home
11:30   High School Spanish
12:00   Driver Education (NET)
12:30 p.m. Farm Facts (agricultural news) *
12:45   Let's Learn More
1:00   Junior High Art
1:30   General Music (enrichment for high school courses)
2:00   Improve Your Reading
2:30   Advanced Chemistry (NBC)
3:00   Advanced Physics (NBC)
3:30   Adventure (film) *
4:00   Face of the Earth (NET film) *
4:30   Girl Scouts Program *
5:00   Design Workshop (NET) *
5:30   Know Your News *
6:00   Greek and Roman Mythology (college credit course)
6:30   Wonder of Words (audience program on vocabulary) *
7:00   Historical Alabama *
7:30   Children Growing (NET—child-rearing problems) *
8:00   Counseling and Guidance *
8:30   Stones and Bones *
9:00   Take 60 (program assigned this evening to the Birmingham studios) *

Looking back over this list, you will see that more than half of the station's day (7:15 out of 13:30) is given to classroom or credit broadcasts, slightly less than half (6:15 out of 13:30) to community broadcasts. The whole school day is used for classroom broadcasts; most of the rest of the day for adult education. This is a packed, businesslike schedule, concentrating on servicing public education and on serious problem-solving, self-improvement programs for adults. It is interesting that almost 75 per cent of the program time should be filled with local productions. Only 3½ hours come from outside—2½ from NETRC, 1 from films of NBC science programs.

DIFFERENCES BETWEEN EDUCATIONAL
AND COMMERCIAL PROGRAMING

One of the ways to describe a noncommercial television station is to contrast its typical structure of programs with that of a commercial station.

A typical educational station is on the air five days a week, about 8 hours and 45 minutes a day. A typical commercial station is on the air seven days, 14 hours or so a day. The commercial station signs on early in the morning and continues until late at night; the educational station usually broadcasts for schools in the morning and afternoon, in many cases signs off the air during the noon hours and after school, then broadcasts programs for home viewing beginning in late afternoon.

About half the commercial station's hours are typically given over to network productions; a little over one-fourth of the program hours of the educational station are filled by programs from NET, the service of the National Educational Television and Radio Center. About 20 per cent of the commercial station's hours are programed live by the station; the educational station, or its academic and community affiliates, programs locally about 60 per cent of its hours.

Less than 25 per cent of the programs of a commercial station— news, weather, information, orientation, etc.—can be classified as "information." The rest is entertainment. In contrast, no more than 15 per cent of the educational station's program hours can be classified as entertainment, and three-quarters of all its time will be spent on either formal or informal education.

Roughly half the program hours of a commercial station will be given to some kind of drama, including domestic serials and old movies. Another quarter will be made up of variety, sports, quiz

shows, personalities, and so forth. In contrast, three-quarters of the educational station's program hours will be given to lectures, talks, and discussion. Roughly two-fifths of its hours will be used for programing material directly into schools or to home students.

The educational station is thus typically a serious, "talky" station, inclined rather to challenge than to invite and soothe its viewers, concerned with ideas, learning, courses, rather than fantasy, entertainment, and escape.

What we have said about the content of commercial television stations is based on the NARTB survey of 1955, and the Smythe and Remmers studies of New York television between 1951 and 1954.[2] What we have said about the programs of educational stations is based on the data presented in this report.

Comparing Smythe's 1953 figures, on a week of New York commercial television, with the current ones for the educational stations, we have some interesting contrasts (Table 7).

TABLE 7

Percentage of Program Time for	New York Commercial Television [a]	U.S. Educational Television
News	7%	3%
Sports	6	1
Children's (drama, variety, etc.)	7	8
Music	4	9
Other entertainment (drama, variety, quiz, stunts, contests, etc.)	62	1
Information (classes, information and orientation, weather, etc.)	14	78

[a] Source of this column—D. W. Smythe, *New York Television*, Urbana, Ill.: NAEB, 1954.

These differing emphases on entertainment and information point up the differences between the two kinds of television in a most impressive way.

[2] Smythe, *New York Television*; H. H. Remmers *et al.*, *Four Years of New York Television*, Urbana, Ill.: NAEB, 1955. See also L. Bogart, *The Age of Television*, New York: Frederick Ungar, 1956.

DIFFERENCES IN PROGRAMING AMONG EDUCATIONAL STATIONS

Let us now try to sum up some of the differences between types of educational stations, so far as we can infer them from our sample.

The state network stations in our sample are, on the average, longest on the air. A much smaller share of their programs comes from NET than is the case with the other stations. They concentrate to a greater degree than any of the other stations on in-school and credit-course broadcasting, consequently less on informal adult education or out-of-school programing for children. They use the lecture-demonstration form to a greater extent than other stations. Curriculum-wise, they tended, at least at the time of our composite week, to concentrate on natural science.

The school-system stations in our sample generally show the same direction of variation as do the network stations, but are less extreme about it. That is to say, they do more in-school broadcasting, on the average, than community and university stations, but not so much as the network stations. They take a little less from NET than the community and university stations, but still a great deal more than the network stations take. Contrary to the science concentration of the network stations, these school stations concentrated on language and literature.

University stations, as might be expected, program more talks than the other types of stations, and they concentrate on natural science. They program more entertainment than either the school or network stations, but less than the community stations. The same is true of their children's programs.

The community stations program the most drama, the most fine arts, the most entertainment. They seem to stand at the opposite end of a continuum from the network stations, a continuum that may be illustrated by abstracting two lines from Table 5.

Percentage of Program Time for	Community Stations	University Stations	School Stations	Network Stations
Entertainment	15.0%	12.4%	6.4%	2.0%
Teaching and information	67.2	72.3	84.2	91.8

In a sense, the community stations are the *most* like, and the network stations *least* like, commercial stations. The community stations feel the greatest need to appeal to widely different groups of people; in increasing measure, as one moves across the continuum, the other types of stations feel the need to service school systems. The community stations have rich cultural resources to draw upon; the other stations can draw on rich academic resources. And therefore we have a continuum stretching from the kind of station that tends to program in the *most* varied manner to the kind that tends to program in the *least* varied manner.

But let us not, as we sort out these differences among educational stations, lose sight of the greater difference, which is that between educational and commercial stations. The two educational stations that are most unlike each other in programs are still more alike than either is like a commercial station.

*The audience of the 45 educational television stations is small compared
to that of the more-than-500 commercial stations. Compared to the usual
audiences of education, however, the audience of educational television is
enormous. This paper reviews the results of 3 national and 16 station surveys, commissioned by NETRC, and presents the best estimates now
possible to make concerning ETV audiences. It also reviews the evidence
on the kinds of persons who view ETV. The educational stations have
many kinds of viewers, but they also have a typical kind. The typical ETV
viewer has, on the average, more education than the nonviewer. He tends
to operate on norms different from those of the nonviewer. He is more likely
to take part in civic organizations and public-affairs activity. He is more
likely to exhibit "high-brow" cultural tastes. And he is also more likely to
be an "influential." This paper is by the Director of the Institute for Communication Research at Stanford University.*

THE AUDIENCES OF EDUCATIONAL TELEVISION

by Wilbur Schramm

The audiences we are talking about are those of the 45 noncommercial educational television stations which were operating in
the United States in the autumn of 1959.

These are not the total audience of educational television. At
least three other audiences are extensive and important. These are
(1) the many schools that use television lectures or demonstrations,
by broadcast or closed circuit, as a part of their teaching; (2) clubs
and study groups that view films made from educational television
programs; and (3) the audiences that view educational programs
on commercial television stations. These groups clearly belong to
the audience of educational television, but for them, unfortunately,
we have as yet no accurate count and only the roughest of estimates. Therefore, of the *total* audience of educational television
in the United States, we can say only that it is larger than the audiences described in the following pages.

Concerning the audiences of the educational television stations,
however, we are now in position to speak with some confidence.[1]

----

[1] Let us point out that educational television stations are not necessarily
identical in program. The preceding study is the first broad examination of ETV

Ten of the 45 stations have been the subject of audience surveys, some several times. These surveys have included new stations and old ones; large cities, suburbs, and small towns. Three national samples by a commercial program-rating agency have estimated the national audience of these stations. Certain special aspects of their audiences have also been studied—among them children's viewing, contributors' viewing, and the viewing patterns of influentials and opinion leaders. A comparison has been made of the use people thought (six months in advance of air time) they would make of a new station, and the use they actually made of it after it had been on the air six months. As a result, we are now able to speak with some assurance of how many and what kinds of persons are in the audience when the educational stations are on the air.

SIZE OF THE AUDIENCE

By the standards of commercial television, the audience of the educational stations is not large. By the standards of education, it is enormous.

At the end of 1959, only about 8.5 million homes—a little less than one out of every six television homes in the United States—were able to receive a noncommercial educational station (17). There are surprising gaps in the coverage of these stations. Twenty-two states have no such station. There are only two stations in all of New England, and only a handful in the western half of the country. There is no such station in some of the largest markets in the country, among them New York, Los Angeles, Cleveland, Washington, Dallas, Fort Worth, Kansas City, Nashville, Providence, and Portland. Such major cities as Philadelphia, Detroit, Atlanta, Buffalo, Cincinnati, and Madison are served by educational stations only in the UHF band, which have to be received on special UHF equipment, thus greatly reducing the potential audience. The communi-

----

content, and there is no corresponding content study in existence for the dates of these audience studies. Since the audiences of a station obviously bear some relation to the content, it may be that what we consider to be the "audience of educational television" may really be the audience of several different kinds of television. We shall have to assume, however, in the absence of evidence, that the variations between stations are much less significant than the difference between educational and commercial television; and therefore that it is legitimate to talk about an audience for ETV.

ties where noncommercial educational television stations are located at the time of this writing are the following:

ALABAMA
　　Three-station net-
　　work, headquar-
　　ters at University
ARIZONA
　　Tucson
CALIFORNIA
　　Sacramento
　　San Francisco
COLORADO
　　Denver
FLORIDA
　　Gainesville
　　Jacksonville
　　Miami
　　Tampa
GEORGIA
　　Athens
　　Atlanta (UHF)
ILLINOIS
　　Chicago
　　Urbana
IOWA
　　Des Moines

KENTUCKY
　　Louisville
LOUISIANA
　　Monroe
　　New Orleans
MASSACHUSETTS
　　Boston
MICHIGAN
　　Detroit (UHF)
　　East Lansing
MINNESOTA
　　St. Paul–Minneapolis
MISSOURI
　　St. Louis
NEBRASKA
　　Lincoln
NEW HAMPSHIRE
　　Durham
NEW MEXICO
　　Albuquerque
NEW YORK
　　Buffalo (UHF)
NORTH CAROLINA
　　Chapel Hill

OHIO
　　Cincinnati (UHF)
　　Columbus (UHF)
　　Oxford (UHF)
OKLAHOMA
　　Oklahoma City (2 chan-
　　nels)
　　Tulsa
OREGON
　　Corvallis
PENNSYLVANIA
　　Philadelphia (UHF)
　　Pittsburgh (2 channels)
TENNESSEE
　　Memphis
TEXAS
　　Houston
UTAH
　　Salt Lake City
WASHINGTON
　　Seattle
WISCONSIN
　　Madison (UHF)
　　Milwaukee

These are the stations that have a potential audience of about 8.5 million homes, which means perhaps 25 million individuals.

This is the *potential* audience. The *actual* audience is smaller. How much smaller depends on the unit of time over which the act of viewing is counted.

For example, there must be very few homes in the coverage area of an educational station where the television receiver has not at some time, either by accident or out of curiosity, been tuned to the educational channel. Counted this way, the actual audience would be very close to the potential audience in size. But this is not a very meaningful way to delineate an audience.

Suppose we count the audience of persons that view the educational stations at least once in a test week. A program-rating service has done this for us (17). In a week of November, 1959, these stations appear to have delivered programs to about one million homes.[2] If we now assume, conservatively, that 2.5 people in each

----

[2] The ARB estimate for 40 out of 45 stations, as of November, 1959, was 962,900 (17). Unfortunately, the UHF stations have as yet little audience.

home make use of these programs at some time during the week, then these stations each week are reaching about 2.5 million different persons.

Some of these individuals will view one program; some will view many. Our best evidence as to how often people tune in these stations comes from surveys of individual station audiences. In Pittsburgh, 72 per cent of respondents said that they had viewed educational station WQED at least once a month, and 52 per cent at least once a week (15). These 52 per cent were divided as follows:

Once or twice a week	21 per cent
Three or four times a week	14 per cent
Just about every day	17 per cent

There is some reason to think that these percentages may be a bit higher than the common practice of ETV viewers. In Houston, 21 per cent reported that they had viewed educational station KUHT-TV at least twice in the last week; 62 per cent had done so in the last six months (3). In Minneapolis and St. Paul, 59 per cent of the people viewed KTCA-TV during the first six months of its existence, and 25 per cent viewed two programs or more a week (10). In Madison, where UHF cuts down the number of potential viewers, nevertheless 29 per cent said they had viewed the station in the last month (7). In San Francisco four audience studies have now come out very close to the same figure: the average viewer of educational station KQED sees 2.7 programs a week (6) and KQED enters each week into 18 to 20 per cent of Bay Area homes (6, 17).[3]

In one way or another, audience surveyors have tried to arrive at a figure for the total number of viewers who make some fairly regular and purposeful use of these educational stations. Three studies in the San Francisco Bay Area all came out with figures very close to 40 per cent as the measure of the population who use station KQED with enough regularity to be considered "viewers" (6). One of these studies was a survey of KQED's audience; the other

---

Furthermore, because their audiences are so small, they are hard to find with a small sample diary such as ARB used in each community. Thus seven UHF stations were credited by ARB with only 8,500 total viewers per week. This means that 18 per cent of the educational stations were furnishing less than 1 per cent of the audience. At the other end of the scale, two large community stations—Chicago and San Francisco—contributed 27 per cent of the total audience of the educational stations as measured by ARB.

[3] The ARB national diary study agreed quite closely with the KQED figures but gave a considerably lower estimate than either the Pittsburgh or Houston studies. The Madison study cannot readily be compared to the ARB figures.

three were probability sample studies on quite different topics, into which a few questions on television behavior had been inserted. This figure of 40 per cent is as conservative as any corresponding figure, except in the case of some of the UHF stations. It is considerably lower, for example, than Pittsburgh's 72 per cent who have said they use the educational station at least once a month, and the 52 per cent who say they view it at least once a week (15). It is only a little higher than the 29 per cent of Madison's viewers who had tuned in the UHF educational station at least once in the last month (7). Therefore, it seems reasonable to assume that at least 40 per cent of the potential audiences make some regular and purposeful use of the educational stations. Projecting this conservative figure against the total number of potential viewers as measured by ARB, and assuming at least 2.5 viewers per average home, we arrive at what is probably our best estimate of the stations' audience at the end of 1959: about 8.5 million persons.

We have talked about the potential audience, the actual audience of fairly regular viewers, and the weekly audience. But what is the program audience? What kind of ratings do the programs of these educational stations earn?

This is the point where we begin to see a difference between the audience of the educational stations and the audience of commercial stations. One after another, the studies of educational audiences have come in with approximately the same report: unlike the commercial audiences, viewers of educational stations seldom "just let their sets run." They go purposefully to the educational channel for a program or programs they know in advance they want. They read the station program guide or the TV programs in the newspapers. They remember the schedule, and turn to the station at a certain time with a certain purpose. The program completed, they usually turn off the set or tune it elsewhere. This pattern of highly selective viewing makes for attentive audiences and station loyalty, but also for lower program ratings.

The average rating of an educational station program (meaning the percentage of sets tuned to the program) is comparable to that of most daytime commercial television—that is, usually between 1 and 5 per cent. The average ETV program in San Francisco in the spring of 1957 was a little over 1 per cent (6). Some programs apparently got about 5 per cent of sets. A few ratings very much higher have been reported in other communities. In Pittsburgh, for example, ratings of 20 and 21 per cent were reported for two very popular presentations of the educational station (15). This is in excess of all but the most popular evening commercial programs, and the figure may be an artifact of time or sample. But suppose that a program from the National Educational Television and Radio Center, which serves the educational stations in somewhat the same way as a network headquarters, were to receive a program rating of only 1 per cent throughout the communities which now have ETV. This would mean that the program was seen by at least 200,000 viewers. If it earned an average rating of 5, then it would be seen by a million viewers. In a single community, like the San Francisco Bay Area, a rating of 1 would mean about 17,500 viewers, and a rating of 5 would mean about 87,500. These are the kinds of figures that lead us to say that the ETV audience is small in terms of commercial television, but enormous in terms of education. For many commercial television programs in the Bay Area attract more than 5 per cent of the viewers, but what teacher ever, outside of educational television, gets a chance to teach a class of 87,500 persons?

To sum up, then, our best estimate is that the 45 educational stations have a potential audience of over 20 million, and an actual, fairly regular audience of at least 8.5 million. In a week they reach at least 2.5 million viewers. But highly selective viewer patterns keep most of their program ratings below 5 per cent of sets.

NATURE OF THE AUDIENCE

The chief problem that has concerned most of the audience studies, however, is not size of audience, but rather the audience's nature. What is it that distinguishes the 40 per cent who make use of educational television from the 60 per cent who do not? Who is the educational television viewer?

Let us make it clear that in the following pages we shall be talking about "typical" viewers. There are many kinds of ETV viewers. We are going to describe a composite or most typical kind.

One of the accomplishments of these audience studies has been to sort out some of the distinctive differences between typical viewers and nonviewers, and in so doing to correct a few of the assumptions made concerning the probable ETV audience in the days when educational television was only a set of proposed channel allocations. For example, the studies have made clear that the ETV viewer does not spend more time over-all on television than does the nonviewer. If anything, he spends less. Madison, Denver, and Syracuse studies (7, 9, 14) found that ETV viewers had somewhat less *total* television time; Houston, Carrboro, San Francisco, and Pittsburgh found no significant differences (2, 4, 6, 15). Educational television, therefore, seems not to be something merely added on to commercial television, but rather something that meets a different need and *replaces* the time which might otherwise be given to something (e.g., commercial television or print) which satisfies the need less well.

There is nothing so far in the findings to indicate that the educational television audience is predominantly male or female. The Madison study and one Boston study (7, 5) found men slightly more likely than women to be in the audience; San Francisco and the other Boston study found the opposite (6, 8). No other significant differences were reported.

With regard to age, Madison (7) found a slight positive but curvilinear relationship, but Boston (5) found younger people slightly more likely than older ones to be in the audience. No other significant differences were reported, and the safest assumption is that the changing likelihood of ETV viewing in the adult years is not far different from the changing likelihood of *any* television viewing.

There is little evidence that educational television meets any special need of racial minorities, as was once thought possible. The Houston study found that Negroes were slightly more likely to view ETV (2), but the other southern study, in Carrboro (4), found no significant differences. No other significant findings on this subject have been reported.

Several studies have reported a positive relationship between educational television viewing and income. Among these are Madison, Denver, Salt Lake, and Syracuse (7, 9, 13, 14). In each case, the persons with higher income were found more likely to be in the ETV audience. However, income is highly related to education and occupation, and is perhaps more meaningfully considered as one of the elements of status or social class.

The most broadly supported and significant differences that have been found, however, are along four lines, which we might describe as education, social status or class, public participation, and "high-brow" communication behavior. These seem closely related to each other, and appear to be dynamically rather than descriptively related to ETV viewing. Therefore let us try to say precisely what we mean by each, and how they seem to be related to the use of educational television.

Education

Most of the studies find that more highly educated persons are more likely to be in the audience of educational television. The greatest difference seems to be between persons who have had some college and persons who have not. Tables 1 and 2 are presented for comparison, from cities on opposite sides of the continent.

TABLE 1. SAN FRANCISCO: PERCENTAGE OF VIEWERS AND NONVIEWERS OF ETV BY EDUCATION [a]

Education	Viewers	Nonviewers
College	61.5%	39%
High school	35.8	52.4
Grade school	2.7	8.6
N =	(298)	(105)

[a] Source—Schramm, *The Audience for Educational Television in the San Francisco Bay Area* (6).

TABLE 2. WINCHESTER, MASSACHUSETTS: PERCENTAGE OF ETV FANS BY EDUCATIONAL ATTAINMENT [a]

Education	Nonfans	In-betweens	Fans	N
Eighth grade or less	64%	22%	14%	36
Some high school	62	24	13	45
High school graduate	56	19	25	140
Some college	39	27	34	77
College graduate	39	24	37	91
Graduate school	27	30	42	66

[a] Source—Sokol, *The Popularity of Educational Television in a Suburban Community* (12).

These are impressive curves, and are supported by 9 of the 12 studies where this information is reported. At a later point in this paper, we shall have to face up to the question of why the other three studies did not find similar evidence. But supposing that this is indeed a genuine and general difference between viewers and non-viewers, how can we explain why more education should make people more likely to seek education on television? The explanation seems to be that learning inculcates the habit, the skill, of learning, and respect for learning. More highly educated persons are thus able more easily to absorb the content of ETV, and more in the habit of seeking learning experiences. We know, for example, that they are more likely to hear serious lectures, to read informative rather than relaxing material, and to take part in discussion groups. Education evidently breeds the desire for education.

Social Class and Status

An individual's social class membership apparently has something to do with the television he watches because a person internalizes the values and norms of the groups to which he belongs. He learns to play the social roles expected of him, and to value the kind of behavior those around him value. Now it happens that a great deal of commercial television runs counter to one of the most common middle-class norms in America—the idea that a person should be active, striving, achieving, trying to better himself, participating in social interaction and public affairs, and dedicated to what Geiger and Sokol call "a productive concern with the tasks and things of the real world" (5). In sharp contrast, most commercial television encourages chiefly passivity and minimum effort rather than activity, a minimum of social interaction, a concern with fantasy rather than real life, and living in the present rather than concerning oneself either with self-improvement or the problems of tomorrow. Therefore, anyone who holds strongly to the norms described above will not be able to express his values through watching commercial television, and will probably feel a certain amount of unease or guilt if he devotes a great deal of time to it.

Educational television, on the other hand, is in much closer agreement with the social norms described above. That is, it is concerned chiefly with the problems of the real world rather than with fantasy; it is intellectually active; it invites its viewers to work, to achieve, to better themselves. And therefore anyone who holds the values we have described ought, other things being equal, to feel less uneasiness in viewing educational television than in viewing commercial television.

Then the question arises: Where in our society are such values strongly held? We called them middle-class values, but might just as truly have called them American values, because they are associated with upward mobility and were certainly held by a large number of the men and women who built the American civilization. And perhaps it is misleading to speak of middle-class values at this time when such a large proportion of Americans are in the middle class. But it is clear that these values are held much more strongly above than below the middle of our socioeconomic scale. The groups we call the upper-middle and lower-upper are perhaps the ones in which the achieving, realistic, problem-centered constellation of norms are most easily perceived.

Geiger and Sokol have been chief advocates of this point of view (5). They hypothesized that men rather than women, young and middle-aged adults rather than elderly ones, and members of higher social class groups rather than members of lower ones, would feel the pressures of the "achieving" norms most strongly, and therefore would be most uneasy over time spent on commercial television, most attracted to educational television. The hypothesized sex difference they were never able to prove, and the results of other studies on this point are equivocal. On the age difference they also found contradictory evidence, but the weight of other studies at least suggests that middle age is a time when commercial television is generally of less importance than in youth or the older years; and therefore the hypothesis may be true. When the hypothesis concerning class difference was tested, however, Geiger and Sokol found large and significant differences.

Table 3 presents some of their figures for commercial television viewing by persons of different socioeconomic status.

Their figures on differences by education and by occupation were parallel to these, and contribute to the already strong evidence that viewing commercial television is a less valued and less engaged-in behavior in higher social class groups. Their results with respect to educational television will be found in large part in their paper reprinted in this volume, and there is no need to repeat them here, except to say that they found the predicted result: educational television was *more* popular, *more* often used, in higher status groups.

In this finding they are impressively supported by three-quarters of the ETV audience studies. Parts of the San Francisco data were reanalyzed in such a way as to obtain class measures, and highly significant differences were found (6). Similar differences seem to be coming out of the Stanford study on children's viewing of television. The Madison audience study concluded that attitude toward educational television is "a more or less linear function of social class" (7). Most of the studies have found positive correlations between education, occupation, income, and ETV viewing, and there is little doubt that these could be restated in terms of social class. The weight of evidence, then, is in favor of the idea that educational television is likely to be most used and most highly valued in higher social status groups, where commercial television is likely to be least valued and least used.

TABLE 3. TELEVISION BEHAVIOR BY SOCIOECONOMIC STATUS [a]

Evening Hours Spent Watching Television	High	Middle	Low
Less than 2 hours	37%	16%	12%
2–3.9 hours	41	45	35
4 or more hours	22	39	53
Amount of Pleasure They Say They Receive from Television			
A great deal	51	67	71
A medium amount	34	29	25
A small amount	15	4	4
Proportion of Spare Time Spent Watching Television			
All or most	11	17	33
About half	25	37	28
A very small part	64	46	39
N =	(110)	(215)	(121)

[a] Source—Geiger and Sokol, *The Normative Significance of Television Viewing* (5).

Public Participation

A very common finding in these audience studies is that viewers of educational television are more likely than nonviewers to belong to civic organizations and to take part in public-affairs activity.

Thus, for example, in Houston, frequent viewers were found also to be more frequent voters (2). Viewers belonged to more civic and social organizations than did nonviewers. In Carrboro it was found that ETV viewers were more likely than nonviewers to belong to "community, welfare, or civic organizations," but *not* to social organizations (4). This was approximately the San Francisco finding also (6). In Madison, the amount of ETV viewing and favorable attitudes toward ETV were positively related to the amount of "voluntary community activity" (7). In Salt Lake the prospective viewers were more likely to belong to civic organizations (13). In Syracuse the viewers were more likely to belong to community organizations, and to be leaders (14). In Boston and Winchester, it was found that viewers of ETV tended to be "influentials" in the community (5, 8, 12).

In other words, the typical viewer of ETV is likely to be an active person, a public-spirited individual, and very possibly a community leader.

"High-brow" Communication Behavior

The San Francisco Bay Area study was the first one to point out that the viewing of educational television seemed to go with more reading of books and of high-quality magazines, reading of editorials and public-affairs news in papers, viewing of serious non-fantasy materials on commercial television, listening to good-music radio, owning classical records, going to opera and symphony, and other high-brow cultural behavior (6). This report concluded that the audience of San Francisco could perhaps best be described—without any uncomplimentary overtones—as a "culture" audience.

Other studies have since confirmed this relation of ETV to cultural behavior. Houston found that its viewers were more likely to go to lectures and to seek other informative recreations (2, 3). Carrboro found that viewers were likely to read more, to listen often to music, to read more newspapers, and to seek out the serious informative programs on commercial television (4). Madison too found more serious reading among its viewers, more listening to educational radio, and more likelihood of selecting cultural programs on commercial television (7). Syracuse found more book and serious mazazine reading, more frequent attendance at lectures and concerts, more nonlocal newspapers in the home and more serious items read in newspapers generally, and more frequent selection of serious and informative commercial programs (14).

It should also be pointed out that Houston, Carrboro, San Francisco, Madison, Denver, and Syracuse all reported that ETV viewers spent less time than non-ETV viewers on commercial television (2,

4, 6, 7, 9, 14). No study reported findings contrary to this. It seems, therefore, that the viewing of educational television is perhaps less of a piece with the viewing of commercial television than it is with certain other kinds of communication behavior we generally think of as "high-brow."

Let us now review the extent of support we find in the audience studies for these four characteristics of the ETV audience. In Table 4 we have listed the studies by cities. In cases where the findings

TABLE 4. DISTINGUISHING CHARACTERISTICS OF ETV AUDIENCES

Study	Education	Class	Participation	"High-brow" Communication
Lansing	Slight	Slight	?	?
Houston	No	No	x	x
Carrboro	No	No	x	x
Pittsburgh	No	No	?	?
Madison	x	x	x	x
San Francisco	x	x	x	x
Boston (Winnick)	x(?)	x(?)	?	x
Boston (Geiger & Sokol)	x	x	x	x
Winchester	x	x	x	x
Minneapolis	x	x	x(?)	?
Denver	x	x	?	?
Syracuse	x	x	x	x
Salt Lake	x	x	x	x

support the generalization we have written x; where the findings contradict our generalization (e.g., where no significant differences are found) we have put No; and where the findings are unclear or do not touch upon the particular topic we have put a question mark.

So far as numbers go, the evidence is overwhelming. But we are still under some obligation to explain why the first four studies, in particular, should show slight results or negative results on education and class differences. We can perhaps explain away the Lansing results on the grounds that this was a study of a UHF station at a time when only 17 per cent of the television households were equipped to receive UHF; and therefore the possession of a UHF receiver, rather than any other personal or social characteristics, was the dominant factor in determining who viewed ETV (1). The author of the Carrboro study speaks of the homogeneity of the town's population. "This lack of variation in demographic characteristics . . . is equivalent," he said, "to holding demographic variables such as education, occupation, and income more or less constant" (4). It is not surprising then, that education and class differences should fail to distinguish viewers from nonviewers in Carrboro, and all the more significant that the differences in participation and high-brow communication should show up. In connection with the Pittsburgh study it is worth noting that the Pittsburgh station has shown some very high program ratings, and presents a more widely varied program than the average educational station— for example, repeats of university athletic events, questions and answers on law, and so forth. It is entirely possible that programs like these attracted a broader spectrum of interest and a more diverse audience than the average ETV station. So far as Houston is concerned, that study was apparently done meticulously and with awareness that some of Houston's programs (e.g., broadcasts of city council meetings) might attract atypical ETV viewers (2, 3). Even when a correction was made for viewers of these special programs, differences in education, occupation, and similar demographic qualities did not turn out to be significant. It may be that the Houston station simply attracts a wider variety of viewers by a wider variety of programs, or that the social structure of Houston is somewhat different from many of the other cities, or that we are dealing with one of the variations in data which keep plaguing social researchers.

In any case, it is clear that there is broad support for this picture of the educational television viewer. It is also clear that the four characteristics are related. Higher education tends to be a component of higher social class. The norms of upper-middle class and lower-upper encourage participation in public affairs and civic organizations. And both education and class norms encourage what we have called "high-brow" communication behavior—concern with problems, preference for serious materials in the newspapers and magazines, enjoyment of fine arts rather than popular arts, and so on. These fit together. The picture is coordinated.

But having said that, let us add a word of caution. This pattern is not intended to describe every viewer of educational television, but only the most typical viewers. There are undoubtedly many variations among viewers, and many different reasons for viewing educational television. No station audience is entirely homogeneous. Furthermore, we have found that the majority of viewers of ETV apparently go to the station for a particular program, or a few programs; therefore the program, rather than the station, selects the viewer. The pattern here discovered is merely a central point around which variation occurs.

To have discovered that centroid, however, in a mass medium so new, is a considerable accomplishment. And let us summarize what we believe we know about this typical viewer of educational television. He is likely to be better educated than the average man in his community. There is a good chance that he has at least some college education. There is a high probability, also, that he is a professional, managerial, or self-employed type (or a member of the family of such a person), that he has an above-average income, and that he has internalized the upwardly mobile values of the middle class. This means that he places a high value on self-betterment, on actively striving toward the solution of problems, on doing something rather than merely being entertained, on realism rather than fantasy, on deferring his gratifications and seeing events in a long time perspective rather than living in the present. Because he holds these kinds of values, he is likely to be civic-minded and to participate in public affairs. He is likely to belong to the P.T.A. if he has children; his wife is likely to belong to the League of Women Voters. He is more likely to be seen in these activity-oriented and problem-centered organizations than in fraternal or other social organizations. In his communication behavior he is more high-brow than the average person. He is more likely to read books, more likely than the average person to read public-affairs news and newspaper editorials, more likely to go to hear good music, more likely to select the serious and informative programs on commercial television. In other words, his behavior is an example of what the present writer once called "delayed reward" as opposed to "immediate reward" seeking. The "immediate reward" person is more likely to be found with the fantasy material on commercial television, the feature and entertainment material in magazines and newspapers, the popular arts rather than the fine arts, social rather than public-affairs activities. The "delayed reward" person has learned to live with a longer time perspective, to value active striving toward improvement and problem solving, to value the communication experiences that challenge him to work harder and keep his mind on social problems rather than distracting him from them. In communities where there is educational television, that tends to become a part of his life because it helps to meet the needs he considers important.

This is not every viewer of ETV, but according to the best knowledge we now have it is the most typical viewer.

EDUCATIONAL TELEVISION AND EDUCATION

One of the interesting items that emerges from these audience studies is the fact that educational television is sometimes evaluated chiefly as education, sometimes as television. This point is developed fully in the paper by Geiger and Sokol reprinted in this volume, and there is no reason, therefore, to say much about it here. But let us at least record that many of the audience attitudes toward educational television seem to be related to this point. The early and widespread effectiveness of commercial television led it to be considered chiefly a medium of entertainment. When the medium is used for educational purposes a conflict is set up. When individuals go to ETV chiefly as *television,* they are likely to think it is *not very good* television. The people who evaluate it highly are usually those who go to it as education rather than as television. This group does not insist that ETV entertain—rather, that it be informative. The former group compares it unfavorably with the artistic smoothness and excitement of commercial television; the latter compares it rather with classroom teaching and public lectures. But it is difficult to dissociate attitudes appropriate to commercial television from the act of viewing ETV, and vice versa. These conflicts are developed interestingly in the Geiger and Sokol paper.

INFLUENTIALS IN THE ETV AUDIENCE

One further note on the educational television audience: we know the audience is relatively small, and we think it is generally loyal, which is evidenced by the fact that it donates the entire annual budget of the community stations; but what makes the smallness less discouraging and the loyalty more significant is that the audience apparently contains a high proportion of influential persons and opinion leaders.

It would be strange if such persons were not in the audience. We know that the viewer of educational television is more likely to participate in public affairs and civic organizations, that he is likely to have more than average education, that he is likely to select realistic mass-media content that tells him about current problems. Sokol, in the Winchester study, however, tested it directly by developing an index of opinion leadership and another index of what he called "personal power" (12). He set these against his "fan index" which measured a person's interest in and use of general television and educational television. Table 5 presents the results of setting the opinion leadership index against the fan index.

TABLE 5. PERCENTAGE WHO ARE GENERAL TV FANS AND WHO ARE EDUCATIONAL TV FANS BY EDUCATION AND BY OPINION LEADERSHIP [a]

Leadership	Noncollege		Some College		College Graduates	
	General TV Fans					
Opinion leaders	70%	(23)	42%	(12)	31%	(32)
In-betweens	63	(67)	52	(29)	42	(45)
Nonleaders	58	(131)	53	(36)	44	(78)
	Educational TV Fans					
Opinion leaders	35	(23)	58	(12)	44	(32)
In-betweens	30	(67)	24	(29)	42	(45)
Nonleaders	14	(131)	33	(36)	35	(78)

[a] Source—Sokol, *The Popularity of Educational Television in a Suburban Community* (12).

The figures in parentheses are in each case the total number of cases on which the percentage is based. The table should therefore be read: Of the 23 persons who had not gone to college and who were opinion leaders, 70 per cent were fans of general TV and 35 per cent were fans of educational TV, etc. What the table actually means is that of people who have gone to college and have become opinion leaders, a much larger percentage are likely to be fans of educational than of general TV. In the case of people who have not gone to college, the situation is reversed. It appears, therefore, that general television comes nearer satisfying the informational needs of a noncollege opinion leader, but that the college-trained opinion leader needs other sources of information such as educational television and some kinds of print.

Sokol's index of "personal power" was a series of questions designed to find out whether the person had been an officer in a club or organization, had been a committee member, had ever been elected to public office, knew people in positions of power, and felt he had something to say about what goes on in the community. Putting this scale against the educational level of his respondents, he came up with the figures presented in Table 6.

TABLE 6. PERCENTAGE WHO ARE EDUCATIONAL TV FANS BY PERSONAL POWER AND EDUCATION [a]

| Education | Personal Power | | |
	High	Medium	Low
Noncollege	36% (28)	28% (93)	10% (101)
Some college	13 (15)	39 (38)	37 (24)
College graduate	57 (37)	36 (97)	25 (20)

[a] Source—Sokol, *The Popularity of Educational Television in a Suburban Community* (12).

This table should be read: Of the 28 noncollege persons who had high personal power in their community, 36 per cent were fans of educational television, and so forth. The meaning of these figures is that in two of three comparisons the more personal power an individual has, the more likely he is to be a fan of educational television. The single exception to this conclusion may well be an accident of sampling; the percentage which is out of line with the others is based on only 15 cases.

Therefore, there is good reason to believe that the educational television audience contains a more-than-usual proportion of influentials and opinion leaders. Through them, the educational stations may be distributing their information and exerting an influence far beyond the restricted circle of their viewers.

The Audience Research Program of NETRC

This paper is based on audience studies commissioned and financed by the National Educational Television and Radio Center. The research heads of these studies are therefore really co-authors of this paper. They are listed below, along with some indication of the nature of their samples. The number before each study is the one by which it is referred to in the text.

1. LANSING, 1956. I. R. Merrill, Michigan State University: *Benchmark Television-Radio Study, Part I; Lansing.*

Someone in every fourteenth dwelling in Lansing was interviewed to find out whether a television receiver was available in the home, and if so whether it would receive the local ETV station. It proved possible to reach 2,103 homes. Of the 167 homes with radio only, 118 were interviewed. Of the 1,901 homes with television, 1,582 were able to receive commercial television only; 291 of these were interviewed. Of the 319 households able to receive ETV (on a UHF channel), 298 were interviewed. For interview purposes the household was considered a unit.

2. HOUSTON, 1956. R. I. Evans, University of Houston: *Psychological Identification of the KUHT-TV Viewing Audience; an Analysis of Some Demographic and Psychological Characteristics of an Educational Television Audience.*

500 homes in Houston were chosen at random, using a "grid density" method of sampling. The adult who answered the door was interviewed.

3. HOUSTON, 1957. R. I. Evans, University of Houston: *Examination of Various Demographic and Psychological Characteristics of the Audience of KUHT.*

From the sample of 500 television homes used in the 1956 study, 42 frequent viewers and 72 infrequent viewers were selected and given a number of psychological tests and other questions.

4. CARRBORO, 1956. J. S. Adams, University of North Carolina (now General Electric Company): *A Study of Viewers and Non-Viewers of Educational Television.*

50 viewers and 58 nonviewers over 18, and living in one of the telephone homes of Carrboro, North Carolina, where a TV set was capable of receiving the nearby ETV station, WUNC-TV, made up the sample. Every telephone household was interviewed, and viewers selected on the basis of having viewed six or more ETV programs in the last two weeks; nonviewers from those who had viewed one or no programs in the last two weeks.

5. BOSTON, 1956. K. Geiger and R. Sokol, Tufts University: *Educational Television in Boston.* (Also in this report: *The Normative Significance of Television Viewing.*)

519 residents of Boston were interviewed. Their households were selected at random (an equal sex quota determining who in the household was interviewed) from 29 census blocks chosen so as to maximize representation at extremes of the status hierarchy.

6. SAN FRANCISCO, 1957. W. Schramm, Stanford University: *The Audience for Educational Television in the San Francisco Bay Area.*

3,428 telephone interviews were completed with persons representing every nth name in four chief Bay Area phone books. 302 viewers of ETV were selected by random-number choice from among the viewers turned up by the telephone interviews, and 132 nonviewers were chosen by random sampling among the viewers' neighbors. 25 large-sum contributors and 45 other contributors were also interviewed.

7. MADISON, 1957. B. H. Westley, University of Wisconsin: *Attitudes Toward Educational Television.*

799 interviews were completed out of a probability sample of 977 drawn from the Madison city directory.

8. BOSTON, 1957. C. Winnick (visiting professor), Massachusetts Institute of Technology: *A Study of Viewers and Non-Viewers of an Educational Television Channel.*

Probability sample of households in the Greater Boston area. Facts on the number of interviews and the source of sampling data are not presently available.

9. DENVER, 1957. G. J. Willsea, Denver Public Schools: *The Educational Television Audience in Denver.*

492 interviews were made, being a probability sample of 10 per cent of the blocks in each of the city's census tracts. 487 additional interviews were conducted with known viewers of station KRMA-TV, chosen from lists compiled by station personnel.

10. MINNEAPOLIS, 1957–58. W. A. Mindak, University of Minnesota: *Community Reaction to Educational Television.*

488 residents of Minneapolis and St. Paul, selected on a probability basis, were interviewed in April, 1957, about six months before station KTCA-TV came on the air. 368 of these were reinterviewed in April, 1958, when the station had been on the air about six months.

11. MINNEAPOLIS #2, 1957–58. W. A. Mindak, University of Minnesota: *Supplementary Study to Measure Community Reaction to Educational Television.*

15 contributors, 15 teachers, and 10 media men were interviewed six months before and six months after KTCA-TV came on the air.

12. WINCHESTER, 1958. R. Sokol, Tufts University: *The Popularity of Educational Television in a Suburban Community.*

500 names were drawn randomly from a list of the residents of Winchester, Massachusetts. 453 of these were interviewed, and 40 follow-up interviews were made to study the effects of a newspaper campaign.

13. SALT LAKE, 1958. O. J. Gordon, University of Utah: *A Study of Public Opinion Toward Educational Television Prior to the Opening of Channel 7, KUED.*

Interviews were made in 450 households, some of the names being chosen at random from the telephone book, others obtained by moving n houses to the left of the original choice; equal sex quota determined the choice of the person for the interview. These were *pre*-ETV. If corresponding interviews were made *after* the station came on the air, they have not been reported.

14. SYRACUSE, 1958. L. Myers, Jr., Syracuse University: *Books and Ideas: The Impact of an Educational Television Program on Its Audience.*

Telephone survey on various programs in an educational television series. Personal interviews were conducted with 200 viewers and 200 non-viewers of the program, identified by these telephone calls.

15. PITTSBURGH, 1958.

Grid density sample of 465 households in Pittsburgh, and 120 from Mt. Lebanon, a nearby high socioeconomic status community. The household was considered as a unit for interview purposes.

16. DETROIT, 1958–59. H. Sharp, Detroit Area Study, and J. B. Haney, University of Michigan: *A Study of Public Attitudes Towards Tax-Support for Educational Television Activities in the Detroit Metropolitan Area.*

Questions added to the 1958–59 Detroit area study, which made 767 interviews in an approximation to simple random sampling of adult residents of Detroit. Findings are not yet reported.

17. ARB SAMPLES, 1958, 1959.

In November and December, 1958, and November, 1959, the American Research Bureau collected information on the viewing of all educational TV stations from its viewer diaries placed in the counties where the stations are located.

Most Americans think of home television as principally for recreation. As such, they value it highly. Remembering that Americans value education highly also, one might think that the combination of television and education in "educational television" would be a happy fusion of ideas and activities. But it hasn't happened that way. Rather, the emergence of ETV set up an attitudinal conflict, which has implications of the very greatest importance for ETV stations and program makers. These two authors, who are on the faculty of the Department of Sociology at Tufts University, explore this conflict and its implications.

EDUCATIONAL TELEVISION IN BOSTON:
Memorandum #3

by Kent Geiger and Robert Sokol

As we have pointed out in an earlier memorandum, there is reason to believe that the pattern of TV viewing, when taken as a unitary and homogeneous pattern,[1] comes into conflict with some strongly held general value orientations in America. The essentially passive, isolated, and receptive rather than productive behavior of the TV viewer clashes with the characteristic commitment of "middle-class America" to activity, sociability, and productive, goal-directed concerns.

If the reader will accept this as a rough depiction of the cultural setting of TV viewing, then he will perhaps also have been prepared to anticipate the present stage of development in the unfolding of events. For out of the clash of such nonsympathetic forces as these one may expect the emergence of syntheses, and it seems to us that the idea of educational television constitutes just such a synthesis. In other words, one of the responses of our society to the

----

[1] It should perhaps be emphasized that this level of analysis passes over the matter of differential program tastes. Obviously, when program preferences are taken into account, television viewing is no more unitary and homogeneous in nature than such a pattern of behavior as book reading or movie attendance. There is a very considerable difference between reading a work of fiction and reading a learned treatise or between watching a western film and watching a documentary. The point made here is simply that it is useful to take book reading, movie attendance, and (as done in our reports) television watching as patterns which merit systematic analysis at a higher level of abstraction.

ingression of television into the homes has been the attempt to re-fashion television and television viewing into a form more har-monious with the active, striving, goal-directed component of our national ethos.

It was at this point in the development of television watching in America that we assigned our interviewers the task of investigat-ing various aspects of the behavior and state of mind of the viewing public. The results permit a discussion of two basic problems: first, what are the sources of resistance to the proposed synthesis? And second, who in the TV audience of our society finds educational television most welcome? The first section to follow thus deals with the criticisms of ETV offered by our sample, and the second is concerned with the social characteristics of those respondents who are more and less likely to watch ETV. In a final section we pre-sent some data and ideas focused on the broader question of the ultimate meaning of educational television in America. Before turn-ing to the findings, however, let us interpose a few words about the situation and survey materials with which we are dealing.

At the time our data were collected there were four channels oper-ating in Boston, two commercial VHF stations, one VHF educa-tional station, and one commercial UHF station. The UHF station had practically no audience, a plight similar to that of many such channels throughout the country. WGBH-TV, the educational unit, has been in existence since the spring of 1955, and our data were gathered in the spring and summer of 1956. Thus, one year's time is the upper limit for the exposure of the present sample to the programs of Channel 2. It should be pointed out that Channel 2 is the only source of ETV for Boston residents, albeit some of them may have become acquainted with ETV in other parts of the coun-try. It should also be stressed that our sample of 519 persons is not a representative sample of the Boston area, but a sample chosen from within some of the highest and some of the lowest rental areas in the metropolitan region. Consequently, the results must not be taken as characteristic of the behavior and attitudes of the popula-tion of Greater Boston as a whole.

SOURCES OF RESISTANCE TO ETV

In America, television viewing is a remarkably popular pastime. Another component of the structure of value commitments by which we all live is the general favor which education finds in the eyes of the American people. At first sight, therefore, one might be tempted to predict that educational television would constitute a happy fusion of these two popular realms of activity in American life, and that watching ETV would quickly seize the imagination and capture the spare time of large numbers of TV set owners. In fact this has not occurred, and in most homes ETV is quite generally out of the running as competition for commercial television. Perhaps this may be explained simply as a function of the novelty of ETV. On the other hand, it is possible that a more fundamental obstacle is involved; perhaps the ETV audience will not be much larger ten years hence than it is today.

What, then, are the sources of resistance to ETV? In this section of the report our respondents have a chance to speak critically about ETV. At approximately the mid-point in the interview this open-end question was asked: "Some people feel that television has great educational possibilities. The fact is, however, that most people do not spend much time watching educational TV. What do you feel is the reason for this?" The reader will notice that there is no specific reference to Channel 2 in this question. The intent of the item was to draw out general reactions to the concept and practice of educational television, and it was felt that a specific reference to Channel 2 might severely restrict the number of responses with which we would have to work.

Notwithstanding the general form in which the question was phrased, the answers to the question indicate that the great majority of those who gave any indication of their frame of reference in answering were responding in terms of Channel 2. This is partly because WGBH-Channel 2 is explicitly identified as an "educational station" operated by the "WGBH Educational Foundation." However, it is also due to the fact that the two questions which preceded this one in the interview both dealt explicitly with Channel 2 and thus often served to focus the respondent's attention on that channel. Nevertheless, although most respondents had in mind the productions of Channel 2, others clearly had in mind the educational material of the commercial stations, while still others had both sources in mind.

Another methodological point which should be discussed before presenting the results of this question concerns the meaning of the respondents' answers. Our approach was an indirect one; the respondent was asked to tell the interviewer why he thought *other people* did not watch educational TV. This was felt to be necessary for two reasons. In the first place, we anticipated that a considerable portion of the sample would never have watched Channel 2, and might, therefore, have been reluctant to speak critically of programs they had never seen, although if the subject were posed in more general terms they would be perfectly willing to divulge their views. Secondly, as we have noted above, "education" is a highly regarded symbol in our society, and we felt that a direct invitation to criticize *educational* television might induce blocking

TABLE 3.1. RESPONDENTS' EXPLANATIONS FOR LACK OF POPULARITY OF ETV

People want entertainment, recreation, relaxation from TV	33% [a]
ETV requires too much attention, effort, brains	8
ETV is too deep, too "high-brow"	7
ETV is for children, most interesting to children	7
Program hours of Channel 2 are inconvenient	6
People are lazy, "in a rut"	6
People do not know about Channel 2, poor publicity	5
Poor reception, picture	4
Poor technique, "amateurish" programs	3
Reiteration of question—not interesting, people do not like it, dull	25
Other answers	18
No answer or don't know	11

[a] The percentage base was the total number of respondents in the sample, and since some gave more than one codable answer, the percentages do not total to 100.

or misleading bias. We hoped that the "projective" form in which the question was presented would constitute a vehicle for tapping the respondent's own reasons for being reluctant to watch Channel 2, but of course we have no systematic way of distinguishing between an objective depiction of "why people don't watch ETV" and the respondent's own reasons for not watching more regularly. Had the interview schedule not already been of considerable length, we would have done well to follow up the "projective" form with a more specific question asking the respondent why he himself did not watch ETV (or did not watch more frequently than he reported himself as doing).

Table 3.1 contains a summary of the pattern of responses to this question. Note that 11 per cent of the sample were unable or unwilling to answer this question, and that an additional 25 per cent of the respondents offered as one of their answers, or as their only answer, no more than a rephrasing of the question, saying in effect that the reason "most people do not spend much time watching ETV" is that "they don't like it." Our interviewers were instructed to attempt to push further than this by confronting such respondents with additional probes, and were usually able to induce them, after further reflection, to be more specific.

In order to portray in more concrete form the flavor of the respondents' thinking, two specific examples of each category of the responses appearing in Table 3.1 follow.

Specific Reasons

People want relaxation, recreation, entertainment, and ETV does not provide this

People who work want to rest. I know I want to laugh when I finish work and I can't get it on [Channel] 2.

For most grown people, when they watch TV they're watching for entertainment instead of educational programs. After a day's work, you don't come home to see an educational program.

ETV requires too much attention, effort, brains from the viewer

They don't want to think too much.

I imagine it requires more concentration and a good many people, especially adults, feel when they're relaxing, they don't want to be taught anything.

ETV is too deep, too profound, too "high-brow"

Well, I guess it's too deep for some and too far advanced for some. If they studied more, they'd take advantage of it.

They don't understand them. You always get something out of TV even if you don't like it, but if you don't understand it—know what I mean? They just don't understand them.

ETV is suitable for, or interesting mostly, or only, to children, designed for children

The average rule is that most who don't watch it are adults who have gone through education, and most who watch are high school and grammar school kids so they can get an education.

Not too much adult appeal. They strive to hit the child.

Inconvenient program hours of ETV

The programs are on at the wrong time, conflicting with children's programs.

Don't broadcast it at the right hours. The time that I watch TV there is no educational program . . . in the evening.

People are lazy, "in a rut"

People get in the habit of watching certain programs and they don't want to miss them by watching educational programs. They should have come out with them right at the start.

It's mental laziness, that's all.

ETV is too new, not enough publicity, people don't know about it

If a program was put on for a kid, and people were informed of it, they'd watch it. People don't know. They don't even know what's on there.

You never know what's on. You don't see it in the paper.

Cannot get the channel, poor reception

They don't have it on the main channels like 4 and 7. People can't get 2.

Anything educational on TV . . . if I know it's coming and I'm interested.

Most people can't get Channel 2 around here. I can't get it. That's the only reason. . . . I can't get it.

Poor technique, "amateurish" programs

Because it hasn't gotten on the main channels with popular artists. If you get a popular artist, there can be a little educational stuff in a lot of programs.

Stars and actors are not polished or finished because of money. Background and script writers are so mediocre and hackneyed. Presented on a child's level.

Other Categories

ETV is not interesting, people do not like it

People tell me they fall asleep watching it.

Few are worth watching. They missed the boat.

Other answers

I can only speak for myself. I am too old to become educated. Education comes from experience and work, not TV.

You gonna test my I.Q.? Maybe people like me who sleep a lot. I usually wake up about 10 or 11 o'clock and watch the rest of the night.

Such is the range of answers which our respondents offered. The most prominent fact about them is the clarity and force with which they reflect the sentiment explicit in the most frequently chosen category and implicit in a number of others: *Home television should provide entertainment rather than learning.* One-third of the entire sample, a rather high proportion for an open-end question, chose this specific response, and the next two responses in order of frequency also give much the same impression—that people expect pleasure and relaxation from TV rather than the hard work of learning.

It is clear, therefore, that home TV is defined by the bulk of this sample as a recreational facility, and that the tendency is to visualize ETV as a violation of this expectation. It is as if to say, "Education and entertainment just don't mix." Psychologically, of course, there may be some truth to this point of view; there are realms of human activities which in a sense are mutually repellent. One of the best documented of these to be found in the literature of research on the mass media is the incongruity of "sacred" as opposed to "secular" reasons for buying war bonds during World War II.[2] It is possible that the juxtaposition of television, a "recreational medium," and education, a "serious matter," both highly valued in themselves, may constitute, when the attempt is made to unify them in one medium, another form of a mutually incompatible expression of coexistent cultural values: "expressive" as opposed to "instrumental" concerns. If this is so, the implication for ETV is that it should not attempt to merge or unify entertainment and education, but should instead maintain a firm commitment to *educational* aims which do indeed place certain demands upon the audience. For if education and recreation are somehow inherently at odds with each other, the attempt to combine them will be ill-starred, and will probably result in the deterioration of quality in each of them rather than a new and attractive synthesis.

There is an additional line of interpretation. A basic structural pattern of American life may be at work. Home television watching seems to be closely tied in with the way in which American family life is organized. "Family life," that is, being together in the family, is highly valued. But, paradoxically, the small amount of time the members of the average family are able to spend together constitutes one of the dominant features of contemporary urban life. In this age of specialization, work, schooling, and a great number of other activities are most typically carried on by family members as individuals in extrafamilial physical and social contexts. This development, roughly coincident with the rise of industrial civilization and its great urban centers, has not taken place without a considerable amount of strain. There is strong popular feeling to the effect that in modern times the family has "grown apart," and that the home has become little more than a dormitory.

In view of this state of affairs, and in view of the fact that the areas of interest and concern of the individual members of the family do actually take many different directions during the day-

----

[2] R. K. Merton, *Mass Persuasion*, New York: Harper and Brothers, 1946, pp. 45–64.

time hours, it has evidently come to be somewhat of a problem for them to find areas of common interest which they can all share. Such a "vacuum" conflicts strongly with the still-vigorous cultural ideal of the family as a solidary unit, as more than just a collection of individual personalities who hang their hats in the same place overnight. It is at this juncture that television enters the picture, and surely one of the reasons why TV has become so popular so quickly is precisely that it affords the members of most families an opportunity to share regularly a common experience. This is reflected in the widespread feeling that TV has "brought the family closer together."

The final question in our interview was: "One last question on television. How would you say TV, which is a relatively new invention, has changed your family life or your own life?" In answer to this question, the set-owning respondents not only gave an overwhelming vote of confidence to TV for a variety of beneficial effects, but 13 per cent of the sample of 490 specifically mentioned that TV had increased the closeness, mutual understanding, etc., of family members. Whether this is actually true is, of course, irrelevant; the point is that so many people *think* it has had this effect.

Let us now, within this framework of the role of television in family life, emphasize the likelihood that the desirability of having all family members share together the experience of watching television places a rather severe restriction on the type of program that is considered eligible for common consumption in the evening. In fact, we are here most probably confronted with the demand that family members of different ages, interests, and levels of intellectual or aesthetic development all be satisfied simultaneously. Small wonder, then, that the dial is set for entertainment-type programs, and that the more specialized and demanding programs of ETV are passed over. It would indeed appear that the desire of the commercial sponsor to find a "least common denominator" which will maximize the size of his audience is complemented in the home by the joint desire of the members of the family to take into consideration the TV appetites of all family members to the extent that they too must arrive at a private "least common denominator." And let the person who insists upon using television for educational purposes go off somewhere by himself and study a book or enroll in an evening course!

Of course, for families small in size and homogeneous in age composition, or with spacious living quarters and/or more than one television set, such an interpretation loses some of its relevance. In general, the larger the family and the more varied the ages, other things equal, the less likely is the TV set to be used for educational purposes. Our data corroborate this tendency. We divided the set owners in our sample into six subgroups, by sex and a three-way social class break, and found that within each subgroup, respondents living in families with one or more children present were more likely to use their TV sets exclusively for "general" rather than for educational TV watching [3] than were those with no children in the home.

At the present time, the most educational of the Channel 2 programs, "French Through Television," and "Spanish Through Television," are both listed as "a beginning course for the whole family." In subsequent surveys it might be worthwhile to compare the family situation of those who watch these programs regularly with those who do not. Our feeling is that it is most unlikely that an entire family would watch such a program regularly, and that a disproportionate number of its viewers are in fact individuals rather than families.

Whatever the relative importance of these interpretations of the main pattern of response to our question on the lack of appeal of ETV, there is no doubt but that its absence of entertainment appeal is the most prominent idea in the mind of the public. In comparison, the other explanations listed in Table 3.1 are insignificant. However, a few comments on the less frequently given responses do seem in order.

Seven per cent of the sample suggested as an explanation of ETV's lack of broad appeal the idea that it is primarily oriented toward children. In Boston a rather large proportion of programs are devoted to children, but to hold that Channel 2 is directed *primarily* to an audience of children, or is *more interesting* for children than for adults, hardly squares with the facts. It is quite likely that the "public image" of the general TV viewing pattern, which

----

[3] The test measure used was the ratio of respondents who were "TV fans" but "never" watched Channel 2 to all respondents for whom measures on both characteristics were available. Referring ahead, it was the ratio of cell frequencies a to zero order frequencies as in Table 3.7, but separately for each of the six subgroups.

points to children as the most enthusiastic sector of the audience,[4] has been generalized in the thinking of these respondents to include educational television. Of course, one can also point to the association between education and youth and hence to the probability that any activity smacking of "education" would be connected with younger persons. On the other hand, analysis to be described below suggests that WGBH-Channel 2 is not at all likely to be seen as a children's station by the sample as a whole. Consequently, we might suppose that the few respondents who feel that ETV is for children are those who are not acquainted with Channel 2, or who watch its programs less frequently. This, however, is not the case; the likelihood of giving such an answer is quite unrelated to the respondent's own particular experience with Channel 2. The other explanation which occurs to us involves the notion of rationalization. Perhaps the respondents who conceive (falsely) of Channel 2 as a channel "for children" are thereby distorting reality in order to diminish their sense of guilt for failure to take advantage of easily accessible educational opportunities.

The next category of responses in Table 3.1 deals with the matter of program hours. Since the Channel 2 hours at the time ran from 5:30 to about 9:00 p.m., it is hard to see any alternative to present policy. Some of the respondents emphasized that the programs were on too early in the evening, but later telecasting hours probably would lead to an even larger number of complaints about inconvenience on the part of those who go to bed earlier. It might be worthwhile in a future survey to compare systematically evening routines of the individuals and families who watch ETV with those who do not.

In the next category we come upon the respondents who apparently are committed to the idea that ETV deserves support, and who choose to criticize the viewer rather than the source. The fact that so few responses fall into this group is rather surprising, and lends some support to the main conclusion to be drawn from the general pattern of responses to the question—education is not yet institutionalized in the context of home television viewing. If it were, we would expect to find considerably more than 6 per cent

----

[4] See K. Geiger and R. Sokol, *Report of the Tufts Television Project*, Ann Arbor, Mich.: ETRC, 1957, Memorandum #1, "The Public Image of the Television Fan," pp. 3–12.

of the sample finding fault with the nonviewers for missing out on a good thing.

The final three substantive categories of response deal with the novelty and "growing pains" of Channel 2, and are probably of less permanent significance than the others. The small over-all proportion of complaints about "amateurism" must in fact be quite gratifying to Channel 2 personnel in view of the fact that student technicians and unpaid performers are widely utilized. On the other hand, it is those who watch Channel 2 most frequently (Table 3.2)

TABLE 3.2. EXPLANATION FOR LACK OF POPULARITY OF ETV RELATIVE TO FREQUENCY OF WATCHING CHANNEL 2

Reason for Lack of Popularity	Frequency of Watching Channel 2 [a]		
	Regularly	Occasionally	Never
People want recreation	20%	34%	33%
Requires too much intellect	10	6	8
Too deep, "high-brow"	5	5	8
For children	10	6	7
Inconvenient program hours	10	8	9
People are lazy	10	7	4
People do not know about it	5	6	5
Poor reception	0	6	4
Amateurism	15	7	1
Other	15	15	20
Percentage totals	100	100	99
Total reasons [b]	(20)	(144)	(317)
Total respondents	(16)	(127)	(340)

[a] The question was: "What has been your own experience with Channel 2—do you watch it regularly, occasionally, or never?"
[b] Percentage base.

who are most likely to be critical of amateur technique in presenting programs, so perhaps this criticism deserves more attention than the figure of 3 per cent would suggest.

The next section is oriented to the question: Who watches ETV more, and who watches it less? First, however, let us emphasize most strongly that the discussion just finished in this section is a one-sided one, and is not meant in any sense to constitute an impartial evaluation of the merits and demerits of ETV. It has rather constituted a deliberate attempt to mobilize the critical resources of our sample, and to spell out the sources in contemporary urban social structure of antagonism to both the idea of ETV and its concrete embodiment in the form WGBH-Channel 2 in Boston. No attempt was made to elicit praise for the idea of ETV in general or for the Boston ETV station in particular. Indeed, we have even neglected thus far to mention that a number of respondents took issue with the loaded nature of our question and said that "most people do watch ETV." Moreover, if we had included in our interview a question such as "What, in your opinion, are the main faults of [commercial] television programs?" it is quite likely that the complaint "You don't learn anything from it" would be not infrequently heard.

THE VIEWER OF ETV

In this section of our report the reader will find a tentative portrait of the educational television viewer in the Greater Boston area. We used the following question to distinguish such a person from the individuals who do not watch educational television: "What has been your own experience with Channel 2? Do you watch it regularly, occasionally, or never?" In response, 3 per cent of the sample characterized themselves as regular watchers, 26 per cent as watching occasionally, and 67 per cent indicated that they never watched Channel 2.[5] Since this question was preceded by two others dealing with Channel 2 or with ETV in general, the responses represented by these proportions are probably fairly valid for our sample. But our sample is not representative of the Greater Boston population; well-to-do respondents, for instance, are considerably overrepresented. Since, as we shall see below, they are most likely to watch Channel 2, the figure of 3 per cent, the proportion of regular viewers, and probably also the 26 per cent figure, should be taken as an upper limit for the area as of the time the interviewing was completed.

To facilitate comparison of the ETV enthusiast with the general TV fan as depicted in our second memorandum [6] we have used the same categories: sex, age, education, etc., to describe the ETV

----

[5] Two per cent gave no usable reply to the question, and an additional 2 per cent indicated only that they were unable to get Channel 2 on their TV sets.

[6] See pp. 3–13, especially Table 2.6, in Geiger and Sokol, *Report,* Memorandum #2, "The Normative Significance of Television Viewing."

fan [7] that we used earlier to describe the general TV fan. In Table 3.3 are presented the proportion from each category who were "regular" or "occasional" viewers of WGBH-Channel 2 at the time of interviewing, March-June, 1956.

TABLE 3.3. PROPORTION OF ETV FANS AMONG DIFFERENT CATEGORIES OF RESPONDENTS [a]

Sex			Age		
Men	34%	(223)	21–40	33%	(221)
Women	27	(251)	41–60	30	(159)
			60 and older	27	(89)
Education			Monthly Rental		
13 years and more	51	(122)	$110 and more	48	(92)
12 years	23	(163)	$70–109	25	(132)
0–11 years	21	(183)	$50–69	24	(116)
			$49 and less	25	(76)
Occupational Level of Head of Family			Socioeconomic Level [b]		
Prof. and business	46	(85)	High	50	(116)
Semi-prof. and white collar	36	(93)	Middle	24	(214)
Skilled worker	22	(78)	Low	21	(116)
Semi- and unskilled worker	20	(125)			

[a] Respondents were considered "fans" if they chose the responses "regularly" or "occasionally" rather than "never" in answer to the question: "What has been your own experience with Channel 2—do you watch it regularly, occasionally, or never?"

[b] Index composed of monthly rental and occupational level of head of family. See Geiger and Sokol, Report, Memorandum #4, "Research Procedures and Analysis Problems," for a more complete description.

The most singular fact about the table is clearly the significantly greater attraction of Channel 2 for respondents with more educational background, higher monthly rental, and so on, rather than for respondents with the contrary characteristics. In striking contrast to the patterns shown in Table 2.6, ETV viewing is directly, instead of inversely, related to social class level. It is perhaps equally interesting to note that, although the differences by sex are quite small, again the direction is in contrast to the pattern for general television; men apparently watch ETV more than women do. On the other hand, in regard to differences according to age, the pattern is similar to that for general TV; the younger persons are some-

[7] We will use the term "fan" or "enthusiast" to aid the exposition, and ask the reader to remember that it refers to the respondents who watch Channel 2 regularly or occasionally.

what more likely to report themselves as watching Channel 2 than are the older respondents. In general, though, the rather symmetrical contrast of the patterns of relationship of sex and social class to educational TV viewing as opposed to general TV viewing serves roughly to locate the ETV enthusiast in the urban social structure. Indeed, the most "typical" ETV fan in the Boston sample seems to be an upper-class male, but as we saw in Memorandum #2, the upper-class male is least likely to be a general television enthusiast.

Let us, therefore, formulate the following hypothesis: Watching educational television programs constitutes an activity which coincides more closely with male sex role expectations than with female, and more closely with higher social class level role expectations than with lower-class role expectations. Apparently the ingression into the television-watching situation of the idea of "education" carries the implication of active, goal-directed behavior, and actually reverses the pattern of normative expectations found to characterize general TV viewing.

A partial and admittedly inadequate test of this idea can be provided with the data we collected in our follow-up interviews. Eighteen respondents, who had already been interviewed once during the preceding spring, were reinterviewed. One of the questions asked was: "Which of the following groups would you say most enjoys watching Channel 2, that is, educational TV?" The respondent was then handed a card on which appeared a list of different social groups similar to that which had been presented to him in the earlier interview.[8] The results are presented in Table 3.4. For convenience, the results from the earlier interview (for the entire sample) are presented in parentheses alongside the new pattern.

The sample size here is only 18, so from this point of view, too, the results can only be seen as suggestive. But the reversal is a decisive one. Even in respect to the factor of age the 18 respondents felt that ETV received the attention of the more active and productive "young adults" and "middle-aged persons" to a significantly greater extent than the sample as a whole felt their attention was drawn to general television. Indeed, the extent of this shift is quite interesting. The label "educational" apparently has a sufficiently

----

[8] Responses to this earlier question on the respondents' opinions about the location of enthusiasm for general TV viewing are discussed at length in Geiger and Sokol, *Report,* Memorandum #1.

serious ring about it to suggest that the children definitely would *not* be interested in watching. Evidently ETV, at least in its home viewing variety, is clearly pictured as involving adult education. This impression is also given by the kinds of programs our respondents were most likely to associate with Channel 2. These results will be discussed below.

TABLE 3.4. RESPONDENTS' CONCEPTIONS OF THE SOCIAL CHARACTERISTICS OF ENTHUSIASTIC ETV VIEWERS [a] (N = 18)

Sex			Financial Status		
Men	44%	(18) [b]	People very well off econom-		
Women	22	(57)	ically	17%	(1)
Don't know	33	(25)	People in comfortable circum-		
Percentage total	99		stances	28	(25)
			People who can just barely afford to buy a TV set	11	(48)
			Don't know	44	(25)
			Percentage total	100	
Age			Education		
Older persons	17%	(17)	College-educated people	33%	(6)
Middle-aged persons	39	(12)	High school–educated people	17	(25)
Young adults	17	(3)	Grade school–educated people	11	(29)
Teenagers	6	(8)	Don't know	39	(40)
Children	0	(53)	*Percentage total*	100	
Don't know	22				
Percentage total	101				

[a] The question read as follows: "Which of the following groups would you say most enjoys watching Channel 2, that is, educational TV?"
[b] The figures inside the parentheses are from Table 1.3, p. 10, in Geiger and Sokol, *Report,* Memorandum #1, and refer to the public image of the *general* TV fan.

THE MEANING OF ETV TO ITS VIEWERS

The meaning of WGBH-TV to the Greater Boston population as a whole is influenced by a number of considerations. Among them three seem to stand out. In the first place, it is clear that the reactions of the respondents in the sample to Channel 2 are closely linked to the idea that it is an "educational" channel. The notion, and the embodiment in the form of a concrete station, of "educational television" is in turn influenced by the experiences, emotions, and images engendered by formal education itself. An exploration of the assets and liabilities of ETV in Boston should therefore be prefaced by a few comments about the place of education in American life in general and in the Greater Boston area in particular.

While education is a positive symbol in American culture, the actual practice of education in the formally organized system of educational institutions means different things of different people. To some it implies invigorating challenges and welcome new experiences; to some it implies frustration or boredom which is scarcely endurable; to still others the idea and experience of education may be closely connected with status striving and social mobility. These things are true of education in America. Education in the Boston area may bring another association—an association between higher education and invidious social class differences. Resistance to educational TV may therefore come to constitute another, perhaps quite subtle, version of the clashing between town and gown.

Second, it is quite obvious that the image and expectations of ETV are governed to an important extent by the actual programs sent out by the local station. Educational television is, after all, in large part "local television," both in the sense that a large proportion of the programs originate in the local area, and in the sense that the programs must be tailored to the cultural level and needs of the local population. It is doubtful, for example, if the directors of WGBH-TV would be interested in sponsoring a program on cattle raising, or irrigation techniques, or even on how to teach illiterates to read and write. This fact stimulates immediately the thought that the characteristics of the "typical ETV viewer" in a particular area are in a significant degree a function of the specific program content of the local station, rather than the label "educational television." Symbols, we must remember, are remarkably flexible; the word "educational" can be used to refer to many different types and levels of programs. Hence, to understand the meaning of differences in social characteristics between viewers and nonviewers, a systematic content analysis of the programs broadcast in a given ETV area is quite important. We have done this for the telecasts of WGBH-TV (Channel 2) during the period March-June, 1956.

Finally, we would like to bring up again the idea suggested by the results presented in the first section of this memorandum. We discussed there the possibility of an inherent contradiction between

TV viewing for educational purposes and TV viewing for recreational purposes.

Let us return to further inspection of our survey data. We can use them to develop further some thoughts discussed in the preceding paragraphs.

To many people an admirable characteristic of ETV is its "worthwhileness." That is, the viewer is expected, in rather strong contrast to commercial TV, to get "something of permanent value" out of his viewing time. This may be designated as information, self-improvement, or, as most frequently happens, simply "education." When one brings to mind the close association in America between education and social mobility, it does not appear unlikely that the feeling that it is worthwhile to watch ETV is closely linked to the pattern of striving for personal success. We might propose, then, that the more success-oriented or ambitious person is more likely to watch ETV than the person who is less ambitious. In the hope that he will benefit in the future, he takes a basically utilitarian view toward television watching, using it as a kind of investment to further his aspirations for personal success and higher social status.

We think there is an item in our interview schedule which may serve to differentiate such persons. It is: "We are not going to ask you how much your income is in this survey, but we would like to know what you would like your income to be in the future to feel satisfied—about the same you have now, a little more, or a lot more?" [9] Clearly there are many other ways in which ambition can be directed. But the indication of a strong desire for more income is likely to include about as large a proportion of such individuals as can be hoped for with the use of a single question.

Results of the test of this hypothesis are presented in Table 3.5. The number of cases in some of the subgroups is quite small, but the pattern of responses is definite enough and the differences large enough to merit some comment. Among higher-status respondents our hypothesis seems to be corroborated: ambition does tend to be associated with a greater tendency to watch Channel 2. But in the middle-status level there is no relationship to be found, and

----

[9] We are indebted to Dr. Eleanor E. Maccoby for suggesting this question to us.

in the lower level it is the unambitious, satisfied person who is more likely to watch Channel 2. Possibly there is something about ETV which arms the upper-class individual in his struggle to get ahead, but which leaves the ambitious lower-class person cold. To see and report upon a demonstrated talk on science by an M.I.T. professor, or to take French lessons, may bring prestige in higher-class circles, but go unrewarded or even be seen as deviant behavior by the associates of lower-class persons.

TABLE 3.5. INCOME ASPIRATIONS IN RELATION TO WATCHING WGBH-CHANNEL 2 FOR DIFFERENT SOCIOECONOMIC LEVELS

| Socioeconomic Level | Proportion of ETV Fans Among Respondents Who | | |
	Are Satisfied	Want a Little More	Want a Lot More
Higher	39% (33)	49% (43)	57% (35)
Middle	26 (35)	20 (107)	30 (71)
Lower	35 (17)	19 (69)	18 (28)

Consider now the rather self-evident point mentioned above—that the question of who watches ETV in a given area is a function of the kinds of programs available on the local ETV station. We have seen in an earlier section of this memorandum that the ETV fan in the Greater Boston area tends to demonstrate characteristics which distinguish him from the general TV fan. He is more educated, of higher social status, and more likely to be a male.

How can we set about explaining this fact in terms of the program content of WGBH-Channel 2? A moment's glance at the Channel 2 program schedule suffices to convince us that this is TV fare of a relatively high-level, intellectual nature. Not only are there no westerns, mysteries, or comedy and variety shows, but sports programs, quiz shows, and even dramatic productions are missing. It does not surprise us, then, to see that Channel 2 has educated (and ambitious?) followers; it is perhaps more surprising that so many individuals with little formal education also indicate that they watch it. In Table 3.6 we have a precise breakdown of the amount of time devoted to different program types by WGBH-TV in the March-June, 1956, period,[10] which corresponds to the time span in which our interview data were collected.

----

[10] We are indebted to Miss Sheila Baker for this analysis.

TABLE 3.6. PROPORTION OF TIME DEVOTED TO DIFFERENT TYPES
OF PROGRAMS ON WGBH-CHANNEL 2

Type of Program	March	April	May	June	March-June
Child care	6%	0%	2%	5%	3%
News	7	7	8	8	8
Language lessons	8	9	8	0	6
Children's songs, stories	19	19	15	8	15
Music, opera, art	16	22	23	25	21
Medical and scientific	19	18	19	11	17
Panel discussions, forums	14	12	10	14	13
Other	10	13	16	29 [a]	17
Percentage totals	99	100	101	100	100
Total program hours	(83.75)	(74.50)	(91.00)	(78.50)	(327.75)

[a] Due primarily to an increased number of ETRC films and lectures by academic persons.

How does this breakdown of the amount of time given to different programs by Channel 2 compare with the actual desires of
the people who watch it? We can get a rough estimate by comparing the program preferences of the most dedicated ETV viewers with the preferences of the respondents who watch television
primarily for recreational reasons. To do this we first divided the
respondents into the TV fans and those less enthusiastic about
general television viewing. We then subdivided each of these two
groups into two more groups, those who watch Channel 2 "regularly" or "occasionally" and those who "never" watch Channel
2. This procedure eventuated in four groups of respondents, as
shown in Table 3.7. Cells *b* and *c* were subsequently combined
to form a middle category which bridges the respondents who quite

TABLE 3.7. ENTHUSIASM FOR GENERAL TV VIEWING IN RELATION TO
ENTHUSIASM FOR ETV

TV Attitude	ETV Abstainers	ETV Fans [a]	Totals
TV fans [b]	177 (*a*)	70 (*b*)	247
Less enthusiastic TV viewers	152 (*c*)	73 (*d*)	225
Totals	329	143	472

[a] Respondents who watch Channel 2 "regularly" or "occasionally" rather than "never."
[b] As measured by the scale described in Geiger and Sokol, *Report*, Memorandum #2, p.
12, and in more detail in Memorandum #4, pp. 9–10.

definitely favor general TV and do not watch ETV at all (cell a) on the one side, and the respondents who are less enthusiastic about general TV and who watch Channel 2 regularly or occasionally (cell d) on the other side.

The differences in program preferences among these three groups appear in Table 3.8, where we have computed the percentage of times each of ten different TV program types was chosen as favorite by each group. The order of preference in the sample as a whole for different types of TV programs is of some interest in itself, but

TABLE 3.8. MODE OF UTILIZATION OF TV IN RELATION
TO PROGRAM PREFERENCES

| Preferred Programs | Mode of Utilization of TV | | |
	Emphasis on General TV	Uses Educational and General TV Equally	Emphasis on Educational TV
Comedy and variety programs	59%	54%	52%
Complete dramas	36	38	51
Mystery and crime dramas	46	32	22
Quiz programs	36	36	33
News	23	31	36
Sports programs	27	27	31
Westerns	28	23	16
Talks or discussions about public issues	10	21	34
Religious programs	21	21	4
Daytime serial programs	8	6	7
Percentage totals	294 [a]	289 [a]	286 [a]
Total respondents	(177)	(222)	(73)

[a] Each respondent was asked to make three choices, which accounts for the high percentage totals.

is similar to that previously found in a number of other studies of TV and radio program preferences, and hence does not constitute information of any particular novelty. As to our own interest, though, the differences in program preference for the viewers with different orientations toward the use of television are quite revealing. One of the most striking differences is the strong preference of the general TV fans for mystery and crime programs, and the relative lack of interest in such programs of the ETV-oriented respondents. Another involves the strong interest of the ETV viewer

in talks and discussions about public issues, and the lack of interest of the general TV fan in such programs. The pattern of differences in preference for western programs and news programs is
smaller, but similar in direction. It is again evident from the structure of choices in regard to these four types of programs that the
general TV enthusiast wants entertainment from his set, and is
likely to give short shrift to the more educational or informative
type of program. However, the reverse is apparently not true; ETV
viewers as a group are not uninterested in entertainment. This is
clear from the high proportion of ETV viewers who like comedy
and variety programs, sports programs, and complete dramas. But
they are significantly less interested in that kind of entertainment
offered by mystery and crime dramas and by westerns.

TABLE 3.9. FREQUENCY WITH WHICH DIFFERENT TYPES OF PROGRAMS
ARE ASSOCIATED WITH WGBH-CHANNEL 2

Type of Program	Frequency
Child care	7%
News	7
Language lessons	21
Children's songs, stories	6
Music, opera, art	14
Medical and scientific	14
Panel discussions, forums	9
Other	22
Percentage total	100
Total references	(214) [a]

[a] Given by a total of 122 respondents.

What more can be said about the relationship between the offer-
ings of Channel 2 and the tastes and expectations of our Boston
sample? Unfortunately, not much; we have no information as to
preferences among the different types of programs telecast by
WGBH-TV. But we do have some data showing the kinds of programs that our respondents associate with WGBH. This was obtained by use of the following sequence of questions: "Do you
know what kind of program Channel 2 has here in the Boston
area?" And, if the respondent indicated he did know something
about this, he was asked: "Will you name a few, please?" In response to the first part of the question, 49 per cent of the 490

set-owning respondents indicated that they knew what kinds of programs were on Channel 2. Of these 238 respondents, 29 per cent were unable to come forth with any additional response; 19 per cent replied "educational" but could mention no specific programs; and 122 respondents, 51 per cent of those who said they knew what kinds of programs appear on Channel 2, gave a total of 214 references to specific programs. These references have been broken down into categories comparable to the code categories used in our content analysis of the WGBH-TV programs during the March-June, 1956, period (Table 3.6). They appear in Table 3.9. The frequency with which the respondents refer to language lessons ("French Through Television") is important, particularly when we compare this frequency with the actual proportion of time taken up by the program, which is not great. This comparison was done through a measure of salience, by which we mean the ratios of the proportions in Table 3.9 to those in Table 3.6. These

TABLE 3.10. SALIENCE OF DIFFERENT TYPES OF PROGRAMS ON WGBH-CHANNEL 2

Type of Program	Salience [a]
Child care	2.0 [b]
News	1.0
Language lessons	3.4
Children's songs, stories	.4
Music, opera, art	.7
Medical and scientific	.9
Panel discussions, forums	.7

[a] "Salience" was computed from the data sources for Tables 3.6 and 3.9. It refers to the ratio of the relative frequency with which the different types of programs were mentioned by the respondents in the sample to the relative amount of time spent by WGBH-TV on each type of program in the March-June, 1956, period.
[b] The figures are computed on the base of the "mention" and "time unit" totals for all specific program types excluding the "other" category.

ratios appear in Table 3.10. Their meaning is as follows: the higher the figure in Table 3.10, the more likely were the respondents to associate the corresponding type of program with WGBH-Channel 2 to an extent greater than that warranted by the actual proportion of the total broadcast time occupied by that program type. Conversely, the lower the figure, the less was the time directed to that type of program likely to be reflected in the respondents' associations between Channel 2 and its specific content.

Quite interestingly, it is the most purely "educational" of all the programs broadcast, "French Through Television," which seems to be most readily associated with Channel 2, not only in terms of being mentioned more than other types of programs (Table 3.9), but also in terms of the measure just discussed. When this fact is placed side by side with the fact that child-care programs are also markedly salient, it is apparent that Channel 2 has come to be associated in public thinking with the kinds of programs *least* likely to be found on commercial television. Here, then, is the public's view of WGBH-Channel 2; it is visualized as a station dealing with learning in much the same sense as that associated with the system of formal education—as a long-term process providing permanent benefit. Table 3.10 also reveals that while WGBH-TV is readily identified as an educational station, it does not seem to be commonly pictured as a "children's station," for the salience of children's programs is the lowest of all the program types.

The final portion of this memorandum of educational television in the Greater Boston area deals with the most controversial of our ideas. In the first section our attention was focused on the nature of the popular resistance to ETV. The idea was presented that such resistance hinges in part upon the contradiction or incompatibility which results when the attempt is made to combine in the same medium two culturally valued goals, recreation and education. This, however, is precisely what ETV tries to do. Watching TV in the home is obviously defined by most people as "entertainment." Yet education is "serious business." In the long run the fortunes of ETV in themselves will constitute a test of the hypothesized incompatibility; if ETV as presently constituted becomes increasingly popular with an ever greater proportion of the set-owning population, the incompatibility hypothesis must be rejected. This assumes that ETV will retain a substantial "educational" component. Such an eventuality would imply that the chief reason for ETV's relatively small audience at the present time lies in its novelty.

On the other hand, if the hypothesis of incompatibility is true, then there seem to be two distinct possibilities for the future. The total ETV audience will continue to be highly specialized and will not become significantly larger than it is now. Most set owners, if faced with the choice, will choose to be entertained rather than educated, for reasons already discussed. The second possibility lies in the direction of "popularizing" ETV by omitting or diluting educational programs and adding entertainment programs or "devices." If this is done, the audience will doubtless grow in size, but this will occur at the expense of educational quality, and thus would also shift the patronage of some of the present audience, seriously interested in gaining knowledge from TV, over to media sources other than television.

An examination of the policies of WGBH-Channel 2 as these are reflected in program content shows quite clearly that such a popularization or dilution has not taken place as of the present time in Boston. This suggests that ETV in Boston occurs in a relatively pure form, so to speak, and thus affords, in terms of the behavior of the Boston TV audience, a most appropriate context in which to test our incompatibility hypothesis.

The notion of incompatibility of recreation and education in the sense in which we have used it does not involve the idea that during their free hours some people are in general interested only or mostly in recreation, and other people only or mostly in education. This of course is true. But our hypothesis lies beyond; it involves the assumption that most people are interested in both, but seek to satisfy these interests with the use of different media or activities rather than through the same medium or activity.

We propose the following test. We predict a negative association between the use of TV for recreation and the use of it for education *among viewers in which the relative weights of the general desire for recreation and the general desire for education are equivalent.* To carry out a test of this notion we must first confront and solve two difficult measurement problems. First, how to "hold constant," in the terminology of survey analysis, the tendency for the ratio of "interest in recreation" to "interest in education" to vary from person to person. A second difficulty has to do with the task of devising a sufficiently pure measure of "the use of TV for recreation" and "the use of TV for education."

As the reader will readily appreciate, the first of these problems presents in general a very difficult obstacle. In particular, we have in our sample data no direct and independent measures of the strength in each respondent of the desire to be entertained relative to the desire to become better educated or informed. If we did have such information, we could then introduce some degree of control over this variable, and proceed to deal with the second problem. As will be seen below, we can offer at this time only an unsatisfactory substitute, in the form of the respondent's estimated amount of spare time per day. As to the second problem listed above, how to develop a measure of the use of TV for "recreational" as opposed to "educational" purposes, we are perhaps a little better off, but still not on very firm ground. We have used a scale of enthusiasm for TV watching [11] as a measure of the strength of the use of television for recreational purposes, and we have used our ETV fan index, described elsewhere in this memorandum,

TABLE 3.11. ENTHUSIASM FOR GENERAL TV IN RELATION TO ENTHUSIASM FOR ETV FOR RESPONDENTS WITH DIFFERING AMOUNTS OF SPARE TIME

TV Attitude	Spare Hours per Day		
	Less than 2		
	ETV Abstainers	ETV Fans	Totals
TV fans	25 [a]	5	30
Less enthusiastic	38	19	57
Totals	63	24	87
	2 to 5.9		
	ETV Abstainers	ETV Fans	Totals
TV fans	109 [a]	41	150
Less enthusiastic	92	42	134
Totals	201	83	284
	6 and more		
	ETV Abstainers	ETV Fans	Totals
TV fans	40 [a]	20	60
Less enthusiastic	17	7	24
Totals	57	27	84

[a] Estimated tetrachoric coefficients of correlation, based upon Pearson's "cosine method" and uncorrected for nonmedian dichotomization, are $-.29$, $-.08$, and $+.06$, reading from top to bottom. These were computed in accordance with the procedure described in A. L. Edwards, *Statistical Methods for the Behavioral Sciences,* New York: Rinehart, 1954, pp. 190–93, 510. None of the associations is significant at the .05 level.

as a measure of the use of television for educational purposes. Obviously, neither of these are very pure measures of the theoretical variables. In addition, we have used the respondents' program preferences as indexes, taking the choice of "talks or discussions about public affairs" as an indication of the use of television for educational purposes, and the choice of "comedy and variety programs" as a measure of its use for recreational purposes.

----

[11] See Geiger and Sokol, *Report,* Memorandum #2, p. 12, and Memorandum #4, pp. 9–10.

We ask the reader's indulgence for the inadequacy of these indexes, particularly that of each respondent's "recreation-education balance," and hope that this problem of such vital interest to educational television will receive further refinement and a more thorough test in the future.

In Table 3.11, 2 x 2 tables show the relationship between the use of television for recreation (i.e., the TV fans) and its use for education (i.e., the ETV fans) for respondents with three different quantities of spare time per day. As stated above, the amount of spare time is taken as a measure of the strength of the general desire for recreation in relation to desire for education—the more spare time, the greater the relative desire for recreation, the less spare time, the greater the relative desire for education. This is based on the assumption that a strong desire for education is an important consumer of the individual's extra hours, but that he does not tend to consider these hours as "spare time." A strong desire for recreation, on the other hand, takes up hours which, we assume, are quite likely to be defined as spare-time hours.

The tables indicate that the hypothesis of incompatibility is not substantiated. Significant negative associations do not appear. Some TV fans are also ETV fans, and substantial numbers of these who are less interested in TV watching as a recreational pattern are also relatively uninterested in ETV.

It is, however, interesting to note that the extent to which the incompatibility hypothesis is verified is apparently a function of the strength of the respondent's desire for education relative to the strength of his desire for recreation. The more prominent his general devotion to education at the expense of recreation, the more does the hypothesis of incompatibility find support.

We now offer another test of the hypothesis, using the same theoretical argument, but with program preferences instead of general viewing habits as indexes of the use of TV for (1) recreation and (2) education. The results of this test may be inspected in Table 3.12. In none of the three groups is there a substantial negative association between orientation toward comedy and variety programs [12] as compared with orientation toward talks and dis-

----

[12] This seemed the most appropriate program choice with which to work because of its relatively "pure" entertainment value, and also because the choices for this type of program are uncorrelated or only weakly correlated with social characteristics and with orientation toward the use of television (see Table 3.8).

TABLE 3.12. PREFERENCE FOR COMEDY AND VARIETY PROGRAMS IN RELATION TO PREFERENCE FOR TALKS AND DISCUSSIONS ABOUT PUBLIC ISSUES FOR RESPONDENTS WITH DIFFERING AMOUNTS OF SPARE TIME

Attitude Toward Comedy and Variety	Spare Hours per Day		
	Less than 2 [a]		
	Do not Like Talks and Discussions	Like Talks and Discussions [a]	Totals
Like comedy and variety	37 [b]	8	45
Do not like comedy and variety	30	14	44
Totals	67	22	89
	2 to 5.9		
	Do not Like Talks and Discussions	Like Talks and Discussions [a]	Totals
Like comedy and variety	71 [b]	95	166
Do not like comedy and variety	41	90	131
Totals	112	185	297
	6 and More		
	Do not Like Talks and Discussions	Like Talks and Discussions [a]	Totals
Like comedy and variety	21 [b]	29	50
Do not like comedy and variety	12	24	36
Totals	33	53	86

[a] The group with less than two hours of spare time per day was dichotomized differently from the other two groups on the variable, orientation toward talks and discussions about public issues, in order to get a closer approximation (still not very close) to the theoretical median of the distribution. This dichotomization was done by considering not only program preferences, but also program "dislikes," thus making it possible to assign each respondent a score of 3 (R likes a particular program), 2 (R indicates neither like nor dislike), and 1 (R dislikes the program) for each of the ten indicated program types. A cut similar to those made for the other two groups would give: 12   33
3   41.

[b] Uncorrected estimates of tetrachoric r are —.29, —.19, and —.15, reading from top to bottom.

cussions about public affairs. Thus, the hypothesis of a contradiction between recreational television and educational television is again not supported. However, it is again supported most strongly in the group with the least amount of spare time per day.

We will conclude this section of our report by again reminding the reader that the empirical measures with which we have been working are in need of refinement; we would prefer that these last few pages be seen as heuristic. But we do feel strongly that the idea we have tried to bring out is a most important one, and that it deserves careful consideration by those concerned with educational television. It is certainly on the basis of this kind of information that intelligent policy decisions can be made in the realm of program content. Let us assume, for example, that with the use of better measurement techniques the small inverse relationships shown in Tables 3.11 and 3.12 could be demonstrated in more convincing fashion. What would this mean to ETV? In the first place, it would imply that since people watch TV either for recreation or for education, *but not for both reasons,* that those who do watch ETV will expect *educational* programs from ETV and not a mixture of both education and entertainment. If the individual chooses to use his TV set for entertainment, he goes elsewhere, to lectures, to books and other printed media, etc., for his educational experience. Conversely, if he chooses to use his set for educational purposes, he wants a "strong dose" of education, and he tends to seek elsewhere for his recreation.[13] This clearly would suggest that ETV does not, and cannot, compete with commercial television for the same audience.

The second mode of relationship shown in these last two tables indicates that the more tipped the individual's "recreation-education" balance is toward the educational pole, the greater will be his tendency to use TV for specialized purposes, that is, for either one or the other of the two main desires television can satisfy. In other words, some of those individuals who are quite devoted to the idea of becoming more educated will nevertheless use television purely for recreation and probably not watch the typical ETV program, while others who feel equally strongly about education will watch the ETV programs but not the entertainment-oriented com-

----

[13] If this formulation of the situation were correct, a number of interesting research problems would come to mind. For one, what are the crucial differences between those individuals who watch television to learn from it, and those (with an identical general orientation toward education relative to recreation) who watch television only for recreation? Similarly, if it is true that the ETV fan tends to use his TV set only for educational pursuits, where and how does he find his recreation? An initial guess (which of course is based on a relationship which may not exist in fact) is that persons of limited educational background but considerable financial resources use TV for educational viewing, and that persons with extensive educational training and small financial resources watch TV for rather more purely "recreational" purposes.

mercially sponsored programs. Another way of putting this is to say that the stronger an individual's desire for education and information is, the more he will tend to treat his home television set as a functionally specific medium.

This implies in turn that those persons who are most devoted to the idea of becoming educated or informed will watch television only if they can see exactly what they want. Conversely, those least interested in education and information are definitely less selective in their television behavior and seem to be willing to watch programs of the most divergent kind. Therefore, if an educational television station wants to attract the former kind of audience it will need to produce highly "educational" programs, whereas if it wants to reach the second kind, the limitations on eligible types of programs are much less narrow.

During the first six months of an educational station's operation in Minneapolis–St. Paul, educational television lost some of its rosy glow. Attitudes toward it were still predominantly favorable, but far more realistic about what kinds of programs it would carry and the process of learning from it. This is a report of interviews made with the same individuals six months before and six months after the station went on the air. The author is a member of the faculty of the School of Journalism at the University of Minnesota. The facilities of that school's Research Division were used in the study.

EDUCATIONAL TELEVISION COMES TO MINNEAPOLIS – ST. PAUL

by William A. Mindak

This report presents some of the results of an extensive study of how residents of a midwestern metropolitan center reacted to the introduction of a new educational television station (KTCA-TV) in their community. This study is unique in that it was the first to measure reactions of the *same* panel of respondents both prior to and after an ETV station went on the air.

The data reported were collected from a probability sample of the residents in Minneapolis–St. Paul and suburbs. Individual households were chosen by multistage probability methods and one respondent from each household was interviewed. A stratification control was placed on sex of respondents.

A total of 448 respondents was interviewed on the first wave of the study in April, 1957, approximately six months before KTCA-TV went on the air. The questionnaire used in that wave followed these areas of inquiry: (1) Respondents' media use, both print and broadcast; program preferences on commercial television. (2) Respondents' information about educational television in general and KTCA-TV in particular. (3) Respondents' attitudes toward educational television and their conception of what KTCA-TV would likely be. (4) Respondents' expectations regarding KTCA-TV's programing and their intentions to make use of ETV. (5) Respondents' personal and social characteristics.

Of the original 448 respondents a total of 368 (or 82 per cent) "survived" the second wave of interviews in late March and April, 1958, about six months after the station began a full schedule.

Most of the panel's second-wave mortality was caused by people moving out of the city or state. There were no differences in personal or social characteristics of respondents in either wave except that the second wave tended to be a bit older on the average than the first. This was felt to be a function of younger group mobility.

The second-wave questionnaire had the following main divisions: (1) Repeat of wave 1 questions on media use, both print and broadcast; attitudes toward ETV in general and KTCA-TV in particular; information questions about KTCA-TV. (2) Respondents' total and general viewing of KTCA-TV; specific program viewing during presurvey week of March 24–28, 1958 (via Roster Recall technique). (3) Respondents' opinions about KTCA-TV and suggestions for changes in programing, hours of operation, etc. (4) Effect of KTCA-TV viewing on other media use; KTCA-TV as a topic in interpersonal discussion; extent of television course registration; mechanical reception of KTCA-TV; preferences regarding program listings in newspapers; how respondents chose programs for viewing; opinions on, and preferences for, University of Minnesota and private college programs.

Additional efforts were made to find out why certain television set owners had remained *nonviewers* even after the station had been broadcasting for six months.

It is, of course, impossible to present all the questionnaire data in the space here available. Therefore, let us concentrate on answering the following questions: (1) What was the audience for KTCA-TV after six months of operation? (2) How did viewers differ from nonviewers? (3) What effect did information about the station have on viewing? (4) What did residents think about KTCA-TV (before and after operation)? (5) What did viewers think about KTCA-TV's program content and range? (6) What did viewers like or dislike about KTCA-TV?

WHAT WAS THE AUDIENCE FOR KTCA-TV?

All 368 second-wave respondents were questioned as to when they had last viewed KTCA-TV and were classified into regular, occasional, and nonviewers according to Table 1.

A further look at the viewing classification shows that nearly a fourth (23 per cent) of the KTCA-TV viewers watch *less* than once a month while only 4 per cent watch five or more programs per week. Using the entire Minneapolis–St. Paul metropolitan area as a base, it can be said that about one-third (35 per cent) of area residents view at least one program a week on KTCA-TV.

TABLE 1

Total Sample: 368	Number	Percentage
Have viewed KTCA-TV within the last six months	216	58.7%
Regular viewers (at least two programs per week)	(91)	(24.7)
Occasional viewers (less often than twice a week)	(125)	(34.0)
Have never viewed KTCA-TV	140	38.0
Do not own television sets	12	3.3
Totals	368	100.0

The pattern of KTCA-TV viewing seems clear. It is highly selective and its appeal to viewers is strictly on a program-to-program basis. There are no favorite nights. The characteristic of commercial television viewing, leaving the dial set for blocks of programs or consecutive programs, was nonexistent when it came to KTCA-TV viewing. For the most part viewing of KTCA-TV had very little effect on use of other media.

HOW DID VIEWERS DIFFER FROM NONVIEWERS?

There were no significant differences between regular and non-viewers of KTCA-TV by (1) sex, age, income, occupation of bread-winner, size of family, length of residence in the Twin Cities; (2) number of club memberships, hobbies pursued, social and business organization memberships; (3) viewing commercial television, listening to radio, reading newspapers, going to movies; total daily or weekly hours spent with mass media. There *were* significant differences between regular KTCA-TV viewers and nonviewers with regard to (1) *education*—regular viewers had significantly more schooling than nonviewers; (2) *magazine and book reading* —regular viewers spent significantly more time with these "media" than did nonviewers; (3) *"cultural"* orientation—regular viewers had attended cultural activities such as talks and lectures, concerts and operas and plays more frequently than had nonviewers. They were also more likely to verbalize preferences for more "cultural" types of television programs, such as "Omnibus," "Voice of Fire-stone," etc.

WHAT EFFECT DID INFORMATION ABOUT KTCA-TV HAVE ON VIEWING?

As might be expected, awareness of the station before it began broadcasting did have a definite relationship to viewing habits. Of those who were to become regular viewers 44 per cent had heard of the station at the time of the first-wave interview, while only 26 per cent of the nonviewers had heard of the station.

However, the level of *correct* information about such factors as the station's financial support, its relationship to the University of Minnesota, need for special equipment to receive the station's signal, had little pronounced effect on regularity of viewing.

There was a substantial increase in informational levels among the panel members between the two measures, as Table 2 indicates.

TABLE 2

Average Number of Correct Responses on Information Items	Totals	Regular Viewers	Occasional Viewers	Non-viewers
Prebroadcast	4.0	4.3	3.9	3.8
Postbroadcast	5.5	5.9	5.6	4.8

All three groups knew more about KTCA-TV after six months of broadcasting, although even regular viewers exhibited some confusion about how the station was to be supported (contributions from individuals and organizations), the extent of "competitive media" support (local newspapers and broadcast stations had contributed to KTCA-TV), and the role of the University of Minnesota in KTCA-TV's operation. As a point of fact the University produces its own programs and feeds them to KTCA-TV, whose studio is located on the University's St. Paul campus, but beyond this it has no control or influence over KTCA-TV's operations. To the extent that the University of Minnesota is looked on favorably by the respondents this confusion could be helpful to KTCA-TV. To the extent that the University connotes high-level, "egghead," lecture-classroom programs, such a confusion could be detrimental, particularly to the nonviewer who has not looked in at the program fare.

Practical applications of the "awareness" data seem obvious and pretty much common sense. A new educational TV station should try to make people aware that it is going on the air even though a high level of correct specific information is not necessarily related to subsequent regular viewing.

WHAT DID RESIDENTS THINK ABOUT KTCA-TV (BEFORE AND AFTER OPERATION)?

Generally speaking, Twin City residents were favorably disposed toward plans and prospects for KTCA-TV before it began telecasting. Education, just as morality, is rarely an issue to be "against."

Nevertheless, 74 per cent of the sample could be classified as being extremely or moderately favorable toward the station and the remainder were neutral or noncommittal. Almost no one could be classified as being unfavorable at the time of the first wave of interviews.

This verbalized enthusiasm settled into a more realistic and less extreme pattern after broadcasting ensued, although favorable responses still outweighed the unfavorable. Of the second-wave respondents, now only 46 per cent of the sample could be classified as extremely or moderately favorable (a drop of 28 per cent), 51 per cent neutral, and 3 per cent actually unfavorable.

This shift did not come from the hard core of regular viewers (i.e., those who watched at least two programs per week), who had the most experience with KTCA-TV and who seemed to have the most valid expectancies of programing range. Changes were caused primarily by the "disenchantment" of the occasional viewer and the almost "militant" neutrality of the nonviewer. In all probability the so-called nonviewer had actually looked in to sample, found programs different from expectancies (if he had had any to begin with), and now shifted more to a point of neutrality.

WHAT DID VIEWERS THINK ABOUT KTCA-TV'S PROGRAM CONTENT AND RANGE?

Respondents were asked in both waves of interviewing to rate seven statements covering three areas on a five-point scale going from "strongly agree" through "neutral" to "strongly disagree," with the following results.

1. *Inherent interest of programs*—"Most educational TV programs are likely to be boring." (On the second wave this read: "Most ETV programs are boring.") Only a minority of viewers agreed with this statement on the first wave (14 per cent), and this percentage decreased after six months. There were interesting differences between regular viewers (19 per cent agreed on the first wave, only 8 per cent on the second) and occasional viewers (7 per cent agreed on the first wave, increasing to 15 per cent on the second). Again this might be caused by the less realistic ideas of KTCA-TV's programs, which caused occasional viewers to be more dissatisfied.

2. *Target audiences of KTCA-TV*—"KTCA is of interest only to those persons who have college educations." "Nearly everybody can get something out of educational TV." As might have been anticipated, nearly all of the viewers (92 per cent) disagreed with the "college education" statement and agreed with the idea that ETV was for everyone (96 per cent). These levels remained high, both for regular and occasional viewers.

3. *Control over discussion of "controversial" subjects*—"Since people who appear on KTCA-TV may be talking about religion [sex and politics were also substituted], the things they say should be carefully checked." Viewers showed interesting differences in the extent to which they thought these three subjects should be controlled between the two waves of interviews, as Table 3 indicates.

TABLE 3

Per Cent Agreeing on the Checking of	Total Sample		Regular Viewers		Occasional Viewers	
	First Wave	Second Wave	First Wave	Second Wave	First Wave	Second Wave
Sex	79%	67%	75%	61%	83%	72%
Religion	68	54	66	47	69	63
Politics	63	55	61	49	66	62

It is apparent that the majority of KTCA-TV viewers on the first wave of interviews wanted some check exercised on the discussion of these subjects, particularly on sex education. Note how experience with KTCA-TV's handling and treating of related subjects

caused a shift in attitude on the part of regular viewers who became much more "permissive," while occasional viewers still wanted
considerable restraints put on the speakers.

WHAT DID VIEWERS LIKE OR DISLIKE ABOUT KTCA-TV?

Viewers were asked to rate particular characteristics of KTCA-
TV's operation on another five-point scale, with the results shown in
Table 4.

TABLE 4

Per Cent Saying "Liked Especially" or "Liked Slightly"	Total Sample	Regular Viewers	Occasional Viewers
Absence of advertising commercials	87%	94%	82%
Program range and variety	72	81	63
Way programs are presented	69	76	62
Lecturers reading from scripts	34	41	27

Any fear of a "halo" effect on the part of viewers about KTCA-TV
seems dispelled by the gradations in liking of specific characteristics.
Although almost no viewers volunteered as a reason for liking ETV
the absence of advertising commercials, this factor received an extremely high rating, especially from the regular viewer. It is necessary to note, however, that a few respondents in each group com-
mented that they would not be adverse to advertising on KTCA-TV
if it were oriented toward getting contributions and support for
KTCA-TV itself.

The low "liking" score for lecturers reading from scripts or "hiding
behind lecterns" is a reflection of the occupational disease of ETV
stations with limited budgets and financial resources, and lack of
adequate prompting equipment. The often stilted and formalized
lecture-type formats received low ratings from the occasional
viewer.

OVERVIEW

Minneapolis–St. Paul residents as a whole verbalized quite favorable attitudes toward KTCA-TV before it began telecasting. Most
of them seemed receptive and evidenced enthusiasm toward the

idea of an educational television channel in the community. There was even anticipation on the part of the sample interviewed of rather frequent viewing of KTCA-TV once it came on the air.

Second-wave interviewing brought in evidence of substantial differences between expressed intentions and resultant behavior. Viewing was selective, on a program-to-program basis, and compared with commercial television viewing (which finds the average household watching television some six hours per day), rather light. The viewing of KTCA-TV follows rather closely the pattern established in other cities in which educational television was introduced.

Prebroadcast enthusiasm for the station, although still high, settled into a more realistic and less extreme pattern after actual broadcasting began. Often this shift was expressed more in attitude change toward a more qualified or neutral response. This was especially the case for the occasional and nonviewer.

The amount of information the community had on KTCA-TV before it began broadcasting was quite modest, and although it improved after the station was on the air, the relationship between awareness of the station and regular viewing would seem to indicate that more attempts at "grass-roots publicity" and door-to-door canvassing should have been undertaken.

In respect to contrasting KTCA-TV viewers with nonviewers, it would seem useful to relate the Minneapolis–St. Paul variety to other cities where previous studies have been done.

In an admittedly oversimplified fashion, one might categorize the results of three leading studies thus:

Lansing (Merrill)—indicated no significant differences between ETV viewers and non-ETV viewers in regard to demographic variables (age, sex, income, education, occupation, etc.), desire for "self-improvement" (education would "improve their lot," help them "get ahead"), or "cultural orientation" (attendance at plays, concerts, etc.).

Houston (Evans)—indicated no significant differences demographically, "cultural" differences were not dramatically different, although he did suggest that the ETV viewer was more likely to be "outgoing" or interested in self-improvement (i.e., joins clubs, has hobbies, etc.).

San Francisco (Schramm)—indicated that an ETV viewer, although not significantly different demographically, or "outgoing," is much more likely to be culture-oriented, have a better education, attend lectures, and read books than a non-ETV viewer.

Naturally, there is always the "chicken and egg" problem of ETV stations selecting their audiences, but it would seem that the typical

Minneapolis–St. Paul ETV viewer is much more akin to his San Francisco confrere than he is to the others. That is, although there are no differences in terms of demography, self-improvement, mass-media consumption, etc., the ETV viewer is different in that he has more education, consumes more magazines and books, and pays more homage to "cultural" values than he does to "practical" values.

As a by-product of this research, the "before" and "after" type of panel study proved quite useful in this case and would seem to offer many advantages to others interested in researching reactions to educational television stations.

This is a progress report on the most extensive research yet undertaken to find out how people decide whether to view or not to view an educational television program, and how they decide whether they like the program if they do look at it. Against what yardsticks of interest do they measure the program? Into what pigeonholes do they put programs? And what is the relation between characteristics of people and the kinds of programs that interest them? These are the questions tackled by the three authors of this paper, who are on the staff of the Communications Research Center at Michigan State University. A potential viewer seems to make up his mind primarily on whether he likes what a program is about, secondarily on whether he expects it to be useful and understandable. Once into the program, he decides whether to continue watching partly in terms of how much he likes the performance and how clearly the performer presents the material, and partly on how varied and exciting he finds the pace of the program.

WHAT MAKES AN
ETV PROGRAM INTERESTING?

by Malcolm S. MacLean, Jr., Edgar Crane, and Donald F. Kiel [1]

What leads anyone to watch an educational TV program? And why might a particular person watch a particular program? We began looking for answers to these questions in the summer of 1958 in a study to discover something of the viewer reactions to NETRC programs. We assumed that most men who produce programs for educational TV want to know what their potential viewers will watch and that the same is true of the men who arrange program schedules. It is often suggested, for example, that some people sometimes watch ETV for immediate pleasure and others because they expect to benefit, directly or indirectly, from the new things they learn. What kinds of programs are needed for a varied diet on ETV, and how do people decide that a particular kind of program

---

[1] This was a team research project. Among the research workers who have been most helpful on the phases of the project reported here are William D. Tarrant, Richard R. Goerz, Todd W. Kaiser, Daniel C. Dodge, Joseph H. Roberts, Dennis P. Scholtz. We have also been helped considerably by Brice H. Howard, Jr., Daniel F. Wozniak, and Ryland Crary, who got us started on the project in the first place.

is well done, or that the "cook" has badly burned another? Our study sought answers to questions like these. This report, preliminary to a more complete report in the future, concerns three aspects of the study: (1) How do viewers judge programs? Do they just think them "good" or "bad"? Or do they find different kinds of goodness? In short, what *yardsticks* do they apply to the educational TV fare? (2) Given viewers' judgments of each program in a heterogeneous group, do programs cluster together in terms of common interest of viewer segments? When these yardsticks are applied, how are programs grouped together by the viewer? In commercial TV, for example, "westerns" and "quiz programs" have been prominent. What are the important *pigeonholes* into which ETV content can be put? (3) Do some viewers prefer programs on art and music, and others programs on history, and, if so, can such differences be related to any demographic characteristics?

We hope that better understanding of the world of the viewer—his decisions, his ways of judging programs and the pigeonholes that he uses—may help ETV policy makers test certain rules of thumb they have been using. For example, does the "wow" introduction win an audience by its attention-getting qualities, as many seem to think, or does the contrast between introduction and body repel an audience? In what ways might ETV stations focus their audience-building publicity techniques? Before such questions can be answered, we must know much more than we have known in the past about how the world of ETV looks to the potential viewer.

A NOTE ON METHOD

Since George Gallup got his doctor's degree, one of the most popular methods of research in communications and the mass media has been the audience survey. Results of such surveys have been used widely to convince prospective advertisers that a particular medium or a particular publication is best for their purposes. We have been looking for data which might assist the men who produce educational TV programs and the men who draw up program schedules for ETV stations. We had three reasons for not using audience-survey techniques: (1) The survey can provide information only as to persons in the present audience for an educational TV station and cannot tell us much as to how nonviewers would react if they were to look at existing programs or if programs were to be created to meet their needs and interests. (2) The survey reports behavior which depends upon many variables extraneous to the quality of the program itself, among them the hour of broadcast, the nature of competing programs, etc. (3) Even if a survey could get reactions to programs as a whole, it still would not specify what it is within programs which makes one popular and another unpopular.

We chose to bring into a laboratory setting for three-hour viewing sessions of ETV program samples a variety of persons. The first phase of the study drew upon a cross section of the general adult population of the Lansing, Michigan, area. Thus we were able to obtain reactions from persons who would ordinarily not view ETV programs as well as those of persons who would. Through laboratory control over our captive audiences, of course, we eliminated extraneous influences. We sought to find what it is within programs which affects popularity by dividing our program samples on a time dimension, by asking subjects to rate them in 20-second segments, and on content dimensions, by asking that subject matter, performer, and quality of production be rated separately. Our ratings, moreover, consisted not only of the "keep on, turn off" dimension tapped in the usual survey, but of such other dimensions as usefulness, program pace, and the like.

The method we used, of course, may have its own limitations. It is possible, for example, for subjects, out of a desire to be "cooperative" or to please the experimenter, to indicate a higher level of liking for ETV in laboratory viewings than they really felt. This was not a major drawback, however, since the absolute level of liking which they reported was irrelevant to our principal interest, which was to find out relative liking for the programs we showed.

To get reactions to a wide variety of ETV programs—our viewers saw samples of 20 programs during each three-hour session—we showed the first four minutes of each program. It seems safe to assume that if a program can't win a viewer within this period, the viewer is likely to have turned his set off or to have switched to another channel. In any case, we did show a few subjects two additional segments of several programs—the four minutes immediately following the first segment, and the final four minutes. The ratings we got on the later segments differed little from ratings for the first segments.

A major problem, one with which we began and one which still puzzles us, is how much a program's appeal depends upon its subject matter and how much it depends upon the way that subject matter is treated. The two, of course, do merge into one another; a program on chemistry with a first-rate script, first-rate performers, and first-rate production appears somehow to differ in subject matter from another on chemistry whose script, performers, and production are inferior. Still, we find it practical to distinguish between subject matter and its presentation.

STAGES OF THE STUDY

This study has gone through three stages during which the measuring instruments, the programs, and the viewers have changed.

Programs

From 92 available NETRC series we selected two groups of 20 programs each, chosen so as to represent the maximum variation possible in both subject matter and format. Both 20-program samples were used in Stage 1, and the group designated as Sample I was used in Stage 2. In the third stage, on the basis of findings in the first two, we used three different sets of programs: 12 on music, 8 on advice for parents, and 16 that we tagged "intellect."

Viewers

Viewings in Stage 1 drew upon a cross section of the Lansing population, equally divided between men and women. In Stage 2 viewings, we invited science and nonscience high school teachers to viewings. In Stage 3, we chose persons belonging to organizations representing the three types of programs: music clubs, parents groups, and groups discussing "great ideas."

Instruments

From our first exploratory work, we developed a semantic differential rating scale and then asked viewers to rate subject matter, performer, and production quality of each program. In Stage 2 we also used a modification of the program analyzer, developed at Michigan State University and the University of Wisconsin, which gave us continuous ratings for each subject throughout each program; as noted above, readings were taken at 20-second intervals. A questionnaire, filled in outside the viewing session, gave us demographic data and viewers' reactions to a list of programs, both by name and type. A semantic differential study of images of *education, TV,* and *educational TV,* and a list of program descriptions were given viewers before and after viewing sessions.

A major aim of this study has been to see whether viewers distinguish among programs, even among programs equally well liked (or disliked), and if so, whether they do so on the basis of subject matter or format, perceived utility, simplicity, etc. We also wanted to see whether viewers tend to file programs away in different sets of pigeonholes.

YARDSTICKS VIEWERS USE IN RATING ETV PROGRAMS

We began, in our exploratory phase in the summer of 1958, by asking our viewers to mark 14 rating scales on subject matter, 26 on production quality, and 29 on the performer (see copies in Appendixes A, B, and C). From then on, we tried to find the scales which seemed to give much the same results, and from each such group chose one or two to represent the group. Through factor analysis and linkage analysis, we eventually reduced the original 69 scales to 14.

The first summer we showed two full-length programs, one of them a program on bottle feeding and the other a lecture on American history, to viewers recruited from eight Lansing organizations— seven of them churches and one a Negro sorority. Since the electronic computer could correlate only 23 scales at a time, those with low reliability were eliminated from the analysis by inspection, leaving 23 each for production quality (called "program" at this stage but explained carefully at viewing sessions) and 23 for the performer. Factor analysis reduced the original 23 production quality scales to seven factors:

1. *Evaluative:* clustering around like-dislike but with loadings of more than 0.5 on all scales except simple-complicated.
2. *Simplicity: simple-complicated,* easy to understand–hard to understand, clear-confusing.
3. *Information:* informative-uninformative, important–not important, worthwhile-worthless, entertaining-boring.
4. *Technique: smooth-jumpy,* good photography–bad photography.
5. *Apathy:* enthusiastic–not enthusiastic, *fast-slow,* useful for me–useless for me.
6. *Activity:* active-passive, *exciting-dull.*

TABLE 1. ROTATED PRINCIPAL AXES FACTORS. CONCEPT: PERFORMER [a]

Scale	I	II	III	IV	V	VI	VII	h²
4. Easy to watch–hard to watch	.89	.04	-.01	-.04	-.09	-.11	.07	.84
7. Graceful–awkward	.88	-.02	.10	-.02	.25	-.08	.01	.85
15. Good–bad	.86	.02	.10	-.13	.06	-.07	-.11	.77
14. Pleasant–irritating	.83	.11	-.04	-.07	.01	-.20	.07	.74
18. I like (him)–I dislike (him)	.82	-.01	-.08	.01	-.10	.17	-.25	.78
10. Warm–cold	.81	.07	.14	.20	.11	-.01	.19	.77
2. Pleasant to listen to–unpleasant . . .	.80	.02	-.18	.21	-.07	-.07	-.10	.74
9. Exciting–dull	.77	-.11	.00	.07	-.10	.12	.04	.64
13. Impressive–unimpressive	.77	-.10	-.13	.03	-.11	.14	.06	.66
5. Friendly–hostile	.76	.04	.13	-.09	-.01	-.03	.36	.73
12. Entertaining–boring	.72	-.01	.14	-.05	-.30	-.02	-.11	.64
19. Informative–not informative	.70	-.04	-.13	-.10	-.12	.11	.06	.55
3. Easy to understand–hard . . .	.70	.41	.14	.13	.18	.07	-.21	.78
21. Relaxed–tense	.70	-.07	-.04	-.12	.45	-.03	-.02	.71
22. Sincere–insincere	.70	.17	-.22	-.15	.01	.03	.11	.60
6. Strong personality–weak personality	.70	-.40	-.03	.25	.10	.04	-.07	.73
1. Colorful–colorless	.58	-.27	-.01	.12	-.09	.09	-.12	.58
23. Clear–confusing	.64	.53	.05	.07	-.08	-.14	-.05	.71
20. Active–passive	.61	-.18	.08	.06	-.03	.36	-.05	.55
17. Fast–slow	.52	-.05	.01	-.03	-.02	.40	.01	.43
11. Common sense–high-brow	.44	.42	.02	-.01	.01	.13	.26	.46
16. Personal–impersonal	.27	.04	.22	.45	-.11	.01	-.04	.35
8. Gay–solemn	.25	.15	.51	.12	-.04	.03	.06	.37
Sum of variance	11.41	1.00	.54	.49	.50	.49	.43	14.98
Per cent of common variance	77.6	6.7	3.6	3.4	3.3	3.2	2.9	
Per cent of total explained	50.4	4.4	2.3	2.2	2.1	2.1	1.9	

.65 per cent of total variance is common variance

[a] Diagonal elements of correlation matrix: squared multiple correlations.

7. *Educational:* I learned a lot–I learned little, meaningful-meaningless.

A similar analysis of the 23 performer scales gave us six factors:

1. *Evaluative.*
2. *Simplicity:* easy to understand–hard to understand, *clear-confusing, common sense–high-brow,* colorful-colorless, strong personality–weak personality.
3. *Mood: gay-solemn.*
4. *Personality: personal-impersonal.*
5. *Attitude:* entertaining-boring, *relaxed-tense.*
6. *Activity:* active-passive, *fast-slow.*

Finally, analysis of the 14 subject-matter scales gave us four factors:

1. *Evaluative:* eight scales included here.
2. *Importance:* six scales, including entertaining-boring, *meaningful-meaningless, entertaining-educational.*
3. *Simplicity: easy to understand–hard to understand, simple-complicated.*
4. *Controversy: useful for me–useless for me, factual-opinionated,* neutral-controversial.

Three tables of factor loadings are shown as Tables 1, 2, and 3.

The next phase of our study occurred in February, 1959, and brought 44 married couples, drawn from a cross section of the Lansing population, into the laboratory. Husbands and wives were divided so that two audiences, each balanced as to sex, saw the two different sets of 20 NETRC programs described earlier. Each viewer filled out 24 scales selected on the basis of factor analysis of the summer's data.

The eight scales under "production quality" included three for the evaluative factor: money well spent–money wasted, good-bad, and experienced-unexperienced, four others italicized in the list above, and one new scale: varied-monotonous. No scales were included for the "information" and "education" factors, since we felt these would be best measured under the subject-matter concept.

The eight "performer" scales included two for the evaluative factor—easy to watch–hard to watch and friendly-hostile, plus the six italicized in the list above. All factors were represented.

The eight "subject-matter" scales included two scales for each factor: I like it–I dislike it and pleasant-inviting for the evaluative factor, plus the six others italicized in the list above. All factors were represented.

While awaiting factor analysis results from the computer, we used

TABLE 2. ROTATED PRINCIPAL AXES FACTORS. CONCEPT: PROGRAM [a]

Scale	I	II	III	IV	V	VI	VII	h²
16. I like it–I dislike it	.87	−.07	−.08	−.19	.15	−.13	.14	.86
12. Good-bad	.87	.09	−.09	.14	−.03	.11	.16	.81
7. Money well spent–money wasted	.86	−.02	.13	−.09	.02	−.04	.13	.78
19. Pleasant-irritating	.86	.23	.06	.06	−.06	.07	−.04	.81
20. Worthwhile-worthless	.84	−.10	.32	−.07	.00	.02	−.05	.83
21. Pleasant to watch–unpleasant . . .	.80	.05	−.13	.06	.00	.13	−.08	.69
4. Meaningful-meaningless	.79	.01	.08	−.22	.03	.06	−.28	.75
3. Easy to watch–hard to watch	.78	.16	−.06	.18	−.13	.05	.06	.69
17. Exciting-dull	.78	−.05	−.12	.00	.00	−.34	.00	.74
1. Entertaining-boring	.75	−.08	−.44	−.20	.00	.00	−.05	.80
8. Important-trivial	.73	−.05	.32	−.10	.11	.02	−.05	.66
9. Smooth-jumpy	.71	.25	.13	.42	−.07	.05	.03	.77
11. Professional-amateurish	.68	.00	−.13	.16	−.16	.14	.04	.55
6. Active-passive	.66	−.08	−.09	.14	−.08	−.29	−.11	.56
15. Informative–not informative	.65	−.16	.41	−.06	−.14	.06	.04	.64
5. Good photography–bad photography	.62	.10	−.03	.51	−.05	−.05	−.07	.66
23. Enthusiastic–not enthusiastic	.61	−.02	−.06	−.07	.36	−.02	.00	.45
10. Clear-confusing	.59	.56	−.16	.13	.02	−.06	.06	.71
18. Easy to understand–hard . . .	.56	.65	−.03	−.06	.04	.06	−.09	.75
2. I learned a lot–I learned little	.54	−.19	−.17	−.12	.15	−.09	−.38	.53
14. Fast-slow	.52	−.02	−.13	.08	.39	.17	.03	.48
22. Useful for me–useless for me	.51	−.13	.03	−.09	.55	−.03	−.02	.59
13. Simple-complicated	.29	.66	.09	.07	−.13	−.02	.00	.55
Sum of variance	(11.36)	(1.44)	(.77)	(.75)	(.74)	(.33)	(.34)	15.66
Per cent of common variance	72.5	9.2	4.9	4.8	4.7	2.1	2.2	
Per cent of total variance explained	49.3	6.3	3.3	3.3	3.2	1.4	1.5	

.60 per cent of total variance is common variance

[a] Diagonal elements of correlation matrix: squared multiple correlations.

linkage analysis, as a good first approximation, with February viewers' ratings on these 24 scales. In an attempt to reduce the dimensions from the 17 factors found earlier, two sets of linkages were performed, as shown in the accompanying tables.

TABLE 3. ROTATED PRINCIPAL AXES FACTORS. CONCEPT: SUBJECT MATTER [a]

Scale	I	II	III	IV	h²
3. I like it–I dislike it	.90	.07	.03	—.11	.83
8. Interesting-uninteresting	.88	—.03	—.04	—.09	.78
7. Pleasant-irritating	.87	—.02	.04	.20	.80
14. Worthwhile-worthless	.84	.28	.05	.01	.79
5. Entertaining-boring	.84	—.35	—.03	—.05	.83
11. Good-bad	.81	.02	.09	.10	.67
2. Meaningful-meaningless	.79	.35	—.01	.09	.75
10. Exciting-dull	.78	—.29	—.01	—.05	.70
12. Useful for me–useless for me	.60	.02	—.15	—.39	.54
4. Easy to understand–hard . . .	.58	—.01	.52	.05	.61
13. Educational-entertaining	.33	.49	—.04	.06	.35
9. Simple-complicated	.30	—.00	.62	—.02	.47
6. Factual-opinionated	.16	.25	—.02	.41	.26
1. Controversial-neutral	.08	—.04	.04	—.50	.26
Sum of variance	(6.57)	(.72)	(.70)	(.66)	8.64
Per cent of common variance	76.0	8.3	8.1	7.6	
Per cent of total variance explained	47.1	5.1	5.0	4.7	

.62 per cent of total variance is common variance

[a] Communality estimates: squared multiple correlations.

Linkages in Table 4 were based on correlations of all scales, without regard to the concept measured. Six clusters were produced. Each scale is identified by the "favorable" polar term and the initials P for performer scales, PR for production quality, or S for subject matter. Direction of the arrow from each scale indicates with which scale it had its highest correlation. As these clusters indicate, except for the grouping of evaluative scales in cluster I, each cluster tended to be made up of scales for the same concept. Thus clusters II and III are production quality and cluster VI is performer. On the other hand, cluster IV combines performer and subject-matter scales and cluster VI suggests that viewers did not distinguish between a "fast" performer and a "fast" production.

TABLE 4. LINKAGES OF 24 SCALES ACROSS CONCEPTS

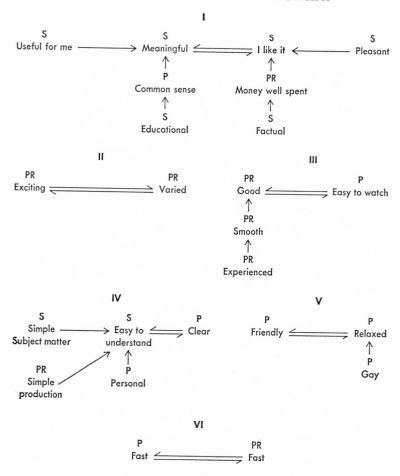

Because of the rather marked clustering of scales by concepts, a second linkage analysis was performed by concepts. It produced the results shown in Table 5: a single cluster for performer and for subject matter, and two clusters for production quality. Apparently viewers did differentiate fast, varied, and exciting productions and simple, good, and smooth productions.

Examination of these two sets of linkages and the correlation matrix from which they were drawn led us to draw up Table 6,

TABLE 5. LINKAGES OF 24 SCALES BY CONCEPTS

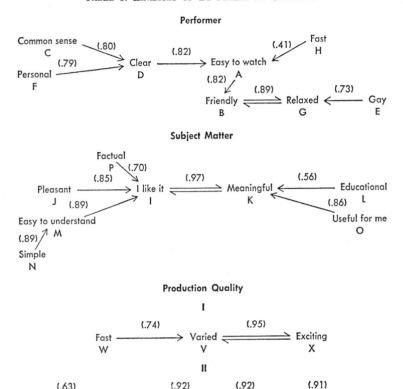

in which scales were grouped into three factors for each concept.[2] Two of these factors were the same for all three concepts: evaluative and simplicity. The third factor was labeled "activity" for performer and production quality and "utility" for subject matter.

[2] The linkages of Tables 4 and 5 did not lead us directly to the scale-concept groupings in Table 7. Other considerations entered in. Despite the clustering into one glob of the meaningful-useful-educational and the I like it–pleasant scales for subject matter in both Tables 4 and 5, we grouped them separately on the grounds that some educational broadcasters like to maintain this distinction. As the reader will see, Table 9 again indicates that these scales form but a single dimension. In Table 5, the "fast" scale links with the other performer scales, but its closer link to the "fast" (production) scale in Table 4 suggests that it would very likely have split away from the main performer cluster had we included another activity scale.

Table 6 is repeated as Table 7, so that scales for similar factors may be compared across concepts.

TABLE 6. GROUPING OF SCALES INTO THREE DIMENSIONS
FOR EACH CONCEPT

Production Quality

Evaluative
Money well spent
Smooth   .92
Good   .92
Experienced   .91

Simplicity
Simple

Activity
Exciting
Varied   .95
Fast   .74

Performer

Evaluative
Easy to watch   .82
Friendly
Gay   .89
Relaxed   .73

Simplicity
Common sense   .80
Clear
Personal   .79

Activity
Fast

Subject Matter

Evaluative
I like it   .85
Pleasant

Simplicity
Easy to understand .89
Simple

Utility
Meaningful
Educational .56   .86
Useful for me

TABLE 7. SCALES ON FACTOR FOR EACH CONCEPT

Factor	Production Quality	Performer	Subject Matter
Evaluative	Money well spent–money wasted Smooth-jumpy Good-bad Experienced–inexperienced	Easy to watch–hard to watch Friendly-hostile Gay-solemn Relaxed-tense	I like it–I dislike it Pleasant-irritating Factual-opinionated
Simplicity; clarity	Simple-complicated	Common sense–high-brow Clear-confusing Personal-impersonal	Easy to understand–hard to understand Simple-complicated
Activity or utility	Exciting-dull Varied-monotonous Fast-slow	Fast-slow	Meaningful-meaningless Educational-entertaining Useful for me–useless for me

The next phase of the study occurred in the summer of 1959, when the set of 20 program segments termed Sample I, which had been shown to 44 "public" viewers in February, was screened for teachers attending M.S.U. summer school. To allow us to check more closely into the relations between concept and scale, only four scales, those underlined in Table 7, were used. Each of the four factors of Table 6 was represented by a single scale: I like it–I dislike it for the evaluative factor, clear-confusing for the simplicity factor, fast-slow for the activity factors, and useful for me–useless for me for the utility factor. The viewer filled out each scale three times—once for subject matter, once for performer, and once for production quality.

In the final phase of the study in the fall of 1959, both the programs and the viewers were changed. In this phase, viewers filled out the same 24 scales which were used in the February viewings.

How can we sum up these findings as to the dimensions of viewers' ratings? Let's put it this way. One can argue that when a viewer watches a TV program, he either likes it or he doesn't, and that, other things being equal, he will watch the program he likes and turn off the program he doesn't like. Or one can argue that when a viewer watches a TV program, there are a great many different scales on which he can judge it, that these can be joined into many different combinations, and that many of these combinations will produce equivalent degrees of liking and/or viewing in the non-captive audience situation of the viewer at home in his own living room. Our study allowed for both of these possibilities.

We asked viewers in February whether they would "keep on" or "turn off" a program, after showing them the first four minutes, and rated each program by the per cent of viewers who would keep it on. (In subsequent sessions we asked them to check their position on a seven-point scale running from "likely to turn off" to "likely to keep on.")

But, as has already been noted, we asked them to break down this over-all rating and rate separately each concept (subject matter, performer, and production quality) by a total of 69 scales. Factor and linkage analysis then showed us that several of these scales apparently measured the same thing, so we reduced the number of scales. The most satisfactory reduction—simple, yet apparently getting at the essential judgments—left us with the nine different dimensions represented by scale-concept combinations.

Apparently viewers can, if they are asked, discriminate among evaluation, simplicity, and activity or utility and do so for subject matter, performer, and production quality. But do these discriminations, these judgments by viewers, have any relation to their over-all liking for a program, as measured by the keep-on ratings? Do some of these judgments have a closer relationship than others?

One way of answering this question was to get correlations among keep-on scores for the programs and ratings of programs on the nine dimensions, three for each concept, obtained through linkage analysis and shown in Table 8.

TABLE 8

Production	Correlation with Keep-on Score
Evaluative	.54
Simplicity	.56
Clarity	.22
Performer	
Evaluative	.46
Activity	.22
Clarity	.46
Subject Matter	
Evaluative	.69
Utility	.54
Clarity	.46

As this table indicates, performer activity and production clarity seemed to bear little relationship to a viewer's decision to "keep on" or "turn off" a program. The evaluative dimension of subject matter bore the highest relationship.

TABLE 9

Factor	1 Presentation Evaluation	2 Activity	3 Subject Evaluation and Utility	4 Clarity
Performer evaluation	.84	.00	.00	.00
Production evaluation	.72	−.14	.36	−.15
Performer clarity	.64	.36	.13	.16
Production activity	.28	.59	.11	.04
Performer activity	.00	.57	.00	.00
Subject utility	.00	.00	.87	.00
Subject evaluation	.15	−.06	.81	.02
Production simplicity	.00	.00	.00	.63
Subject understandability	.22	−.14	.24	.56
Keep-on ratings	.21	.13	.34	−.04

The nine dimensions of Table 8 were subsequently reduced still further, by oblique rotations, producing the Holzinger primary pattern factor loadings shown in Table 9.

As this table indicates, we had by now reduced the 69 scales with which we had started some 12 months earlier to four factors, with the heavy loadings on each factor underlined. Each of these four factors was then correlated with each of the others, producing the matrix shown in Table 10.

TABLE 10. CORRELATION AMONG FACTORS

Factor	1 Presentation Evaluation	2 Activity	3 Subject Evaluation and Utility	4 Clarity
1. Presentation	1.00			
2. Activity	.62	1.00		
3. Subject evaluation	.64	.44	1.00	
4. Clarity	.61	.28	.51	1.00

As this indicates, presentation evaluation was highly correlated and equally correlated with each of the other factors: activity, subject evaluation, and clarity. Our next step was to discover how, using these yardsticks, viewers group programs into types.

PIGEONHOLES VIEWERS USE IN CLASSIFYING PROGRAMS

When our study began, NETRC files listed 225 series comprising 2,899 individual programs. Before we could think of examining such a mass of material, it was necessary to classify it—to arrange a series of pigeonholes, if you will, into which the programs could be placed. The difficulty, of course, was that there were several different systems we might use. Educators, for example, might tend to divide the program universe, as NETRC did at the time, on the basis of subject matter: about 40 per cent of the nearly 3,000 programs were in the social sciences, 20 per cent each in the fine arts, the humanities, and the natural sciences. TV producers, on the other hand, might be interested in program format, differentiating among lectures, interviews, panel shows, etc. Program directors might be interested in classifying programs on the basis of their expected audience: adults generally, women specifically, teenagers, children, etc.

The two programs studied in the summer of 1958 might have been classified by any of these systems. One consisted of a *lecture* in the *humanities,* on *American history,* using a *male performer,* probably intended for an *adult audience.* The other consisted of an *interview* on *child raising;* as for target audience, our viewers that summer suggested the program would be of interest only to a pregnant woman and then only to a woman expecting her first child.[3]

There was, in short, no lack of category systems to be applied to the NETRC output. Our problem, however, was not to pick one of them or even to construct a new set of our own, but to determine the pigeonholing system actually used by the ETV viewer. We wanted to know what the viewer said to himself in those critical few minutes of decision making as he read the program listings in his newspaper or watched and heard the first few minutes of a program.

Our process of discovery was the same used in developing our yardsticks: begin with the widest possible variety of programs and then, through factor analysis, reduce the program types to the smallest number relevant to viewer decisions. We began by breaking the four NETRC subject categories into 20 smaller units, based on the usual academic distinctions. Thus fine arts was subdivided into art, music, and a catchall category of opera, theater, and the dance.

These 20 we listed down the left-hand side of a page. Across the top we put 21 categories based on program format. Building on the basic distinction between lecture, interview, panel, and a catchall category including demonstrations and "real life," we made further distinctions on the basis of the sex of the performers. As a rough indicator of quality, we divided production units into thirds, on the basis of the number of series produced for NETRC: 1 or 2, 3 to 7, 10 or more. Our hunch was that the units with a large number of series, even if not originally chosen solely on the basis of superior quality, might have developed such quality through the experience.

The 20 x 21 table gave us 420 pigeonholes. Many of these had no entries, of course. We found no "panel discussions on biology," for instance. (Programs using women performers were so few that the 33 theoretically possible columns listed at the top of the page had already been reduced to 21 when we constructed the table itself.)

----

[3] For more details on these two programs, see M. S. MacLean, Jr., and H. H. Toch, "The Group Interview as an Audience Reaction Measure," *Audio-Visual Communication Review,* 7 (1959), 209–19.

TABLE 11. CORRELATION MATRIX FOR PUBLIC RATINGS ON UTILITY OF 20 PROGRAMS IN SAMPLE I (N = 44)

	1	2	3	4	5	6	7	8	9	10	11	12	13	14	15	16	17	18	19
1 Religions																			
2 Tragedy	25																		
3 Insurance	04	05																	
4 Space Doctors	10	21	31																
5 Dinosaurs	−01	06	01	25															
6 Carbon	−10	30	35	19	30														
7 Prairie Towns	36	03	22	48	−00	17													
8 Puberty	−09	04	10	35	26	22	20												
9 Education	11	23	20	08	28	50	19	31											
10 Friends	06	01	45	12	03	23	15	12	28										
11 Agriculture	14	07	48	19	−01	29	27	24	43	61									
12 Guatemala	13	21	36	44	−15	47	32	37	33	23	45								
13 USSR	28	45	09	27	20	14	12	13	21	−20	21	35							
14 Archeology	11	23	25	13	23	37	19	15	25	03	21	22	41						
15 Sculptor	−00	14	−06	28	21	08	09	52	06	23	22	35	29	−01					
16 Rondino	40	46	23	15	17	43	17	11	34	28	22	36	37	46	29				
17 La Finta	13	−03	10	14	30	10	23	26	01	31	16	13	07	33	48	44			
18 Quill	41	33	10	10	25	33	02	10	42	16	30	34	49	33	13	39	10		
19 Witness	13	42	10	35	29	11	21	24	25	−19	18	38	53	25	24	00	12	32	
20 French	27	28	20	17	22	27	09	17	21	17	02	43	32	19	20	46	21	42	21

Some pigeonholes, on the other hand, had several entries: that calling for a lecture on history by a male performer had no less than six series in it.

Not all the series entered in our table were available for study. Some had been broken up and others were still circulating. Program data sheets, which we used in classifying series, were missing for still others. We were able to enter 92 series into our table. Because some series fell in the same category, the 92 series actually meant entries appeared in 75 pigeonholes.

We then chose two samples of programs, trying to represent as many different columns and rows as possible; as it turned out, 37 different pigeonholes were drawn upon. Our task in the study thus was to see whether viewers' reactions to all 37 could be explained in less than 37 dimensions. Our analysis, although not yet completed, has at this point reduced the 37 to perhaps half a dozen. This is how the reduction was accomplished.

We rescored each of the 20 programs in Sample I on the basis of the four factors already reported in Table 9, and then correlated each program with every other. We also correlated programs on the basis of their keep-on ratings. Although all five of these sets of "pigeonholes" will be included in our final report, only one will be given here. This is the set based on factor 3 in Table 9, "subject evaluation and utility," which yielded the highest loading for the keep-on ratings (.34). Within this factor, scores for "subject utility" had the highest loading (.87). Each program, therefore, was given a "subject utility score" consisting of the sum of its rating on four scales: meaningful-meaningless, useful for me–useless for me, educational-entertaining, and factual-opinionated. Then the programs were correlated with one another, producing Table 11.

From this table we determined, for each program, with what other program it had its highest correlation. These linkages, shown in Table 12, gave us six clusters, to which we attached the following letters and names:

A. *Natural science and education:* includes four programs: "Dinosaurs," "Carbon," "Guatemala," and "Education." "Dinosaurs" was rated least useful of the group, "Education" most useful.

B. *Social problems:* includes four programs: "USSR," "Witness," "Quill," and "Religions." "Religions" was rated most useful in the group (and second highest in all 20 programs in Sample I); "Witness" was rated lowest in utility.

C. *Culture:* includes four programs: "Archeology," judged most useful; "Tragedy"; "French"; and "Rondino," judged least useful.

TABLE 12. LINKAGES AMONG 20 PROGRAMS OF SAMPLE I ON
"UTILITY" DIMENSION

A. Natural Science and Education

Guatemala
12

|

(.48)

(.30)   ↓   (.50)

5 ————→ 6 ⇄———→ 9

Dinosaurs   Carbon   Education

B. Social Problems

(.41)   (.49)   (.53)

1 ——→ 18 ——→ 13 ⇄ 19

Religion   Quill   USSR   Witness

C. Culture

(.46) Rondino (.46)

2 ⇄ 16 ←——— 14

Tragedy   Archeology

↑ (.46)

20
French

D. Spatial Art

(.52)   (.48)

8 ⇄ 15 ←——— 17

Puberty   Sculptor   La Finta

E. Personal and Family

(.61)   (.48)

10 ⇄ 11 ←——— 3

Friends   Agriculture   Insurance

F. Pioneers and Adventure

(.48)

4 ⇄ 7

Space Doctors   Prairie Towns

D. *Spatial art:* includes three programs: "Puberty," "Sculptor," and
"La Finta." All three programs were among the least useful of Sample I
programs.

E. *Personal and family:* includes three programs: "Friends," "Agriculture," and "Insurance," the last of which had the highest utility rating of
all Sample I programs.

F. *Pioneers and adventure:* includes two programs, "Space Doctors"
and "Prairie Towns," with the former judged more useful.

The labels represent the judgment of the researcher. They are an
attempt, based on what we know of the programs themselves, to
guess why viewers put them into the same pigeonhole. Group D, for
example, might, with equal logic, have been labeled "esoteric culture." In "Sculptor," a man showed how he made three-dimensional
sketches out of clay in planning a larger sculpture. In "Puberty," a
Negro professor lectured on adolescence in different cultures, as
Negro youths interpreted his remarks in dance and pantomime. In
"La Finta," the whole four minutes was taken up in presenting the
cast of a highly artificial, mannered operetta. The labels are based
on at least five to ten viewings of each program, but the reader may
want to fashion his own labels for these clusters, on the basis of brief
descriptions of the programs included in this report.

A somewhat more systematic way of examining the clusters appears in Table 13. To create this table, we took the six pairs of programs forming the "cores" of the linkages, and entered the correlation of each program with the other 11. (The correlations between members of each pair were used as the communality and appear on the diagonal.)

The next step was to enter into Table 14 the sum of each program's correlations with the two programs in each of the groups A through F. For example, program 16 correlated .15 with program 4 in group F and .17 with program 7 in the same group. Summed, this gave us .32 in Table 14.

Finally, we created Table 15 by adding correlations for each of the programs in groups A through F. Thus programs 10 and 11 of group E had correlations of .27 and .46 with group F. Summed, these gave us .73 as the relationship between groups E and F.

Thus the 20 programs of Sample I with which we began have been put into six pigeonholes and we can even, in a manner of speaking, line the pigeonholes up in some kind of order. We know, as shown by the linkages, that the "personal and family" programs of group E seem to be quite remote from the "spatial art" programs of group D, but that the same personal and family programs seem to be near to the science and education programs.

A similar analysis reduced the 20 programs of Sample II to an even smaller number of four pigeonholes:

A. *Natural science and humanity:* includes four programs: "U.N.," "Telescopes," "Atoms," and "Zoo." "U.N." was rated most useful of all 20 programs; "Telescopes" was lowest in utility in this group.

B. *Social science and culture:* includes seven programs: "Seeing," "U.S. Geography," "Middle East," "Greeks," "American Culture," "Music," and "French." "Seeing" was rated most useful and "French" and "Music" least useful.

C. *Art and history:* includes five programs: "Commager" (lecturing on history), "Panel on Art," "Opera," "Oresteia" (in Greek, played by girls), and "Great Ideas" (a talk by Mortimer Adler). These programs were rated least useful of the 20, with "Panel on Art" at the very bottom.

D. *Applied social science:* includes four programs: "Birth," "Insurance," "Social Work," and "Freedom." Utility ratings in this group varied greatly: "Birth" and "Insurance" were second and third highest of the 20, and "Social Work" among the lowest of the 20.

Two tables summarize the findings for Sample II: Table 16, counterpart of Table 12, shows linkages which produced the four clusters just described. Table 17, counterpart of Table 15, shows the

TABLE 13

		E 10⌃11		B 13⌃19		D 8⌃15		A 6⌃9		C 2⌃16		F 4⌃7
Friends E	10	61										
Agri. E	11	.61	61									
USSR B	13	−.20	.21	53								
Witness B	19	−.19	.18	.53	53							
Puberty D	8	.12	.24	.13	.24	52						
Sculptor D	15	.23	.22	.29	.24	.52	52					
Carbon A	6	.23	.29	.14	.11	.22	.08	50				
Education A	9	.28	.43	.21	.25	.31	.06	.50	50			
Tragedy C	2	.01	.07	.45	.42	.04	.14	.30	.23	46		
Rondino C	16	.28	.22	.37	.00	.11	.29	.43	.34	.46	46	
Space Doctors F	4	.12	.19	.27	.35	.35	.28	.19	.08	.21	.15	48
Prairie Towns F	7	.15	.27	.12	.21	.20	.09	.17	.19	.03	.17	.48	48

TABLE 14

Personal App. soc. sci. Family	E	1.22	1.22	.01	−.01	.36	.45	.52	.71	.08	.50	.31	.42
Soc. prob. World events Humanities	B	−.39	.39	1.06	1.06	.37	.53	.25	.46	.87	.37	.62	.33
Art School-classroom	D	.35	.46	.42	.48	1.04	1.04	.30	.37	.18	.40	.63	.29
Sci. education	A	.51	.72	.35	.36	.53	.14	1.00	1.00	.53	.77	.27	.36
Culture Drama-Music	C	.29	.29	.82	.42	.15	.43	.73	.57	.92	.92	.36	.20
True advent.	F	.27	.46	.39	.56	.55	.37	.36	.27	.24	.32	.96	.96

TABLE 15

	E	B	D	A	C	F
E	2.44	.00	.81	1.23	.58	.73
B	.00	2.12	.90	.71	1.24	.95
D	.81	.90	2.08	.67	.58	.92
A	1.23	.71	.67	2.00	1.30	.63
C	.58	1.24	.58	1.30	1.84	.56
F	.73	.95	.92	.63	.56	1.92

Final Linkages for Sample I

relationships among the four groups, with these relationships shown graphically in the attached linkage.

TABLE 16. LINKAGES AMONG 20 PROGRAMS OF SAMPLE II ON "UTILITY" DIMENSION

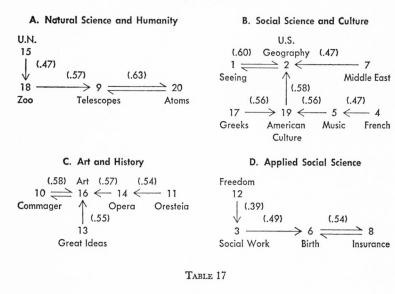

A. Natural Science and Humanity

U.N.
15
| (.47)
↓   (.57)   (.63)
18 ————→ 9 ⇌ 20
Zoo   Telescopes   Atoms

B. Social Science and Culture

U.S.
(.60)   Geography   (.47)
1 ⇌ 2 ←———————— 7
Seeing   ↑   Middle East
              | (.58)
(.56) | (.56)   (.47)
17 ————→ 19 ←—— 5 ←—— 4
Greeks   American   Music   French
         Culture

C. Art and History

(.58)   Art   (.57)   (.54)
10 ⇌ 16 ←—— 14 ←———— 11
Commager   ↑   Opera   Oresteia
           | (.55)
13
Great Ideas

D. Applied Social Science

Freedom
12
| (.39)
↓   (.49)   (.54)
3 ————→ 6 ⇌ 8
Social Work   Birth   Insurance

TABLE 17

	B	D	A	C
B	2.40	1.05	1.85	.73
D	1.05	2.16	.69	.86
A	1.85	.69	2.52	1.18
C	.73	.86	1.18	2.32

Final Linkages for Sample II

C ————→ A ⇌ B ←———————— D
Art-History   Natural science   Social science-Culture   Social science

As we look at these results of our examination of "utility," two questions arise which have still to be answered. The first is how the set of six pigeonholes in Sample I and four in Sample II may be related to one another. Some suggestions will occur to the reader. In both samples, for instance, we have two "cultural" groups, one more esoteric than the other: C and D for Sample I and B and C for Sample II. In both samples, natural science, and social science and utility pigeonholes seem to appear. A more systematic examination of these relationships needs to be made.

The second question is this. The reader will note that the labels for the pigeonholes reflect a subject-matter rather than a format orientation. This may reflect the fact that the researchers are educators rather than TV producers and that correlations are based on ratings of subject-matter utility. Our next step will be to take the groups discovered and see whether they show any common characteristics in our extensive coding of both verbal and nonverbal content. So far we have not been able to discover any such characteristics.

PEOPLE: THE SEARCH FOR TYPES OF AUDIENCES

Few persons in educational TV argue that each of its programs should seek, like many in commercial broadcasting, the largest possible audience. Many persons feel, however, that when the audiences for all the programs on an ETV schedule are added up they should represent a cross section of the population. Many feel, no doubt, that everyone should watch some ETV program sometime during the week.

How does one get a balanced schedule which has something of interest for everyone? If it were true that we have four types of persons—those interested in fine arts or the humanities or natural science or social science—then a schedule which drew upon each of these subject-matter pigeonholes should attract everyone. As we have already seen, the viewer does not seem to use this set of pigeonholes.

It is not enough to find out which programs are the most popular —which have the highest keep-on ratings in our study—and schedule only them. There are several reasons why this would not work. First, because it could be that five programs, each of which won 80 per cent of the audience, all lost the same 20 per cent. Second, because popularity alone tells us little about the educational value of the programs. Finally, such a schedule might be monotonous, like the pages of a newspaper filled with nothing but pictures of Miss America, popular though one or two pictures might be. After a time, it might drive away an audience. But one can take a closer look at the popularity ratings and see which combination of programs appeals to the largest total of different viewers.

Group 1 in Table 18 shows three very popular programs with a total keep-on rating, for the group, of 76. But note that the second and third programs didn't add any new viewers to the 35 (out of

41) reached by the U.N. program. All three of these programs were drawn from the same cluster of Sample II programs, the cluster we called "natural science and humanity." If we define "possible audience" as number of viewers multiplied by number of programs, then these three programs did reach 62 per cent of this possible

TABLE 18. PROGRAMS PACKAGED TO MAXIMIZE NUMBER OF DIFFERENT PERSONS IN AUDIENCE (PUBLIC)

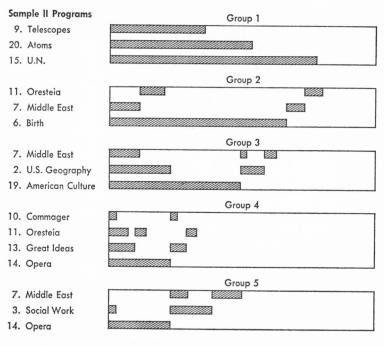

audience. But if we want each program to tap a different segment of the public, rather than duplicate the audience of another program, then Group 1 was not so good as Group 2. Although Group 2 reached only 37 per cent of "possible audience," as defined above, it reached 36 *different* persons—1 more than Group 1! This Group 2 drew its programs from three different clusters. Group 3, made up of programs in the same cluster ("social science and culture"), had a total keep-on rating of 44. Like Group 2, it reached one-third of the possible audience. But it reached only 28 different persons—8 fewer than Group 2.

This problem of gaining the maximum of *different* viewers becomes particularly important when none of the programs available is particularly popular. This is shown by Groups 4 and 5, which have the same core program—"Opera"—with a keep-on rating of 10 viewers out of 41. Adding three programs to "Opera," to make the Group 4 "package," added only 5 new persons, whereas adding only two programs to "Opera" in the Group 5 "package" brought 12 different persons into the ETV audience.

Here, if you will, is a concrete illustration of the utility of finding out what "pigeonholes" the public uses in classifying ETV programs. Once these are known, one has a means of producing and scheduling so as to attract all segments of the population to ETV. Or one can, if he wishes, use the same knowledge to focus upon any single segment of the audience.

It does not seem at all unreasonable to suppose that some day all new ETV programs might be shown before a small audience, of the kind we used, but representing a cross section of the American public, and the results used to assist program directors and publicity men. Indeed, it seems possible that such audiences could be used as a supplement to the viewings by policy makers and other experts, in the viewing of pilot programs.

Until such a plan is put into effect, however, more information is needed about the types of persons who fell into the audiences for our several program clusters. We asked ourselves: Is it possible to predict who will reach into a given pigeonhole when he wants to watch ETV? To answer this question, we devised six indexes based on material which could easily be obtained by an audience survey or, in some cases, from census data—information which any ETV station can obtain about the people in its broadcast area. (Our subjects filled out questionnaires.)

Although audience surveys have failed to agree on any consistent relationship between viewers' education (or other demographic characteristics) and their inclusion in the ETV audience, we suspected that such indicators might be related to differences within the ETV program budget itself. These were the indexes we used:

Cultural behavior: from 0 to 5, with 1 point for each of the following activities: attendance at concerts, plays, or lectures; listening to university FM stations, ownership of symphony records.

Socioeconomic status: maximum of 6 points if professional occupation, income of $10,000 a year or over, 13 years or more of education.

Print media use: maximum of 3 points if read books, magazines, and newspapers.

Hard news readership: 2 points for each of following read regularly, 1 point if read occasionally: foreign news, editorials, news of national politics.

Soft news readership: 2 points for regular readership, 1 point for occasional readership of: comics, news of people, society, and sports news.

Now we sorted out all of the persons who said they would keep on the two programs which formed the core of each of our program clusters. We then averaged the scores of these people on each of the above indexes. Although the differences were not great, we found that in both Samples I and II the utility clusters—E or "personal and family" in Sample I and D or "applied social science" in Sample II—attracted people with a "cultural activity" index lower than those attracted by any other cluster. In both groups, the "cultural" programs—C or "culture" in Sample I and C or "art and history" in Sample II—attracted persons who had an average score on the cultural activity index that was higher than for those attracted to any other program. Here are the results for the other indexes:

Socioeconomic status: here, as in the cultural index, the lowest average score was by persons attracted to the utility clusters—E in Sample I, D in Sample II. But persons with the highest average score were those interested in social problems; that is, those attracted to the B "social problems" cluster in Sample I and the B "social science and culture" cluster in Sample II.

Print media use: in both samples, persons attracted to the cultural and social problems clusters of programs showed the highest use of print media. Low use of media showed a less consistent relationship to program preferences between samples.

Hard news readership: devotees of social problems programs in Sample I had the highest scores on this index but were outscored in Sample II on hard news readership by persons who liked cluster A, "natural science and humanity."

Soft news readership: rather surprisingly, the same persons who liked cluster A programs in Sample II, and had the highest average score on hard news readership, also had the highest average score on soft news readership. The same was true for Sample I. Among our viewers, at least, the hard news–soft news distinction does not separate people. Those who liked a lot of one also liked a lot of the other. This was shown when the two indexes were correlated; they gave us product-moment correlations of .62 in Sample I and .59 in Sample II, much higher than the relationship between the print media index and either soft news or hard news indexes.

Women made up 49 per cent of the viewers of our two 20-program samples, but formed a much larger proportion of the keep-on audience for some clusters. They made up two-thirds of the keep-on audience for clusters C ("culture") and D ("spatial art") of Sample I. In Sample II, cluster C ("art and history") attracted only five viewers, and four of them were women. In only one cluster did women represent a smaller proportion of keep-on persons than they did of the total number of viewers exposed to the programs. This was cluster A ("natural science and humanity") of Sample II.

SUMMARY

Our analysis of the ways in which members of the adult public respond to a great variety of NETRC programs suggests that much of the variation in response rests on whether a viewer likes what a program is about. He asks whether the subject matter is likely to be useful to him and if it is understandable. Once into the program, he decides whether to continue watching or not partly in terms of how much he likes the performance and whether the performer presents the material clearly. His decision to continue watching a program also seems to depend, in part, on how varied or exciting he finds the pace of the program. In the end, however, if he likes the subject matter or anticipates it will be useful to him, and there is nothing around which attracts him more, he will probably continue to watch.

People differ among themselves, however. Hypothetically, each of the 40 programs we studied might have appealed to 40 different segments of a potential audience. In actuality, we found that both our sets of 20 programs divided into four content groups, which might be described thus:

I. *Utility:* practical applied psychology and health advice. Personal and family relations.

II. *Social science and culture:* political, social, and economic problems at the broad social system level. Interpretation of society through art and artifacts.

III. *Art, aesthetics, and history:* the esoteric, "arty," artificial, mannered, stuffy presentation of or talk about some art form.

IV. *Natural science, education, and humanity:* dinosaurs, the zoo, chemistry, astronomy, the atom, education, war and peace.

Each of these groups attracted its own set of viewers, with group III having the fewest viewers. Our report shows how such program groups might be used in drawing up a program schedule to maximize either the number of different viewers or the number of viewer-program exposures.

The reader should be warned that the number of persons who attended our viewings was small and that there may have been types of NET programs which we missed. Although we would not advocate any radical revisions of program policy on the basis of evidence, we would suggest that continuation of this line of study might lead to evidence which would support such revision.

Finally, the report has suggested something about the nature of potential audiences for these program types. As one would expect, the "utility" program is the most likely to attract viewers from the lower socioeconomic stratum—the kinds of people least apt to become viewers of the other programs.

NEXT STEPS IN THE STUDY

The results that have been presented—our findings about yardsticks, pigeonholes, and people—might best be regarded as signposts that suggest directions. We have been searching for hypotheses, for important and relevant questions. Our analysis is far from complete and some highly interesting aspects of the study could not be touched on in this report. Here, in brief review, are some of the directions of our search.

Subject Matter vs. Production

A major problem has been to separate the effects on viewers' preferences of a liking for subject matter from their judgment of the way that subject is treated in a specific program. We have tried to get at this in several ways.

1. Originally, we gave subjects descriptions of each program before viewings and asked them to "vote" for those they would like to watch. We felt these reactions would represent liking for subject matter to a greater extent than reactions after viewing program samples. In later experiments, we substituted for these ballots a series of paired comparisons for subject groups.

2. We held subject matter more constant by taking readings from a program analyzer at 20-second intervals within each program. Although elaborate coding of verbal and nonverbal content so far has failed to distinguish clearly the much-liked program from the disliked program, we suspect coding may give clues to why some programs have ascending and others descending lines of favor on

the graphs or explain the sharp peaks and valleys that occasionally occur.

The Segmented Audience

In this report we have discussed only reactions by a cross section of the "public" of the Lansing area. We are examining other audiences, however. We have found that a sample of high school teachers viewed programs differently from the public. When we asked students majoring in TV production to predict public reaction to programs, we found they predicted correctly low keep-on scores for "Sculptor," "Quill," "Witness," "French," and "Puberty," but fell far short, underestimating the audience by 50 per cent or more, for programs like "Agriculture," "Guatemala," and "Friends." For our final viewings, we selected programs from three of the pivotal clusters—programs on music, on great ideas and books, and on child care. We then looked for groups of people with special interest in one of the areas and invited them to viewings. We are now analyzing results, to see whether a person with high interest and considerable knowledge in a subject area tends to be more or less critical of programs in that area, and whether he does not make finer discriminations within such programs than the person who lacks his special interest.

Predictors of Viewer Reaction

As has already been noted, when we exposed viewers to a great variety of subject matter, they seemed to use rather gross subject-matter classes in their judgments. They may, however, use more format-oriented pigeonholes when they see several programs within a single subject area. If so, then coding the content of programs should help predict viewer reaction to them. Although the cost of regular viewer sessions is not large, relationship between codable program content and viewer reaction would eliminate much of the need for them.

Another possible predictor of viewer reaction focuses upon the viewer himself rather than on the programs. Part of this line of investigation has been reported in this paper—the relationship between demographic indexes and viewers' preference for program clusters. Another part, not reported here, involves giving viewers paper-and-pencil check lists of program types, based on materials used in audience surveys at the Universities of Wisconsin and Minnesota and at Stanford University. Types of viewers, based on these responses, may show a relationship to types of viewers based on responses in viewing sessions. If they do, then any ETV station would find it comparatively easy to gather such data for the population in its area and predict their responses to specific programs.

Anticipations

Throughout the study we have been interested in seeing whether a viewer's feeling about how well he could anticipate what was coming next is related to his liking for a program. In the beginning we looked at viewers' images of educational TV, TV and education, and their images of the audience of educational TV. Later we asked viewers to tell us, on a seven-point scale, after viewing a program segment, how sure they felt of what was coming next. We felt that either extreme on the scale might be associated with low liking for a program—that too much certainty would make a program dull, and too little make it confusing. We hoped that differences in program ratings on this scale could be traced back to differences in content. These data, too, remain to be analyzed.

Appendix A

Performer

1.	Colorful__:__:__:__:__:__:__	Colorless
2.	Unpleasant to listen to__:__:__:__:__:__:__	Pleasant to listen to
3.	Hard to understand__:__:__:__:__:__:__	Easy to understand
4.	Jumpy__:__:__:__:__:__:__	Smooth
5.	Easy to watch__:__:__:__:__:__:__	Hard to watch
6.	Friendly__:__:__:__:__:__:__	Hostile
7.	Controversial__:__:__:__:__:__:__	Neutral
8.	Strong personality__:__:__:__:__:__:__	Weak personality
9.	Graceful__:__:__:__:__:__:__	Awkward
10.	Solemn__:__:__:__:__:__:__	Gay
11.	Exciting__:__:__:__:__:__:__	Dull
12.	Warm__:__:__:__:__:__:__	Cold
13.	High-brow__:__:__:__:__:__:__	Common sense
14.	Boring__:__:__:__:__:__:__	Entertaining
15.	Biased__:__:__:__:__:__:__	Unbiased
16.	Impressive__:__:__:__:__:__:__	Unimpressive

Performer

17.	Pleasant__:__:__:__:__:__:__	Irritating
18.	Bad__:__:__:__:__:__:__	Good
19.	Educational__:__:__:__:__:__:__	Entertaining
20.	Impersonal__:__:__:__:__:__:__	Personal
21.	Fast__:__:__:__:__:__:__	Slow
22.	I dislike him__:__:__:__:__:__:__	I like him
	(her) (them)	(her) (them)
23.	Informative__:__:__:__:__:__:__	Not informative
24.	Active__:__:__:__:__:__:__	Passive
25.	Relaxed__:__:__:__:__:__:__	Tense
26.	Insincere__:__:__:__:__:__:__	Sincere
27.	Snobbish__:__:__:__:__:__:__	Folksy
28.	Confusing__:__:__:__:__:__:__	Clear
29.	Professional__:__:__:__:__:__:__	Amateurish

Appendix B

Program

1.	Boring__:__:__:__:__:__:__	Entertaining
2.	I learned little__:__:__:__:__:__:__	I learned a lot
3.	Easy to watch__:__:__:__:__:__:__	Hard to watch
4.	Meaningless__:__:__:__:__:__:__	Meaningful
5.	Bad photography__:__:__:__:__:__:__	Good photography
6.	Active__:__:__:__:__:__:__	Passive
7.	Money well spent__:__:__:__:__:__:__	Money wasted
8.	Important__:__:__:__:__:__:__	Trivial
9.	Smooth__:__:__:__:__:__:__	Jumpy
10.	Educational__:__:__:__:__:__:__	Entertaining
11.	Confusing__:__:__:__:__:__:__	Clear
12.	Professional__:__:__:__:__:__:__	Amateurish
13.	Bad__:__:__:__:__:__:__	Good
14.	Simple__:__:__:__:__:__:__	Complicated
15.	Slow__:__:__:__:__:__:__	Fast
16.	Informative__:__:__:__:__:__:__	Not informative
17.	I like it__:__:__:__:__:__:__	I dislike it
18.	Too many facts__:__:__:__:__:__:__	Too few facts
19.	Exciting__:__:__:__:__:__:__	Dull
20.	Easy to understand__:__:__:__:__:__:__	Hard to understand
21.	Pleasant__:__:__:__:__:__:__	Irritating
22.	Worthwhile__:__:__:__:__:__:__	Worthless
23.	Unpleasant to watch__:__:__:__:__:__:__	Pleasant to watch
24.	Useful for me__:__:__:__:__:__:__	Useless for me
25.	Enthusiastic__:__:__:__:__:__:__	Not enthusiastic
26.	Factual__:__:__:__:__:__:__	Opinionated

Appendix C

Subject Matter

1.   Controversial__:__:__:__:__:__:__Neutral
2.   Meaningful__:__:__:__:__:__:__Meaningless
3.   I like it__:__:__:__:__:__:__I dislike it
4. Easy to understand__:__:__:__:__:__:__Hard to understand
5.   Entertaining__:__:__:__:__:__:__Boring
6.   Opinionated__:__:__:__:__:__:__Factual
7.   Pleasant__:__:__:__:__:__:__Irritating
8.   Uninteresting__:__:__:__:__:__:__Interesting
9.   Complicated__:__:__:__:__:__:__Simple
10.   Dull__:__:__:__:__:__:__Exciting
11.   Good__:__:__:__:__:__:__Bad
12. Useful for me__:__:__:__:__:__:__Useless for me
13.   Entertaining__:__:__:__:__:__:__Educational
14.   Worthwhile__:__:__:__:__:__:__Worthless

Appendix D

Sample I. Descriptions of Four-Minute Segments of Programs
Shown to Public and Teachers

1. Religions of Man (The Good News)

Title moves from picture of Hindu dancer symbolizing series to drawing of fish for this program. Camera shows speaker before map. Alluding to previous program, Dr. Huston Smith says that Jesus' execution, unlike that of other visionaries before and since, marked the beginning of a movement in which disciples were transformed and went out, eloquently proclaiming the Gospel. Close-up of map shows spread through Mediterranean area. Standing by the drawing of the fish, he says it was not the ethical teachings of Jesus which represented the "good news," but something symbolized by the fish.

2. Measure of Man #3 (Tragedy)

Prof. John Dodds of Stanford University is seated before fireplace with book; he turns pages with program credits as off-camera voice reads them. About 40″ camera shows close-ups of headlines concerning death and disaster as he drops newspapers on desk. Dodds then says that although we accept natural catastrophe, human-made disasters puzzle us. Religion and philosophy have answers, he says, but those of dramatists are more creative. Why is it, he asks, that we can enjoy the stage representation of human misery? Philosophers, he says, give dusty answers, distorted by their preconceptions. He cites Hegel as an example, charging he completely misinterpreted the plays from which he drew his theory of tragedy.

3. Insurance (Comprehensive Home Owner's Policy)

Abstract title leads to Carl Fischer of University of Michigan, in waist shot, as announcer says he will help viewers plan program for selves and family. Fischer says the home, one of largest investments person will make in his lifetime, faces risks other than fire, and introduces lecturer in business administration. As they mention perils, camera shows cartoons of falling trees, landslides, explosion. Camera then returns to two speakers, as they begin to discuss adequacy of coverage.

4. Doctors in Space (Flight Toward the Stars)

Title shows jet-assisted plane taking off, then rocket zooming off, as voice off screen gives credits. Camera then shows M.C. through window, then shifts on his side of window, standing against clouds. Saying that man's urge to explore universe grows as his knowledge of it increases, speaker moves to model of earth and satellites. Unmanned satellites will be put up during the geophysical year, he says. The main obstacle to manned flights, he continues, is man himself. While engineers work on rockets, doctors study physiological difficulties man will meet in space. Only one laboratory, that at Randolph Air Force Base, has a department of space medicine, and its head is in the studio today.

5. Discovery (Age of Dinosaurs)

Screen shows footprint to music background, then off-screen voice with credits, then off-screen voice of M.C., Mary Lela Grimes, who identifies footprint, then the "oldest egg in the world," shown on camera, which predates the dinosaurs. At 1'20" we have close-up of her. Then cartoon of caveman clubbing a dinosaur—which she says could not occur since dinosaurs were dead when man appeared. She says dinosaurs did not appear overnight. At 2'30" we go to close-up of blackboard on which name and dates of Silurian, Devonian, and other periods appear. Pointer points to them, and to cutouts of fish and amphibians, as she traces evolutionary process.

6. Tempest in a Test Tube (Carbon)

Boiling test tube appears on screen, then voice and titles for credits. At 45' we see speaker in laboratory who says program will deal with carbon, one of most common yet rarest elements. At 1' he begins demonstration: pours cane sugar into glass cylinder, then adds sulfuric acid; contents turn black and give off vapor. Camera gives close-up of tube, back to speaker, back to tube, as speaker explains acid releases hydrogen and oxygen from sugar, leaving carbon. Next he lights candle on table, then picks up white dish and holds it over candle so we can see black carbon soot appear on base. He coughs, as he accidentally leans over fumes, and comments on need to avoid effects of previous experiment.

7. Great Plains Trilogy III (Prairie Towns a Boomin')

Picture of buildings on camera as voice says frontier was passing, and best illustration of this was in the prairie towns. Credits then appear on screen. Dr. James C. Olson appears at 1'30" with back to camera, looking at an enlarged picture of business buildings in a prairie town. He turns around, says optimism was the keynote of these towns. Glances now at camera and now to the left or right. At 2'30" close-up of picture, with his pencil pointing to board sidewalk, business signs on building. He sits on table, picks up long wooden box, with glass lid, containing coins and bills, which he says represented the safe of a pioneer county in the days when every town wanted to be the county seat.

8. People Are Taught to Be Different (Puberty in Boys)

Three features suggest unusual program: many type faces in series title, swinging, out-of-focus, masklike drawings of faces, and unfamiliar music. At 45" move to waist shot of Negro speaker, Dr. Henry Allen Bullock, who says puberty is a traumatic experience for boys, with lasting impact on personality. The program, he says, will concern boys of the U.S. and of two African tribes. At 1'30" camera shows Negro boys and girls seated inside a hoop. Music and dance go on as his voice continues, pointing out that at this time young people begin entry into adult world. A rapid rate of growth disturbs personal and social balance, he says, illustrating it as boys rise in silhouette, for living graph of heights from 2 to 18 years. At 3'30" we move to single boy against abstract of room, shown as in distorting mirror, as speaker says irregular growth at this age leads a boy to worry about his looks.

9. Challenge to American Education B

Program begins with shot of table seating 11 persons, as four aides scurry about. The group is identified as Educational Policies Commission. Camera and off-screen voice identify each member in turn, beginning with Herman Wells, Chairman, and ending with James B. Conant. About 2'30" Wells introduces the day's guests, two of the younger members of Congress, one a Democrat and the other a Republican. The former begins by reading his statement.

10. Not in Our Stars #8 (Friends)

Program begins with two small boys wearing boxing gloves who are slugging one another. Camera shifts to Prof. McKinney at desk who calls to boys. They say they are friends and tell what this means to them. McKinney then summons two girls with dolls who tell what friendship means to them. Camera then shifts to two college students drinking milk shakes as McKinney, seated off camera, asks what being friends means to them.

11. Agricultural Policy (So Many with So Little)

Man is looking at photographs as program begins. At 1' we see close-up of two photos. At 2' camera shifts to family of four at table sorting snapshots. Man walks into scene after 15" and explains family went south previous summer. At 1'30" we get close-up of map as he traces route, then see travel folders. At 3'10" we see landscape, as from a moving car, then interior shots of family in car. Then we see movies of southern scenes, from a fixed camera, of cotton in the field and cotton arriving at the gin.

12. America Looks Abroad (Guatemala)

This is Guatemala, says off-camera voice, as hand checks country on close-up of map. At 15″ we see speaker who says this is where Communism made a bid for power in the western hemisphere. At 30″ credits begin. At 1′10″ we are back to Carter Davidson of the Chicago Council on Foreign Relations. On map he shows relation of Guatemala to U.S. and Panama Canal, says country has three million people, half of direct Indian descent. At 2′30″ he says, "For a closer look of what the people are like, let's have a chat with one," and moves to couch where a young woman is seated. For rest of segment they talk about garments she has with her and necklace she is wearing.

13. Dateline USSR (Lifetime of the Soviet Man)

Close-up of newspaper headline as off-camera voice says Russia takes more space in our newspapers than any other subject. We lack information to match our concern for we get only what we can learn from the Russian press, voice says, as Russian newspapers appear on screen. These, voice says, are combed for clues; he gives examples of small items from which we learned of reform of the legal code, deportation of Chechen people. At 1′30″ we see map drawn on glass, with speaker in far distance behind it. Speaker comes closer, then at 1′45″ we shift to credits. At 2′15″ speaker returns, now on camera side of map, to tell who he is and his connection with Columbia University. He says that Russia is a place where cabinet members may disappear overnight and that we lack statistics on their births and deaths, crime, disease, ship tonnage, etc. Russia, he says, is a jigsaw puzzle with many of the pieces missing, but clues can be found in their publications.

14. Science in Action (Religious Archeology)

Behind title and credits are pictures of scientific equipment and workers in what appears to be a chemistry laboratory. At 45″ we see man in laboratory coat before mural photo of an archeological dig. Speaker says that religion and science are not at loggerheads and that the program's guest, Jack Finnegan, is a biblical scholar, pastor, and scientist. Camera shows close-up of book by Finnegan and at 1′50″ he and M.C. shake hands. M.C., taking role of naive stooge, says, "Let's see, archeology means . . . ," and Finnegan agrees. Finnegan adds that archeology shows that ancient peoples were much like ourselves. At 2′40″ we get close-up of table full of finds, some 3,000 years old. Finnegan identifies plowshare, sickle, and grinding stones, and says that men even then had a religion. M.C. picks up bone pendant, which is identified as a magic object worn to make the owner strong. Finnegan then says that magic, like religion, is an attempt of man to relate himself—and the program segment ends.

15. Visits with a Sculptor (Terra Cotta Sculpture)

Camera slowly goes up staircase with sculpture heads behind credits. At 45″ we see hands of sculptor, Merrell Gage, working with clay. At 1′ we see him, and he says he is working on a squeeze-out, a sculptor's sketch; he holds a similar "sketch" against the finished product. Camera shows similar sketches under the eaves, and Gage picks up several in turn, explaining what they are. He explains that an idea not used evaporates but that these three-dimensional "sketches" catch the idea. At 3'35" he explains that these sculptures are in terra cotta clay, which, unlike other clay, can be fired in large masses.

16. Musical Forms #3 (Rondo)

Screen shows names of performers and of selections they are to play. Henry Temianka says subject of program is the rondo, which he compares to a three-decker sandwich or a layer cake. At 1'45" he begins playing violin with piano accompaniment: Kreisler's "Rondino on a Theme of Beethoven." Camera moves in, showing part of Temianka's face and bow on violin, then moves out to long shot with accompanist, then moves in again for close-up.

17. *La Finta Giardiniera*

There is no narrator for this program. Music plays in background as screen gives name, translator, etc., of the Mozart opera. Screen goes black for a moment, then costumed actors move on and off, as their names and roles appear in subtitles. Just as four-minute segment ends, curtain parts on stage and actors, and woman opens her mouth to sing.

18. The Quill #4 (Writing Forceful Sentences)

After title, we see teacher seated at desk. He says he hopes we are ready for work and warns that the lesson will be difficult. We didn't learn to write a sentence in grade school, he says. A professional writer once said *he* hadn't written a half-dozen good sentences in his whole life. At 2'10" camera shows this printed sentence: "I arrived on Saturday night and the city was very busy." Whoever wrote that, says the speaker, wasn't thinking well and will never write a good engineering report or a good short story. Nevertheless, he adds, there isn't much mystery about writing. Like bricklaying or carpentry or football, it is a matter of getting down to fundamentals.

19. Books and Ideas (*Witness*)

Four men apparently conversing in background, although their voices cannot be heard, as we get credits. Off-screen voice introduces four members of panel as camera gives close-up of each. Camera moves in and we hear voices for a moment, then M.C. says "Excuse me" to others and addresses camera. He summarizes the book, Whittaker Chambers' *Witness*, as being one-third the story of his youth, one-third his experiences in the Communist party, and one-third the Hiss case. At 2' camera moves to first speaker, at 3'15" to second speaker, at 3'50" to third. They say that Chambers tells how he came to be a Communist and what it was like being one, and going underground. They add that Chambers does a poor job of explaining why Hiss became and remained a Communist and suggest the book is modeled on that of Jean Jacques Rousseau.

20. French Through TV

Stick figure appears on screen as voice gives credits and explains that by mimicking voice of good native speakers, while stick figures illustrate the meaning, viewer can learn French. Simple phrases follow—"It's me," "I am here," "You are there"—then at 3' phrase appears orthographically while voice and stick figures repeat lesson.

Other Studies of Programs Commissioned by NETRC

1. UNIVERSITY OF HOUSTON. R. I. Evans, project director: *An Investigation of Some Aspects of the Social Psychological Impact of an Educational Television Program.*

Attitudes toward 3 of the 11 concepts in the test program were changed by television viewing. There was no evidence that individuals measured as more dogmatic would be more likely to resist change, or that there would be more change when the program was presented as coming from a commercial network rather than an educational station. It is suggested that the conception that educational television lacks prestige in the eyes of its viewers may be more imagined than real.

2. UNIVERSITY OF HOUSTON. R. I. Evans, project director: *An Examination of the Social Psychological Impact of a Controversial Educational Television Program, and of the Differential Effects of Experience in Viewing Television on Attitudes Toward Telecourses.*

Attitude change was not significant in the case of relatively prejudiced viewers, but was slightly effective on relatively unprejudiced viewers. Individuals experienced in telecourses appeared to be more favorably inclined toward traditional classroom instruction. Other results suggest that this may be the result of peripheral factors rather than of television experience.

3. UNIVERSITY OF WASHINGTON. M. Ryan and Edith Dyer Rainboth, project directors: *Pilot Study of KCTS-TV Programming.*

Results suggest a per-program rather than a per-station viewing. Viewers seem most interested in "cultural" programs; science next; public affairs and social sciences third.

4. UNIVERSITY OF MICHIGAN. D. J. Shettler, project director: *Multiple Evaluations of Films Selected from Educational Television Music Series.*

In progress.

EDUCATIONAL TELEVISION IN THE CLASSROOM

Can filmed ETV courses be used to fill in some of the science which a college freshman should have, but hasn't, learned in high school? In other words, can colleges lift the standards of freshman courses by turning some of the remedial work over to television teachers? Penn State tried it with freshman physics, and found that use of some of Harvey White's television lectures made a significant improvement in the performance of their students. Frank R. Hartman is on the staff of the Division of Academic Research and Services at Pennsylvania State University.

FILMED PHYSICS LECTURES AS SUPPLEMENTARY AND REFRESHER COLLEGE PHYSICS INSTRUCTION

by Frank R. Hartman [1]

A major concern of American colleges and universities in recent years has been the insufficient preparation for mature college work which has characterized many members of the incoming freshman class. Several areas of instruction are especially critical in this respect, among them introductory physics.

Numerous suggestions have been made toward the improvement of this situation: changes in high school curriculum and courses of study, toughening of entrance requirements, increases in the salary, selectivity, and level of training of high school science teachers, etc. But whatever the merits of improving the high school program, it is evident that any advantages accruing from such changes will require several years to alter the college picture even if effected immediately. For this reason it has been necessary to ask what the colleges might do to prevent deterioration of their own standards during the period of time elapsing before revisions at the high school level begin to take effect or in the event that no improvements are forthcoming.

One such solution is that the colleges themselves must take the

----

[1] The author wishes to acknowledge the help and cooperation of the following persons: Dean Clarence I. Noll, Dean William H. Powers, Professor John A. Sauer, Professor Robert L. Weber, and especially the graduate students of the Academic Year Institute who served as assistants in the first study.

responsibility for insuring adequate preparation. This solution requires that an instructional program be introduced which has as its objective the remedying of the existing academic deficiencies of the incoming freshmen. Such a remedial program could be scheduled either preceding or concurrent with the regular academic program.

The primary concern of the studies reported here is the possibility of using filmed lectures for such remedial instruction in physics. Several advantages can be argued for films as an instructional medium: (1) there is not a sufficient number of qualified instructors available to staff a remedial program with live instruction; (2) filmed lectures of good quality prepared by an instructor of national reputation and possessing a high degree of technical proficiency are available; (3) homogeneity of instruction among sections is insured; (4) the cost per student instructed is relatively inexpensive. What remains to be demonstrated is the effectiveness of the filmed physics lecture program in satisfying its remedial educational objectives.

A close scrutiny of the Penn State physical science program revealed that two investigations pertinent to the value of filmed remedial physics lectures could be made without greatly disturbing the program itself. The first was a compulsory orientation course for all freshmen in the College of Chemistry and Physics which permitted the utilization of these students for one hour a week to view selected filmed lectures. Since none of the freshmen involved was scheduled for physics until the following semester, this arrangement permitted the evaluation of the effectiveness of filmed lectures to increase the level of achievement over those areas which they covered *prior* to the introductory course. This constitutes the first experiment to be described.

A second possibility was to schedule evening showings of the filmed lectures concurrent with a physics course and allow student utilization of the opportunity and expressed opinion to be the criteria of the effectiveness of the venture. This is the concern of the second study reported.

The filmed lectures utilized were selected from a complete one-year course, "Introductory Physics," taught by Harvey E. White and produced by Encyclopaedia Britannica Films, Inc. The filming was accomplished simultaneously with the telecasting of the lectures over WQED-TV in Pittsburgh. The process is described in detail by Dr. White in a 1957 article in *Physics Today*.[2] An evaluation of the usefulness of the films for the instruction of rural high school students has now been completed in Wisconsin. Two progress reports [3] are available on this project. An urban high school evaluation was performed in Chicago.[4] Teaching outlines and test items have been prepared by Encyclopaedia Britannica to accompany the films.

THE FIRST EXPERIMENT

Procedure

Approximately 180 students, the entire freshman class in the College of Chemistry and Physics, were randomly divided into two groups which were ultimately reduced by academic shrinkage to 80 and 75 respectively. After measurement on a pretest consisting of the College Entrance Examination Board Test in Physics, each group was placed in a separate lecture room. One group received films selected from the series of films covering electricity and magnetism. The other group viewed films selected from the series devoted to mechanics. Each group viewed a single film at the same hour. Following the film a short quiz was given on the material covered in the film, administered by graduate students in physical science education, who assisted at the class meetings. This assistance was limited to a simple introduction of the film of the day, quiz administration, and the answering questions on the quiz problems if time permitted. The quizzes were graded by the students themselves and were designed to stimulate learning, not as criteria for the experiment. The arrangement described above permitted each group to serve as a control for the other, assuming that electricity and magnetism subject matter is relatively independent of the mechanics subject matter. Thus, two individual experiments were carried out: one on the effect of mechanics films on achievement in

---

[2] H. E. White, "Physics Course on TV," *Physics Today*, Vol. 10, No. 9 (Sept., 1957), pp. 14–19.

[3] Wisconsin Physics Film Evaluation Project, *Progress Report*, May, 1958; Wisconsin Physics Film Evaluation Project, *Progress Report-II*, Nov., 1958.

[4] M. D. Engelhart, E. C. Schwachtgen, and Mary M. Nee, *The Chicago Public Schools Television Instruction Experiment in High School Physics*, mimeographed report, undated.

mechanics, the other on the effect of electricity and magnetism films on achievement in electricity and magnetism.

At the close of the 11-week experimental period during which one film per week was viewed and a quiz administered, an hour examination was given to both groups. This examination consisted of two parts, one concerning mechanics, the other electricity and magnetism. Each part contained 25 questions selected from the questions pertinent to the film subject matter and compiled especially for the films by Encyclopaedia Britannica. The selection of the questions was made by physical science graduate students who assisted in the presentation of the films. Each test was timed for 25 minutes and the order of the tests was randomized in such a way that approximately half of the students in each experimental group took the tests in the order mechanics–electricity and magnetism; the other half in the order electricity and magnetism–mechanics. A questionnaire concerning the value of the films to the students was administered at the last film showing.

Results

The results of the two covariance analyses of the scores on (1) mechanics and (2) electricity and magnetism using the College Entrance Examination Board as an adjusting variable are presented in Tables 1 and 2.

TABLE 1. ANALYSIS OF COVARIANCE OF THE MECHANICS SCORES USING THE COLLEGE ENTRANCE EXAMINATION BOARD SCORES AS AN ADJUSTING VARIABLE

Source	SS	Df	V	F	P
Treatment	72.78	1	72.78	9.59	$<.01$
Error	1153.70	152	7.59		
Total	1226.48	153			

Group	Adjusted Means	N
Mechanics viewing group	15.70	75
Control group	14.33	80

The results of the analyses of both the mechanics and electricity and magnetism achievement scores indicate significant differences in achievement resulting from the viewing of the series of films related to these respective topics.

TABLE 2. ANALYSIS OF COVARIANCE OF THE ELECTRICITY AND MAGNETISM SCORES USING THE COLLEGE ENTRANCE EXAMINATION BOARD SCORES AS AN ADJUSTING VARIABLE

Source	SS	Df	V	F	P
Treatment	77.05	1	77.05	7.75	$<.01$
Error	1510.98	152	9.94		
Total	1588.03	153			

Group	Adjusted Means	N
Electricity and magnetism viewing group	13.26	80
Control group	11.85	75

The results of four relevant questions from a questionnaire administered at the end of the experiment are given in Table 3.

TABLE 3

1. What effect do you think the films have had on your understanding of physics?

	E & M	Mech.	Totals
Very helpful	15%	14%	14%
Somewhat helpful	67	58	62
Not very helpful	16	26	21
Not at all helpful	2	2	3
Percentage totals	100	100	100

2. Do you feel the need for some sort of supplementary work beyond your high school preparation in physics, such as a no-credit physics preparatory course?

	E & M	Mech.	Totals
Yes	43%	39%	41%
Maybe	28	34	31
No	29	27	28
Percentage totals	100	100	100

3. How much high school preparation in physics have you had?

	E & M	Mech.	Totals
One year	90%	85%	87%
None	4	10	7
Two years	3	1	2
Three years	0	1	1
Hardly any	3	1	1
No answer	0	1	1
One-half year	0	1	1
Percentage totals	100	100	100

TABLE 3. (*concluded*)

----

4. Would you like to see a preparatory physics course introduced at Penn State which would be based on these films?

	E & M	Mech.	Totals
Yes	68%	64%	66%
No	20	25	22
Possibly	11	4	7
No answer	0	3	1
Don't know	1	1	1
Use other material also	0	1	1
Course voluntary	0	1	1
Take laboratory trips	0	1	1
Percentage totals	100	100	100

THE SECOND EXPERIMENT

Procedure

An evening showing of two of the series of lecture films on mechanics was scheduled once a week. The time of the film presentation was selected to conflict with relatively few courses and extracurricular activities. Two filmed lectures on mechanics were shown each evening in proper sequence without any supplementary material, either written or verbal.

The nature of the films and the time of showing was announced to approximately 300 students who were encouraged to take advantage of the opportunity to improve their knowledge of mechanics. Approximately 240 of these students were enrolled in the nonengineering course in mechanics (this course does not require the calculus). The remaining 60 were freshmen in chemical engineering who received information concerning the films in a meeting with the head of their department. Attendance records were kept and at the close of the showings questionnaires were sent to all who had attended.

Results

The major criterion for the success of the trial was obtaining a large and continuing audience for the films. The initial showing attracted 34 students, a little better than 10 per cent of the students to whom the films were announced. The attendance was reduced to 15 for the second week. At the fifth presentation only 3 students attended, and the venture was canceled.

Thirty-four of the students who viewed varying amounts of the series were contacted. By means of a follow-up letter a completed questionnaire was obtained from 30 of the 34. Those students who did view the films seemed positively disposed toward them. Results of three pertinent questions from the questionnaire administered at the close of the trial are given in Table 4.

TABLE 4

1. What effect do you think the films have had on your understanding of physics?

Very helpful	30%
Somewhat helpful	40
Not very helpful	30
Not at all helpful	0
Percentage total	100

2. Do you feel the need for some sort of supplementary work beyond your high school preparation in physics, such as a no-credit physics preparatory course?

Yes	38%
No	28
Maybe	34
Percentage total	100

3. Would you like to see a preparatory physics course introduced at Penn State which would be based on these films?

Yes	86%
No	14
Percentage total	100

DISCUSSION

The findings of these rather modest studies indicate that filmed lectures are useful in increasing the knowledge of physics of college freshmen. Significant gains were recorded in both of the areas of subject matter sampled. These gains may be considered impressive in that they were achieved with a small number (11) of lectures without outside preparation or practice on the part of the students and with none of the usual academic incentives such as grades, credits, or honors. The student acceptance of the films is favorable with a large majority supporting a film-based preparatory course.

In regard to the optional attendance of concurrent films it appears that the presentation of the lecture material on a voluntary attendance basis as supplemental to the freshman program is impractical. The students simply cannot find time for this extra activity, and to make it compulsory would constitute a serious imposition.

The studies reported may be considered as tentative evidence that an economical and productive remedial physics program can be based on filmed lectures. The practical and economic advantages of such a program have been previously mentioned. Experimental comparisons with other media of instruction within a formally constituted course are necessary, however, before any strong endorsement of the film lecture is possible. The advisability of a given college or university undertaking any remedial instruction of its freshmen remains, of course, as a policy decision for that institution.

Students at the University of Detroit learned at least as much about Spanish verb forms from television as from classroom teaching. The author discusses the meaning of the results, and is especially interested in television's ability to superimpose one visual stimulus on others, which he regards as an exceptionally promising tool for language teaching. Dr. Bundy was an Associate Professor at the University of Detroit when he made this study. He is now Production Manager of educational station KNME-TV in Albuquerque, and Associate Professor of Speech at the University of New Mexico.

TELEVISION AND
THE LEARNING OF SPANISH VERBS

by E. Wayne Bundy

SUMMARY OF PROJECT

Purpose of the Study

The purpose of the study was to determine the effectiveness of instructional television presentational techniques as compared to conventional classroom procedures in promoting initial comprehension of critical basic Spanish verb form concepts.

So far as could be determined, neither television's effectiveness in the foreign language area nor the effectiveness of the specific techniques employed to project such content had previously been established.

Design

A single variable experimental pattern was followed, with the experimental groups treated alike in all respects save one—the variation in presentational techniques and procedures under investigation.

The primary independent variable was *presentational technique* —television production techniques *vs.* conventional classroom procedures—rather than *mode of presentation* as such. The primary dependent variable was *academic achievement*—demonstrated comprehension of concept following initial exposure, as measured by a teacher-designed test administered to real subjects in a realistic situation. The same concepts were presented over an identical length of time per concept by the same teacher using the same basic methodology of language teaching. After presentation, the same time elapsed before evaluation from the same test, marked by the same grader, with qualitative judgments made by the same teacher. *Equivalent-groups* procedures were employed, combined with *rotation* of the groups to further minimize uncontrolled variables.

SELECTED CONCEPTS

Three critical basic verb form concepts were selected for experimental treatment: (1) form relationship of the irregular preterite to the imperfect subjunctive and hence to the past perfect subjunctive, (2) the irregular future, and (3) the patterns of radical-changing verbs.

PRESENTATIONAL TECHNIQUES

Two differing kinds of techniques and procedures were compared: (1) *conventional classroom procedures* (CR)—regularly possible in a conventional classroom with normal facilities and contributing to the instructor's best face-to-face teaching, and (2) *television presentational techniques* (TV)—utilizing complex mobile superimposition, and capitalizing on the ability of the medium to provide economically and conveniently simultaneous dual and/or sequentially multiple visual stimuli for maximal visualization of language concepts.

EXPERIMENTAL SUBJECTS

The study was conducted during the spring of 1958 at the University of Detroit, with students in two conventional Spanish I sections regularly taught by other instructors serving as experimental subjects. Although the use of existing groups within a course being taught had the disadvantage of limiting experimental manipulation to some degree, it offered the advantage of working within a genuine learning situation with subjects presumably typically motivated to learn.

Procedure

1. In normal sequence in the course, Concept 1 was presented by Gordon Farrell, Associate Professor of Modern Languages—

first to Group A as a unit within a typical teleclass lesson for group viewing under CCTV conditions, and then to Group B as a content unit of equal length within a typical classroom session. Evaluation was conducted 24 hours later with a brief teacher-designed test intended to indicate concept comprehension, graded first quantitatively for over-all score, then qualitatively for concept comprehension as such.

2. Identical procedure was followed for Concept 2.

3. Identical procedure was followed for Concept 3 *except* that the groups were rotated, with Group A becoming the CR group and Group B the TV group.

4. Concept 3 was re-presented in a 15-minute review context, with each group subdivided into TV and CR subgroups, followed by similar evaluation.

5. Statistical analysis of the data obtained was undertaken.

SUMMARY OF FINDINGS

Description of Subjects

Composition of the two sections of Spanish I available for experimentation had been determined by ordinary registration procedures, and student subjects could not readily have been reassigned to experimental conditions. However, statistical analysis revealed no significant differences between the two groups in age, sex distribution, language aptitude, or performance on the final examination for the course, and therefore found them suitably comparable. After attrition, there remained 19 applicable subjects per group.

Comparisons Undertaken

Data both quantitative and qualitative were obtained, allowing both kinds of comparisons, first for unmatched groups and later for matched. Analysis of variance technique was later applied to comparison for the four subgroups evaluated in a review context.

COMPARISONS OF UNMATCHED GROUPS FOR CONCEPTS 1, 2, AND 3

Quantitative. Seven quantitative comparisons were undertaken, dealing with relative achievement on Tests 1, 2, and 3. First, mean scores of the two groups were compared for each of the tests separately. Next, all TV scores were compared with all CR scores over all three tests. Then, intragroup comparisons were undertaken, contrasting performance of each group after rotation to the other presentational technique and circumstances with its previous performance. Finally, a comparison was made of amount of improvement shown by the two groups following rotation to the opposite set of experimental conditions. Table 1 summarizes these comparisons.

TABLE 1. SUMMARY—QUANTITATIVE COMPARISONS—TESTS 1, 2, AND 3

Comparison	Concept	Mn Diff.	Favor TV	CR	Signif.	Nonsignif. Near	Far
Mn scores A vs. B	1	2.04	A				X
Mn scores A vs. B	2	3.14	A			.20	
Mn scores B vs. A	3	1.17	B				X
Mn scores TV/CR	1, 2, 3	1.93	A & B			.16	
Postrotate B Mn diff. vs. prev.	3/1	3.59 [a]	3		.04		
	3/2	0.74	3				X
	3/1 & 2	2.15	3			.17	
Postrotate A Mn diff. vs. prev.	3/1	0.94		3			X
	3/2	−2.08	2			.08	
	3/1 & 2	−0.49	1 & 2				X
Postrotate improvement B vs. A	3/1	2.65	B			.15	
	3/2	2.82	B [b]			.18	

[a] Significant beyond the .05 level.
[b] A—negative on improvement.

Qualitative. Five qualitative comparisons were undertaken, dealing with relative achievement of the two groups over Tests 1, 2, and 3. First, obtained and expected distributions of qualitative scores indicating comprehension or noncomprehension of concept for both groups over Tests 1, 2, and 3 were compared for each of the tests separately. Next, obtained and expected distribution of qualitative scores indicating comprehension or noncomprehension of concept for all TV subjects was compared with that of all CR subjects over all three tests. Finally, individual subject improvement or decline for both groups following rotation in experimental conditions was compared. Table 2 summarizes the comparisons.

TABLE 2. SUMMARY—QUALITATIVE COMPARISONS—TESTS 1, 2, AND 3

Comparison	Concept	Distrib. Yes	Distrib. No	Favor TV	Favor CR	Signif.	Nonsignif. Near	Nonsignif. Far
Y/N distrib. A vs. B	1	11 7	6 11	A			.14	
Y/N distrib. A vs. B	2	9 11	4 8	A				X
Y/N distrib. B vs. A	3	14 10	4 8		B		.17	
Y/N distrib. TV vs. CR	1, 2, 3	34 28	14 27	A & B [a]		.04		
Postrotate	3/1	11 7	6 [b] 9		B		.19	
improvement B vs. A	3/2	7.5 4	10.5 [b] 9		B		.13	

[a] Significant beyond the .05 level.
[b] Categories—improve/decline.

Summary of Findings from Unmatched-Groups Comparisons

1. Direct comparison of the two groups—both quantitatively and qualitatively—on Concepts 1 and 2 revealed n.s.d. (no significant difference) between mean scores and between distributions of qualitative scores. However, there was a consistent—though statistically nonsignificant—trend of differences favoring TV presentational techniques. Some of these differences approached significance.

2. When the groups were rotated in experimental conditions, identical findings resulted: n.s.d. between mean scores and between distributions of qualitative scores of the two groups on Test 3, although with the reversal of group roles came a reversal of relative achievement. Hence, the same trend of differences favoring TV presentational techniques continued and to a comparable degree. The previous conclusion that the two groups came from a common population was sustained.

3. When the mean of all TV scores was compared with the mean of all CR scores for the first three tests, n.s.d. was found. But when

the distributions of qualitative scores from both groups for both techniques for the first three tests were compared, a difference *significant* well beyond the .05 level was found favoring TV presentational techniques over conventional CR procedures.

4. When comparison of postrotation results with those of previous tests was undertaken—in effect matching each group with itself—*n.s.d.* was found between test scores of Group A following CR procedures presentation and following TV techniques presentation. However, comparison of Test 3 with Test 1 provided the only difference found to favor CR procedures (although far short of significance). On the other two comparisons, the differences found favored TV techniques, with one approaching significance.

5. When the same comparison was undertaken for Group B, *n.s.d.* was found between test scores after TV techniques presentation and after CR procedures presentation in two of the three comparisons. However, when Test 3 (post-TV) was compared with Test 1 (post-CR), a difference *significant* beyond the .05 level was found favoring TV presentational techniques. Other differences found also favored TV techniques.

6. When the difference in scores for both groups following rotation was compared, there was *n.s.d.* between the groups in their respective performance differences on Tests 3 and 1, although again a much greater amount of improvement was shown in going from CR to TV. With the same comparison of differences between Tests 3 and 2, there was again *n.s.d.*, with slight improvement shown from CR to TV contrasting with a larger negative finding from TV to CR. Both differences approached significance.

7. When the same comparison of Tests 3 and 1 was made in terms of individual improvement or decline (with 50 per cent expectancy), the same reverse trend favoring the shift from CR to TV developed, but again fell somewhat short of significance. Comparing improvement or decline between Test 3 and Test 2, *n.s.d.* was found, but the amount of decline (in going to the more difficult Concept 3) was considerably greater for the group going from TV to CR.

COMPARISONS OF MATCHED GROUPS FOR CONCEPTS 1, 2, AND 3

Groups were then matched person to person on the basis of their individual language aptitude scores. Confirmation of the suitability of this basis for matching lay in the correlation of final examination grades with aptitude scores, which was significant beyond the

.01 level. Matched, the two groups consisted of 12 subjects each, with group means identical.

Six comparisons dealing with relative achievement of the two groups (matched) over Tests 1, 2, and 3 were undertaken. Four of these were quantitative, two qualitative. First, mean scores of the two groups were compared for each of the tests separately. Next, summed data from all three tests were used for the same comparison. Then, obtained and expected distributions of qualitative scores over all three tests were compared for the two groups. Finally, a similar comparison of high/low distribution of TV and CR scores for all three tests was undertaken. Table 3 summarizes these comparisons.

TABLE 3. SUMMARY—MATCHED-GROUP COMPARISONS—TESTS 1, 2, AND 3

Comparison	Concept	Diff.	Favor TV	Favor CR	Signif.	Nonsignif. Near	Nonsignif. Far
Mn scores A vs. B	1	3.73 [a]	A [b]		.05		
Mn scores A vs. B	2	1.28 [a]	A				X
Mn scores B vs. A	3	1.29 [a]	B				X
Mn scores TV/CR	1, 2, 3	2.13 [a]	A & B			.08	
Y/N Distrib. TV vs. CR	1, 2, 3	23 / 16	9 [c] / 16	A & B		.07	
High/Low Distr. TV/Exp.	1, 2, 3	20.5 / 16	11.5 [d] / 16	A & B		.11	

[a] Mn Diff.
[b] Significant beyond the .05 level.
[c] Yes/no pairs for two groups.
[d] TV superior/inferior (50 per cent expectancy).

Summary of Findings from Matched-Groups Comparisons

1. When matched-groups comparison was undertaken, *n.s.d.* was found between the mean scores on two of the three tests, although the trend continued to favor TV presentational techniques regardless of which group had been the TV group, in all three comparisons. The difference found on Test 1 proved *significant* at the .05 level.

2. When matched-groups comparison of TV scores and CR scores for the three tests was undertaken, *n.s.d.* was found, although a difference approaching significance at the .08 level was found favoring TV presentational techniques over conventional CR procedures.

3. With matched-groups comparison of distribution of qualitative scores on all three tests, *n.s.d.* was found, although the difference favoring TV presentational techniques again approached significance closely. A similar comparison of TV as superior/inferior (with 50 per cent expectancy) revealed the same trend, approaching significance, but *n.s.d.*

SUBGROUP COMPARISON ON REVIEW CONCEPT PRESENTATION

Following re-presentation of Concept 3 in a review context, subgroup comparison was undertaken by analysis of variance technique. *No significant difference* was found among the four subgroups in terms of amount of improvement shown by each individual from Test 3 to Test 4. The reverse trend differences occurring suggest a finding of somewhat better results from a change in presentational technique for review purposes, whichever direction the change.

Summary Statement

Of 24 statistical comparisons made on Tests 1, 2, and 3, 23 indicate a consistent trend favoring TV presentational techniques over conventional CR procedures. The one finding favorable to CR procedures is far from significant, while 13 of the 23 favoring TV techniques approach significance and 3 are statistically significant beyond the .05 level.

CONCLUSION AND IMPLICATIONS

Conclusion

From these findings, it is apparent that in promoting initial comprehension of critical basic Spanish verb form concepts, television presentational techniques utilizing the unique ability of the medium to provide—through *superimposition*—simultaneous dual and/or sequentially multiple visual stimuli are fully as effective as—and probably more so than—conventional classroom procedures.

Discussion

The certainty of at least equal effectiveness for the television techniques seems amply established. The probability of greater effectiveness seems equally clear in view of the overwhelming consistency of the trend favoring television presentational techniques —regardless of which of the experimental groups was thus exposed to the concept material, or what the comparison was.

Moreover, it may well be that this rather conventional conclusion represents only the minimal meaning of the findings. Meaningful interpretation of experimental data and research findings begins with an arbitrarily assigned level of statistical significance, but it should not end there. Its true function must be to reveal the significance of the total data obtained in the context of the particular experiment and in relation to the established findings in the field. Its true concern must be not only with statistical significance but with social significance.

In this instance, it is quite possible that the consistency of trend is more indicative than the finding of some statistically significant differences. Indeed, were the significant differences found relatively isolated phenomena, distinct in direction from those findings which merely approach significance, they should be somewhat suspect despite statistical significance. To a considerable degree, it is their coherence with the whole pattern of the findings that gives them true meaning as more striking expressions of consistent differences.

This consistency is apparent not only in the direction of the trend but also in its continuation in degree through rotation of the experimental groups and bilaterally in both quantitative and qualitative comparisons.

Why, then, in view of the consistency of the trend, were no more of the findings statistically significant? Analysis of probable causative factors provides additional rationale for broader interpretation of the findings.

First, it is obvious that the limited number of experimental subjects available required relatively large differences between groups for statistical significance. Quantitative differences of 2 and 3 points on a scale of some 30 possible failed to produce significance. The same result obtained from rather strikingly varied proportions of qualitative comprehensional scores. With a greater number of subjects available, had anything like the same differences occurred a high proportion of significant ratios should have resulted.

An equally important factor is the probability that it is unrealistic to expect to find dramatic differences in any comparison of teaching methods or techniques when academic achievement is the criterion. The San Francisco State study sums up the rationale:

> When knowledge is used as a criterion to discover the differential effects of two teaching methods, the results are disappointing. Birney and Mc-Keachie, summing up the research on the teaching of psychology during the past 12 years, make the following statement: "In 1942, Wolfle summarized research up to that time by repeating Longstaff's statement of 1932: 'The experimental evidence submitted to the present time tends to support the general conclusion that there is little difference in achievement in large and small classes, and also, that it makes little difference as to what method of presentation of materials of the course is used.' The third decade of research has not outdated Longstaff's statement." This same finding is applicable to the research on the effects of television teaching which has been conducted to date.[1]

A third possibility, commonly proposed as causative in relative effectiveness studies with academic achievement as criterion,[2] is that measuring instruments may not have been truly appropriate to the specialized learning situation involved. The rationale holds that since situation differed, achievement logically should have—and would have been revealed as differing by wholly appropriate instruments.

Moreover, it is evident that the comparison of effectiveness was not—and could not be—of the teacher's television presentational techniques with his own pre-TV conventional classroom procedures, but rather with his TV-modified classroom procedures—as shown in organization of material, tempo of presentation, and even in graphic use of the classroom blackboard. Hence, the inherent differences were to some extent minimized.

Finally, although concept presentation time was equal in the two situations, delay incident to utilization of viewing-room facilities radically reduced drill-discussion time for the TV groups. Since the CR groups had the benefit of a full 50-minute class session with adequate drill-discussion time following the presentation, a

----

[1] R. E. Dreher and W. H. Beatty, *Instructional Television Research, Project No. One: An Experimental Study of College Instruction Using Broadcast Television*, San Francisco, Calif.: San Francisco State College, 1958, p. 48.

[2] Carpenter, Kumata, Miller, and others.

time bias of at least 15 minutes per concept—favoring CR—was unwittingly introduced.

Hence, in view of these probable causatives and ETV research experience, it is clear that the surprising thing is not that no other statistically significant differences were found, but that these were, and that so many others approached significance. Moreover, since each factor tended to militate against the finding of significant differences, the differences found seem more significant and the consistency of trend more meaningful.

While it cannot be said, as warrant for broader interpretation, that the same differences would have occurred with more experimental subjects available, both the evidence on subject population and the consistency of pattern in spite of group rotation suggest that similar differences would have existed.

In any case, there would seem to be social significance in the obtained differences of 2 and 3 points out of 30—whether statistically significant or not. Since the differences appeared in tests in which the message was less than a single class unit long, cumulative differences over a semester's length would achieve considerable magnitude. A similar probability of social significance would seem to exist for concept comprehension differences running two and three to one in the TV groups, compared with generally equal distribution in the CR groups.

Yet another reason for broader interpretation of the minimal conclusion lies in the alternative implications of "promoting . . . comprehension"—which may appropriately refer either to "securing *improved* comprehension" or to "securing the same comprehension *more readily.*" The study sought to determine whether improved comprehension could be secured in equivalent time. However, with the time bias indicated, the fully equivalent and probably superior achievement found was actually obtained in less time and therefore secured more readily.

Hence, in view of the overwhelming consistency of trend favoring TV presentational techniques—and the implications of various other factors—the findings seem reasonably indicative beyond a minimal conclusion that complex language word form concepts can be communicated by specialized television presentational techniques fully as effectively as—and very probably more effectively than—by conventional classroom procedures.

Implications

RELEVANT TO THE TEACHING OF LANGUAGES IN A TELEVISION CONTEXT

The implications of the findings of this study and their interpretation relevant to the teaching of languages in a television context appear obvious:

1. Instruction-production teams teaching Spanish via television can reasonably expect to secure more effective communication of content concepts through these television techniques than through conventional classroom procedures.

2. Teams charged with television teaching of other Romance languages—and hence dealing with parallel concepts—can probably anticipate similar results.

3. Teams charged with such teaching of other languages can very possibly expect similar results, since problems comparable in kind—though not necessarily parallel in concept—ought logically to be susceptible to similar solutions.

The broader implications for administrators responsible for maintaining standards of foreign language instruction to increasing enrollments are equally clear. When a superior teacher taught complex language concepts through specialized TV presentational techniques, students so exposed did fully as well as—and very probably better than—their conventional classroom counterparts. If two experimental classes could so learn the critical and demanding complex verb form concepts of elementary Spanish, a dozen—or a hundred—could have.

1. Hence, when the problem of increased enrollment can no longer be met by scheduling more sections to be taught by more teachers in more classrooms—or when such scheduling will result in lowered standards as the proportion of fully qualified teachers decreases—the alternative of teaching languages by television presentational techniques may reasonably be expected to produce student achievement fully equivalent—and probably superior—to that produced by conventional classroom procedures.

2. Moreover, by implication from the broader interpretation of these findings, there is good reason to believe that improved comprehension of complex word form concepts can now be secured by effective utilization of these television techniques. Hence, the use of television in the teaching of languages—if the abilities of

the medium are effectively utilized—is a presently desirable procedure, not merely an acceptable alternative in time of future need.

RELEVANT TO RECENT CONTRAFINDINGS IN TELEVISION RESEARCH

The appearance of a minority of findings showing less satisfactory achievement for television-taught students than for their conventionally taught classmates at several institutions at about the same time is one of the more significant developments of recent ETV research. Since their trend is contrary to previous findings, it would appear that there had in these instances been factors added, subtracted, or modified in some way within the television-teaching milieu. Identification of these causative factors is obviously of prime importance to educational television activities, and various possibilities have been suggested.

Since the present study concurs with the trend of earlier research, it appears that the causative contrafinding factors were not operative in it. Hence, although for some of the apparent possibilities there can be no meaningful indication from a single study, for others there are relevant implications.

1. The first—*improved measurement of achievement*—is somewhat qualitative to permit meaningful comparison, but its likelihood as a causative factor appears somewhat diminished in terms of this study since the instruments used were carefully designed by a highly experienced and competent teacher, with performance goals clearly in mind, specifically to measure particular content comprehension from a single content unit presentation he himself had taught. The possibility remains, but since the direction of findings derived from intentionally careful measurement differs, this factor is not indicated as causative by this study.

2. However, the likelihood of the second—*use of conventional teaching methods in the television situation, and hence limited utilization of the medium*—as primary causative factor seems enhanced by the present study. Certainly the intent of production concept differed. Just as certainly did the presentational techniques utilized. Since the findings also differ, the possibility of causal relationship clearly remains, with its probability somewhat increased.

3. In itself, however, this explanation cannot account for the fact that earlier mode-of-presentation studies equally limited in production concept found equal or somewhat better effectiveness for television—in comparison with face-to-face. If, however, it be

reasoned that a change in response to the television experience in general were a contributing factor, this possibility too seems enhanced by the present findings. If it be supposed that television itself possessed a general novelty effect initially, and that this effect tended to decline in importance as television became commonplace, then it is quite reasonable that the recent contrafindings should have appeared—*the natural result of such a decline interacting with continued use of minimal production utilization.* Hence, the findings of this study of equal and probably better achievement from its presentational techniques suggest the possibility that only maximum utilization of the medium and its abilities is now likely to produce findings of *n.s.d.* or better.

RELEVANT TO OPERATIONAL APPLICATION OF THE TECHNIQUES

The implications relevant to the use of the specific techniques and the particular ability of the medium seem reasonably clear.

1. The use of complex mobile superimposition is confirmed as an effective device to project complex concept material involving intricate changes and interrelationships. In view of the consistent pattern of the findings, the time differential, and other indicative factors, it appears that such techniques—with their ability to provide teaching devices impracticable in the conventional classroom —can more effectively promote comprehension of such concepts.

2. Moreover, such evaluation is relevant to the larger question of validity of rationale for maximal utilization of the capabilities of the medium—with its implication of equality of production and instruction in team relationship, as well as a conscious attempt to achieve *instructional television* rather than *televised instruction.* There would appear to be indication at least of support for the proposition that improved utilization of the abilities of the medium should result in improved comprehension of concept.

FURTHER RESEARCH NEEDED

Studies on Foreign Language Teaching by Television

The lack of specific inquiry into language teaching in the television context is apparent. Obviously, further investigation is needed. The present study has resulted in three implications for language teaching via TV: (1) fairly positive indication that instruction-production teams teaching Spanish on TV can expect superior results in comparison to conventional classroom presentation if the medium's capacities and abilities are effectively utilized; (2) the strong probability that similar results may be anticipated in the teaching of other Romance languages through exploitation of similar techniques; and (3) a reasonable possibility that similar results should be attainable in the teaching of other languages. Experimental investigation of these hypotheses in various language areas is desirable, although it is suggested that utilization of the medium not wait verification of the present findings. Such investigations are also needed in view of the implications for administrators facing the problem of maintaining or improving standards in teaching foreign languages to increased enrollments.

Again, in view of the paucity of literature in the language-TV field, it is suggested that evaluation studies ought to be conducted wherever television teaching of languages is undertaken. Whenever feasible, such evaluation ought to be threefold—comparing classroom presentation with both classroom and home viewing of television presentation.

To be meaningful, such evaluation ought to go well beyond mere final-grades comparison, both in terms of achievement measurement and in bases of comparison. Specific evaluation should be sought in terms of student performance in reading, conversation, and composition, and even in such specifics as relative performance in language labs where utilized as a normal part of the course work. A battery of studies is indicated to determine optimum methods of classroom utilization, as well as classroom-monitor qualifications, procedures, and preparation. Follow-up studies should be instituted after the initial investigations to evaluate longer-range effects on television-taught students.

Studies based on replication and/or modification of the present study are also needed. Modified repetition in a variety of language contexts would certainly be worthwhile.

In view of the difficulty in securing evidence of improved academic achievement, and the relevant implications of the present study, it might well be more realistic to choose deliberately to investigate the relative time required to secure equal achievement from contrasting presentational techniques and procedures. It seems probable that differences found might be more dramatic than are likely to be obtained in studies of quantitative achievement. Significance of findings—if reduced time requirements for lecture-demonstration should be demonstrated—is obvious, since more course time could then be devoted to lab, drill, exercises, and other activities now curtailed by lack of time remaining after grammatical exposition.

The present study contrasted TV techniques with CR procedures. Its findings seem to indicate that the complex techniques used are more effective than routine TVI techniques, since its findings contrast with those of the minority of studies reporting contrafindings and based on minimum utilization. However, a study similar to Klapper's N.Y.U. "barebones" *vs.* "maximal visualization" approach would serve a useful purpose. It is suggested that specific inquiry dealing with single concept units might be more indicative than semester-long examination.

Similarly, studies seeking to determine the relative effectiveness of different kinds of TV visualization and visual devices are needed. The experimental design might parallel closely that of Brandon or Ulrich, with the three independent variables being instructor with blackboard only, instructor with routine visuals, and instructor with devices and techniques appropriate to full medium utilization.

A secondary element of the present study was to seek evaluation of relative effectiveness of television techniques and classroom procedures in review context, primarily as a further indication of differences of effectiveness that might be found. Since the only apparent finding was an indication that a change in presentational technique for review seemed desirable, replication and additional investigation are indicated. Should the implication of the present study be sustained, significant conclusions as to scheduling of combination TV-CR courses might result.

Television Studies on the Implications of the Contrafindings Studies

The need for research bearing on such findings is evident. Replication in itself will do much to clarify the issues. Additional studies over a wide range of content areas and with various production philosophies will do more.

Once a sufficient number of carefully designed studies have been conducted, it should become clear whether such findings were indeed rare instances of statistical misinterpretation or positively related to other factors. It is of course essential that measuring instruments be as carefully constructed as possible to reduce the possibility of variation there. Production approaches and devices should be carefully defined; since it is almost impossible to verbalize an essentially visual procedure adequately, reports of such research should include illustrative sections to make clear the kind of production effort involved. Then, with measurement and production factors clearly defined, a sufficiency of studies across a range of content areas should establish significant profiles if content area proves critical in its own right.

Finally, it has been suggested that such findings may have resulted from continued use of minimal utilization techniques interacting with a declining general novelty effect of the television experience itself. While it is probable that there have not yet been enough minority findings to prove more than suggestive, survey consideration of all such studies might be undertaken to investigate any possible relationship between their appearance and the duration of general television exposure in their geographical areas.

Television Studies on Effectiveness of Techniques

Obviously, numerous studies are needed to investigate further the effectiveness of *instructional television* techniques as contrasted to *televised instruction* procedures. These might well be either comparisons with each other, or—as in the present study—with class-room procedures. Data should be secured on specific content units as well as from more general comparisons. In some instances, key studies previously concerned with *mode* comparison only might now be repeated with every effort to secure maximal utilization of the capacities of the medium.

Since one of the unfortunate characteristics of current ETV operations seems to be a failure to capitalize on ITV techniques, it might be meaningful to undertake a survey study of significant production techniques utilized in those operations seeking to achieve ITV rather than TVI only.

One of the serious limitations of such a survey would be the fact that the judgments as to what are "significant" techniques would have to be almost wholly subjective. Hence, detailed investigation as to what techniques are really significant in projecting content information is indicated. Such studies need to have the intent of Ellery and of Kale, but manage to avoid the dilemma these studies encountered—the near impossibility of isolating individual techniques sufficiently as variables without divorcing them entirely from the context that gives them meaning.

Finally, if effectiveness of certain techniques can be experimentally established, further study should then be undertaken to explore possible interrelationships of particular techniques and specific kinds of content material.

How does radio compare with television as a teaching tool? The authors of this paper set out to find whether grade school pupils would learn more from a news program on radio or a comparable news program on television. In each case, they tried to get the best possible program produced, using whatever techniques are thought to be most effective for each medium. Result: the pupils learned more from the television lesson. Mr. Westley is an Associate Professor of Journalism, and Mr. Barrow, then a graduate student in the mass communications program at the University of Wisconsin, is now an Assistant Professor in the Communications Research Center at Michigan State University.

"EXPLORING THE NEWS":

An Experiment on the Relative Effectiveness of Radio and TV Versions of a Children's News Program

by Lionel C. Barrow, Jr., and Bruce H. Westley [1]

THE EXPERIMENT

This experiment was designed to compare the effectiveness of equivalent radio and television versions of "Exploring the News," a series of background-of-the-news programs for grade school children produced by WHA-TV for the Wisconsin School of the Air.

Essentially this involved testing the relative effectiveness of transmitting equivalent messages through different media—radio (a single-channel, audio medium) and TV (a two-channel, audiovisual medium).

Prior research indicates that in general the two-channel medium should produce a greater effect than the single-channel medium. Nelson and Moll found that a complete film (A-V) produced significantly higher learning than either the sound track (A) or the visual portion of the film (V) alone. Nelson and VanderMeer also

---

[1] This part of the report of Professor Westley and his colleagues to NERTC was published in substantially this form in the *Audio-Visual Communication Review*, 7 (1959), 14–23, and is republished here by permission of the journal and the authors.

found that the complete film was significantly superior to the sound track alone.

There are at least four ways in which a radio (audio) *vs.* TV (audio-visual) comparison may be made: (1) A radio program with the TV cameras "turned on." (2) A TV program with the sound track piped to the radio audience. (3) A simulcast.

The first method designs the program for radio and thereby handicaps the audio-visual presentation. The second, used by both experimenters quoted above, designs the program for TV and thereby handicaps the audio version. The third attempts to take the limitations of both into account and thereby handicaps both. Another possibility is (4) producing the programs separately.

This procedure permits the use of the full potentialities of both media but it too has drawbacks. It can lead to a high degree of uncontrolled and unmeasurable variation and thereby confound the explanation of any results. In spite of this possibility procedure 4 was chosen for this experiment, primarily to preclude any "unfair advantage" criticisms.

To minimize the possible confounding effects, the same script writer handled both versions, writing the radio from the TV script. The same actors appeared in both versions. The radio version was recorded the night before presentation. The TV version was produced "live." Both were aired at 9:30 a.m., on Thursdays. The facts in both versions were the same. Of course total emphasis (in number of words) differed—one talks, or should talk, more on a radio than on a TV program—but there was an extremely high correlation in relative emphasis.

Subjects

Some 228 pupils in eight classroom groups in four Madison, Wisconsin, public schools took part in the experiment. Classrooms were randomly divided into two equal groups for assignment to radio and TV treatments. Some attrition occurred but it was negligible and did not affect the analysis. Mean total I.Q. for the 228 pupils on the California Mental Maturity Test was 111.93. The radio group mean was 112.19; the TV group mean was 111.67. The I.Q. distribution was approximately normal, with a range of 73 to 149.

Variables

The major independent variables were (1) medium (radio, TV), (2) programs, (3) discussion (of program content by teachers before or after test administration), (4) thematic emphasis (defined as number of words devoted to a theme in the script), (5) visual presentation (in the TV versions, commentator alone *vs.* commentator with visual aids such as film clips, maps, etc.).

I.Q. scores (total and the verbal and nonverbal subscores) and schools were treated as mediating variables.

The major dependent variables were (1) saliency (defined in terms of first-mentioned themes in response to the open-end question: "Now write down everything you remember"); (2) immediate recall of factual information; and (3) delayed recall of factual information.

Programs

Four "Exploring the News" programs were used in the experiment. The programs, all of which were aired in January, 1958, were: the Presidency and the presidential succession; the Eighty-fifth Congress and the issues before it; the Fuchs expedition to the South Pole and living conditions there; and the new United States of the Caribbean and trouble in Venezuela.

The writer was given a free hand in developing the 15-minute programs. The timely nature of the subject matter made it impossible to prepare the scripts more than three days in advance. This prevented pretesting the information tests. It also meant that the program variables had to be "coded out" rather than "built in." Such *post hoc* analysis limits the certainty of the findings.

The themes [2] in a given program were categorized by *emphasis* (the number of words in the commentary used to describe the theme) and *method of presentation* (*visual* if in the TV versions the presentation of a theme by a commentator was supplemented by such visual aids as films clips, maps, etc., *nonvisual* if in the TV versions the theme was presented by the commentator alone. The occurrence of the same themes in the radio version was used as a control).

----

[2] Both the program and the saliency analysis were performed by three journalism graduate students—Lowell F. Brandner, K. Robert Kern, and Fuoad R. Mikhail.

As expected, more words were used in the radio versions of the four programs than in the TV versions—8,315 to 7,540. Relative emphasis of the themes, however, was remarkably close. Rank order correlations for the themes in each of the four programs were: Congress, .92; Presidency, .72; South Pole, .83; Latin America, .86. Visual themes received 52 per cent of the emphasis in the TV versions. The same themes received 51 per cent in the radio versions.

RESULTS

Saliency

Following each program, six of the eight classroom groups received a questionnaire in which the pupils were told, "Now write down everything you can remember from today's program. Try to remember as much detail as you can."

TABLE 1. NUMBER (N) AND PROPORTION (P) OF PUPILS WHO MENTIONED FIRST A THEME WHICH IN THE TV VERSION HAD OR DID NOT HAVE SOME ADDITIONAL VISUAL ELEMENTS SUCH AS FILM CLIPS, MAPS, ETC.[a]

| | Radio Group | | | | | TV Group | | | | |
| | Visual | | Nonvisual | | | Visual | | Nonvisual | | Totals |
Programs	N	(P)	N	(P)	Totals	N	(P)	N	(P)	
Presidency	41	(.55)	33	(.45)	74	50	(.64)	28	(.36)	78
Congress	37	(.52)	34	(.48)	71	40	(.55)	33	(.45)	73
South Pole	49	(.63)	29	(.37)	78	61	(.74)	21	(.26)	82
Latin America	52	(.66)	27	(.34)	79	58	(.74)	20	(.26)	78
Totals	179	(.59)	123	(.41)	302	209	(.67)	102	(.32)	311

[a] Binomial tests for the significance of difference yield a z score of 3.165 for the radio group and 6.010 for the TV group, both of which are significant at the .001 level. A critical ratio between the number who chose visual themes in the TV group and those who chose the same themes in the radio group yields a CR of 2.03, which is significant at the .05 level.

Their responses to this question were analyzed for saliency, for what "came to the top" first; only the first response of each pupil was tabulated for this analysis and the results related to the thematic analysis of the scripts.

Both method of presentation and emphasis were significantly related to saliency.

Visual themes received 67.2 per cent of the first mentions in the TV group. The same themes received 59.3 per cent of the first mentions in the radio group (see Table 1). A critical ratio between the two percentages revealed that the TV visual percentage was significantly greater than its radio counterpart. This suggests that while the visual element is making a difference, something else is also making a significant contribution.

A clue as to what that "something else" is comes from examining the relation of emphasis and saliency. For the purposes of this analysis, the themes were rank ordered and then split into two categories —a high- and a low-emphasis category. The high-emphasis themes received 56.1 per cent of the first mentions in the radio group and 56.4 per cent in the TV group. The differences between first mentions for high- and low-emphasis themes were significant at the .05 level in both cases (see Table 2).

TABLE 2. NUMBER (N) AND PROPORTION (P) OF PUPILS WHO MENTIONED FIRST A THEME WHICH HAD HIGH OR LOW EMPHASIS IN THE COMMENTARY [a]

| | Radio Group | | | | | TV Group | | | | |
| | High | | Low | | | High | | Low | | |
Programs	N	(P)	N	(P)	Totals	N	(P)	N	(P)	Totals
Presidency	24	(.32)	50	(.68)	74	47	(.60)	31	(.40)	78
Congress	34	(.48)	37	(.52)	71	39	(.53)	34	(.47)	73
South Pole [b]	49.5	(.63)	28.5	(.37)	78	47.5	(.58)	34.5	(.42)	82
Latin America	62	(.78)	17	(.22)	79	42	(.54)	36	(.46)	78
Totals	169.5	(.56)	132.5	(.44)	302	175.5	(.56)	135.5	(.43)	311

[a] Binomial tests for the significance of difference yield a z score of 2.072 for the radio group and 2.155 for the TV group, both of which are significant at the .05 level.

[b] This program was coded into an odd number of themes. Therefore scores for the median theme were equally divided between the high- and low-emphasis groups.

Immediate Recall

Three of the four main variables—medium, I.Q., schools-programs [3]—produced significant differences. Only the differences between the discussion groups failed to reach significance. None of the interaction terms was significant. The means, cell sizes, and significance levels for the main effects are shown in Table 3.

----

[3] This is a confounded variable. Scheduling difficulties prevented assigning an immediate recall test to all subjects on every program. The scores for each program, therefore, are from pupils in a different school.

TABLE 3. MEANS, CELL SIZES, AND SIGNIFICANCE LEVELS OF MAIN EFFECTS FOR 24-ITEM IMMEDIATE RECALL TEST

Variable/Subgroup	Mean	Cell Size	F [a] Significant at
Medium			.01
Radio	15.27	111	
TV	16.48	110	
Total I.Q.			.001
High (above 116)	17.81	76	
Medium (107–16)	15.91	70	
Low (below 107)	14.18	75	
Programs			.01
Presidency	14.65	62	
Congress	17.13	55	
South Pole	15.08	51	
Latin America	17.15	53	
Discussion			n.s.
Yes	15.76	109	
No	16.16	112	
Totals	15.96	221	—

[a] Obtained from an analysis of variance with appropriate corrections for disproportionality as suggested by Snedecor.

The superiority of TV over radio was consistent for all I.Q. groups and for all programs.

Delayed Recall

A delayed recall test was administered in the sixth week after the fourth program. The 32-item test was composed of the eight "best discriminators" from each of the four 24-item tests.

An analysis of variance revealed that while the I.Q. and school differences were still significant, radio *vs.* TV was not. Again, none of the interaction terms reached significance (see Table 4).

An analysis of the program by program subscores showed a small but consistent mean difference in favor of the TV group (see Table 5).

SUMMARY

This experiment was designed to compare the relative effectiveness of equivalent radio and television versions of a series of background-of-the-news programs for grade school children. Some 228 sixth graders took part in the experiment. Classroom groups were

TABLE 4. MEANS, CELL SIZES, AND SIGNIFICANCE LEVELS OF MAIN EFFECTS FOR 32-ITEM DELAYED RECALL TEST

Variable/Subgroup	Mean	Cell Size	F [a] Significant at
Medium			n.s.
Radio	19.41	97	
TV	20.02	96	
Total I.Q.			
High (above 116)	22.13	71	
Medium (107–16)	19.78	63	
Low (below 107)	16.75	59	
Schools			.01
1	19.07	42	
2	19.16	50	
3	18.49	51	
4	22.06	50	
Totals	19.72	193	—

[a] Obtained from an analysis of variance with appropriate corrections for disproportionality suggested by Snedecor.

TABLE 5. PROGRAM SUBSCORE MEANS FOR RADIO AND TV GROUPS ON THE DELAYED RECALL TEST

Medium	Presidency	Congress	South Pole	Latin America
Radio	5.01	4.69	5.44	4.27
TV	5.14	4.85	5.68	4.31

randomly divided and assigned to the radio or TV treatment. The TV group made significantly higher scores than the radio group on an immediate recall test of factual knowledge. The TV group's score on a delayed recall test was still higher than the radio group but the difference was no longer significant. I.Q. was significantly related to scores on both the immediate and the delayed recall tests. A teacher-led discussion after the program but before the administration of the immediate recall test did not produce higher scores than no discussion before the test. Message variables such as emphasis (defined in terms of the number of words used to describe a theme) and method of presentation (defined in terms of the use or nonuse in the TV versions of such visual aids as film clips, maps, etc.) were both significantly related to saliency (what a subject was most likely to mention first in response to an open-end question).

Bibliography

McNemar, Q., *Psychological Statistics*, New York: John Wiley and Sons, 1949.

Nelson, H. E., K. R. Moll, and W. Jaspen, *Comparison of the Audio and Video Element of Instructional Films*, Port Washington, L.I., N.Y.: Special Devices Center, Technical Report SDC 269–7–18, 1950.

———, and A. W. VanderMeer, *The Relative Effectiveness of Differing Commentaries in an Animated Film on Elementary Meteorology*, Port Washington, L.I., N.Y.: Special Devices Center, Technical Report SDC 269–7–43, 1955.

Siegel, S., *Nonparametric Statistics*, New York: McGraw-Hill, 1956.

Snedecor, G. W., *Statistical Methods*, Ames, Iowa: Iowa State College Press, 1950.

The great majority of studies that compare television teaching with ordinary classroom teaching come to the conclusion that students taught by television learn as least as much factual material as students taught by ordinary methods. Here are two studies which indicate that this is not always the case. Kumata's advertising study, in its first round, showed that TV students did not do so well as face-to-face students. When he replicated the study, however, the differences virtually disappeared. The second study began as a study of attitude change, but showed its most significant results in learning; and here, again, face-to-face students learned significantly more than television students. Why should this be, in the face of so much contradictory evidence? Kumata suggests that the expertness of the television technique may have much to do with it. The advertising teacher had one semester of experience behind him when the study was repeated, and therefore probably knew better how to use the medium. The second study used conventional classroom methods of teaching, rather than methods better adapted to television, and therefore may not have used television's full potential. Whatever the reason, these studies stand as challenging arguments against assuming that television is necessarily *as good as or better than classroom methods. Kumata is a member of the Communications Research Center at Michigan State University.*

TWO STUDIES IN CLASSROOM TEACHING BY TELEVISION

by Hideya Kumata

Teaching Advertising by Television: A Report on Two Experiments [1]

This report presents the results of two experiments with a term-long course in basic advertising at the college level. The second experiment was a repeat of the first although some new questions were asked. The purpose of these experiments was threefold: (1) to present a class in which the presentation was predominantly visual (a great number of training aids), (2) to assess the feasibil-

----

[1] A condensed version of two reports submitted to NERTC by the Communications Research Center, Michigan State University, 1958.

ity of teaching advertising, which had never been tried before on TV, as a solution to contemplated large enrollments, and (3) to give experience to the instructor in teaching over television.

EXPERIMENT I

Subjects

Two sections of a junior-level course in advertising were used. The morning section of 46 students comprised the face-to-face section. The afternoon session was divided into two parts on the basis of ACE scores. One section of 30 students became the in-studio group and the other section of 30 students became the television group. None of the students knew that the course was to be televised until the first day of class. The in-studio section was set up because the instructor desired a live audience. The three groups were compared on their ACE scores and the means were not significantly different from each other.

Tests

The regular assignments and the mid-term and final examinations were used in analysis. Final quarter grades for the course were also analyzed. In addition, two specially constructed quizzes were given. Two attitude questionnaires were administered. One was a Thurstone-type attitude scale designed to tap acceptance of television. This questionnaire was developed at Purdue University. The second questionnaire was a semantic differential type with three concepts to be rated. These were TEACHING BY TELEVISION, A CAREER IN ADVERTISING, and THE ADVERTISING BUSINESS. Scales used with the concept TEACHING BY TELEVISION were *good-bad, easy-difficult, personal-impersonal, clear-hazy, interesting-boring, active-passive,* and *easy to take notes– hard to take notes*. Scales used with A CAREER IN ADVERTISING were *attractive-unattractive, approve-disapprove, good-bad, high prestige–low prestige,* and *active-passive*. Scales used with THE ADVERTISING BUSINESS were *ethical-unethical, strong-weak, fair-unfair, good-bad,* and *high paying-low paying*. The Thurstone scale was administered during the sixth week of classes and the semantic differential scales were given during the seventh week.

Results

All comparisons were made by simple analysis of variance. There were eight regular assignments during the quarter. Four of these were book reports, one was a letter written by students in which they were to apply for jobs in advertising, one was an analysis of a print campaign, one was an analysis of TV programing and commercial content, and one was a problem in copywriting. This latter assignment was given more weight in the final grade. For the first seven assignments listed above, no significant F's were produced. There was no indication of a trend in these seven assignments— the rank order of grades of the three sections for each assignment varied from assignment to assignment.

In the eighth assignment, which was given more weight toward the final grade, a significant difference was found. Face-to-face students got the highest grades, followed by in-studio students and then by TV students. For the two special quizzes constructed for the study, significant differences occurred. The face-to-face group was highest on both quizzes. In one of the quizzes the TV section got the lowest score, while in the other quiz the in-studio section came in last.

The mid-term examination produced no significant difference. On the final examination, however, the face-to-face group received significantly higher marks. The in-studio section was next, followed by the TV group. The same result appeared for the final grades. Face-to-face was first, followed by in-studio, and then by the TV group. The difference between the face-to-face group and the TV group amounted to about six-tenths of a grade point.

Scores on the Purdue attitude scale were not significantly different among the three groups. All three groups were quite favorable toward teaching by television. The only significant difference on the semantic differential scales for the concept TEACHING BY TELEVISION was on the scale *clear-hazy*. The TV group thought the concept to be *clear* compared with the other two groups. The two other concepts, THE ADVERTISING BUSINESS and A CAREER IN ADVERTISING, produced no significant differences among groups. All groups were very favorable toward both concepts.

EXPERIMENT II

In view of the significant differences favoring the face-to-face group in the previous experiment, it was decided to rerun the experiment using the same materials and instructor. The purposes of the follow-up study were (1) to recheck the findings on course achievement, (2) to stimulate motivation in the television class, and (3) to explore the "irrelevant-relevant" hypothesis. The "irrelevant-relevant" hypothesis was that the face-to-face group, which would see the visual aids (in this case advertisements) in color enlarged upon a projection screen, would remember a great deal of the details of these aids compared with the TV group, which would see these same ads in black and white on a 25-inch TV monitor. However, it was hypothesized that the TV group would remember the principles involved better than the face-to-face group on the basis that there were less distracting, irrelevant cues for the TV group.

Subjects

Two sections of the course were used. There were 111 students, with 57 students in one section and 54 in the other. The latter section was divided into two parts on the basis of ACE scores. One part became the television section while the other became the in-studio section. The three sections were compared on their ACE scores. There were no significant differences among groups.

Tests

Six regular assignments, mid-term and final examinations, and final grades were analyzed. In addition, four special quizzes were made up. Two of the quizzes were taken from the previous study. One of the new quizzes made up was a two-part test, constructed to test a lecture in which 12 types of advertisements illustrating certain advertising principles were given. In one part of the test, questions on details of the ads themselves were presented. In the second part of the test, questions were asked on the principles which these ads were supposed to illustrate.

Pretests and posttests of attitude were made. A semantic differential test was administered. The three concepts were similar to those of the previous experiment—TEACHING BY TELEVISION, A CAREER FOR ME IN ADVERTISING, THE ADVERTISING PROFESSION. The scales used with TEACHING BY TELEVISION were the same as those used in the first experiment except that the scale *easy-difficult* was dropped. The scales used for the second concept were the same as in the first experiment with the addition of the scales *fast advancement–slow advancement* and *unlimited openings–limited openings*. To the five scales used for the third concept in the first experiment the scale *necessary-unnecessary* was added.

Results

Analysis of six regular assignments, the mid-term examination, the final grades, and the four special quizzes produced no significant differences. Only in the analysis of final examination grades did a significant F appear. Here, as in the previous study, TV students did less well than face-to-face students. In the second special quiz, a special analysis was run for "irrelevant" and "relevant" scores. Each subject received two scores on this quiz—one for details of ads and one for principles about the ads. For each of the three sections, students were divided into two groups—those whose details of ad scores ("irrelevant" scores) exceeded their principles scores ("relevant" scores) and those whose "relevant" scores were equal to or exceeded the "irrelevant" scores. Table 1 presents the frequencies and percentages for this analysis.

TABLE 1. FREQUENCIES AND PERCENTAGES FOR THREE GROUPS ON IRRELEVANT-RELEVANT SCORES [a]

Group	Face-to-face		In-studio		Television	
	F	P	F	P	F	P
Irrelevant > relevant	25	75.8%	9	50%	6	31.6%
Irrelevant ≤ relevant	8	24.2	9	50	13	68.4
Totals	33	100	18	100	19	100

[a] Chi square = 10.12. At 2 df P < .01.

The face-to-face group and the TV group perform in the expected manner according to the hypothesis. The in-studio group splits evenly in their frequencies. The interesting point here is that the in-studio group could view the color slide projection or they could view the two monitors which were in the originating room.

On all scales for all concepts, there were no differences among groups on pretest attitudes. All groups thought TEACHING BY

TELEVISION to be slightly good, quite passive, slightly clear, slightly impersonal, slightly hard to take notes, slightly interesting, and slightly easy to learn. Favorability was high on all scales toward the other two concepts.

Difference scores between pretest and posttest were analyzed by *t* tests. For the concept TEACHING BY TELEVISION, no significant differences were found for the face-to-face group. One difference was found for the TV group on this concept. The group shifted significantly toward the *easy to learn* pole on the scale *easy to learn–hard to learn*. The in-studio group shifted significantly on the scales *active-passive* and *easy to learn–hard to learn*. The group thought the concept to be more passive and easier to learn.

On the concept A CAREER FOR ME IN ADVERTISING, no significant differences were found for the TV and in-studio groups. The concept became significantly more attractive, better, faster advancement, and more approval for the face-to-face group.

For the concept THE ADVERTISING PROFESSION, all three groups changed significantly toward the good pole on the *good-bad* scale. In addition, the face-to-face and in-studio groups found the concept more ethical and fairer.

DISCUSSION

The results of the first experiment indicated that TV students did not do so well as face-to-face students. The second experiment, however, finds no difference between these groups. How can this be explained? In the first experiment, no check was made on student attendance or motivation. There was some reason to believe that students in the TV section were absent from class oftener. In the second experiment, an effort was made to spur motivation of TV students. This, plus the fact that it was the second time on television for the instructor, may have accounted for the showing of the TV class in the second experiment.

In the area of attitudes, the second experiment seems to indicate that the face-to-face teaching situation is the better vehicle for getting attitude change in the desired direction. This goes along with what others have stated about the efficacy of face-to-face in comparison with interposed communication situations.

One interesting finding worth pursuing is the outcome of the "irrelevant-relevant" hypothesis. We can only offer this finding as tentative since we cannot attribute the outcome to a specific variable. The face-to-face class received the ads not only enlarged upon the screen but in color. The TV group received the ads in smaller size with the absence of color. Thus our outcome may be the result of size or color or an interaction of both.

Attitude Change and Learning as a Function of Prestige of Instructor and Mode of Presentation [1]

In a great many attitude change studies, it has been found that the perceived prestige of the source significantly affects the amount of attitude change. The higher the perceived prestige, trustworthiness, or expertness of the communicator, the greater the attitude change toward the position advocated in the message. Further, these studies have indicated that attitude change is independent of amount of factual information absorbed from the message.[2]

Such findings have relevance to the classroom teaching situation. If we accept the idea that an important part of formal education is the acquisition of particular mental sets or the restructuring of frames of reference on the part of the student, then the investigation of teacher prestige and its effects upon course-related attitudes becomes highly important. We may find that although two teachers do not differ in terms of student information gain, they differ significantly in the way their students view the world as a result of exposure to their courses. Part of this may be explainable by student-perceived expertness or prestige of the teacher.

With the advent of instruction by television, the possibility is offered for contributing something new in credibility studies. We know that so far as information gain is concerned, no significant differences seem to exist between conventionally taught and TV-taught students.[3] In the area of attitude change in the classroom, not much work has been done utilizing TV. It may be that appearance on the medium confers prestige. If this is the case, we would

----

[1] An abbreviated version of a report submitted to NERTC by the Communications Research Center, Michigan State University, 1958.

[2] C. I. Hovland, I. L. Janis, and H. H. Kelley, *Communication and Persuasion*, New Haven, Conn.: Yale University Press, 1954.

[3] H. Kumata, *An Inventory of Instructional Television Research*, Ann Arbor, Mich.: ERTC, 1956.

expect differential effects on attitudes depending upon whether the teacher appeared on the medium or appeared in a normal classroom situation.

DESIGN AND PROCEDURE OF THE EXPERIMENT

In order to explore the effect of teacher prestige and mode of presentation upon student attitudes and information gain, the following plan was adopted. The experiment was limited to one class period. The class to be used had to have sufficient sections to allow for varying experimental conditions and the subject matter had to be readily amenable for attitude testing. The main independent variables were mode of presentation (television and face-to-face) and expertness of the instructor (national expert, departmental expert, and ordinary instructor). The dependent variables were attitude toward the instructor, attitude toward receiving instruction via television, attitude about concepts presented in the message, and amount of information gain. In addition, data were to be gathered on ability level and amount of prior television instruction received by subjects. These were included to explore the question of intelligence level and learning from television [4] and the problem of the existence of a novelty effect.[5]

Two modes of presentation and three levels of expertness produced six conditions. It was decided to use at least three different instructors in the experiment. This now produced a cube with 18 cells. An after-only design was planned so that a base-line control group had to be utilized. Subjects would receive only one treatment under this design.

Course and Subject Matter

The basic course in social science at Michigan State University was selected. Sixty sections composed of about 40 students each were available. The subject matter in the term contemplated for

----

[4] J. H. Kanner, R. P. Runyon, and O. Desiderato, *Television in Army Training: Evaluation of Television in Army Basic Training*, Washington, D.C.: Human Resources Research Office, George Washington University, Technical Report No. 14, 1954.

[5] P. M. Hurst, Jr., *Relative Effectiveness of Verbal Introductions to Kinescope Recordings and Training Films*, Port Washington, L.I., N.Y.: Special Devices Center, Technical Report SDC 269–7–42, 1955; R. Jackson, *Learning from Kinescopes and Films*, Port Washington, L.I., N.Y.: Special Devices Center, Technical Report SDC 20–TV–1, 1952.

study was government and politics, which offered good possibilities for attitude testing. The department had been experimenting in the two previous terms with teaching over closed-circuit television, thus making available a pool of students who had had prior television instruction.

Subjects

Twenty sections were selected. Eighteen of these became experimental sections and two were used as controls. A total of 840 students was involved. Of this number, 405 were in sections receiving face-to-face teaching treatment, 359 were in sections receiving television instruction, and 76 were in control sections. A check was made on comparability of classes by examining scores on the L component of the ACE intelligence test. A simple analysis of variance comparing 20 sections produced an F ratio of 1.23 which at 19 and 802 degrees of freedom is not significant at our arbitrary 5 per cent level.

The Message

The topic picked after consultation with the department was power politics. This topic came in the second week of the course. Since the experiment was to be run in the first week, use of this topic would not seriously disrupt the normal progress of the course and would still serve as a new and as yet unassigned subject. The topic of power politics had the following teaching points: (1) the neutrality of the term "power politics," implying neither good nor bad, (2) a definition of the term, (3) the distinction between political power and other forms of social power, (4) the distinction between power and authority, (5) an analysis of political power structures, and (6) the characteristics of various power structures such as the oligarchical, the caste, and the democratic.

The purposes of the message were to move students from viewing power politics as something bad toward a position of seeing the reality of power and to make students cognizant of factors involved in various power relations.

Test Materials

To test the three attitude areas, the semantic differential, developed by Osgood and associates,[6] was used as the measuring instru-

----

[6] C. E. Osgood, G. J. Suci, and P. H. Tannenbaum, *The Measurement of Meaning*, Urbana, Ill.: University of Illinois Press, 1957.

ment. It was decided that scales highly loaded on the *evaluative* factor would be used as a measure of attitude. Scales from the *activity* and *potency* dimensions were used also to explore the kinds of changes in these factors. In addition, scales which were thought to be especially appropriate but not found on the list of scales developed by Osgood were included. All *evaluative* scales were summed for analysis. The same procedure was used for *activity* and *potency* scales. Those scales for which factor loadings were not known were analyzed separately.

The information gain test was a multiple-choice type with anywhere from four to six foils per item. Thirty items were constructed and pretested three times. After analysis, the final version contained 15 items.

The concepts selected for attitude testing were TEACHING OVER TELEVISION, FACE-TO-FACE TEACHING, CASTE POWER PYRAMID, AUTHORITY, POWER POLITICS, OLIGARCHICAL POWER PYRAMID, DEMOCRATIC POWER PYRAMID. In addition, some of the classes rated the instructor who had given the presentation.

For the concepts TEACHING OVER TELEVISION and FACE-TO-FACE TEACHING, the following scales were used: *good-bad, fair-unfair, pleasant-unpleasant, valuable-worthless* (these four scales were summed to get an *evaluative* dimension score); *active-passive, fast-slow* (these two were summed to get an *activity* dimension score); *strong-weak, large-small* (these two were summed to get a *potency* dimension score); *interesting-dull, clear-hazy* (each of these scales was analyzed separately).

For the rest of the concepts listed above, the same scales for the three dimensions were used except for the addition of the scale *kind-cruel* to the evaluative set. The scales *interesting-dull* and *clear-hazy* were not used.

For those who rated the instructor, the same scales used for rating the concepts TEACHING BY TELEVISION and FACE-TO-FACE TEACHING were used. The exception was the replacement of the scale *valuable-worthless* by the scale *expert-inexpert*. This scale was analyzed separately.

In all, the test form consisted of seven concepts, each rated on nine or ten scales, a 15-item multiple-choice information gain test, and a page of questions for identification, accuracy of recalling announced expertness, and prior instructional TV experience. Some classes rated an additional concept, their instructor, with ten scales.

Instructors

Three volunteer instructors in the department were used as the experimental teachers. All three had taught several years in the department and were fully familiar with the subject matter. It was assumed that these three were adept and skilled at teaching.

Level of Expertness

Three levels of announced prestige were used. The levels ideally would have been low, neutral, and high prestige. However, it was not possible to introduce instructors as low-prestige sources, and therefore the three levels decided upon were ordinary classroom instructor (no announced expertness), medium expert (announced as the departmental expert on power politics), and high expert (announced as a national authority on the subject).

Procedure

The nine sections of the three experimental instructors plus nine other sections were used as experimental sections. Each instructor appeared before six different sections—in three prestige versions under face-to-face and TV conditions. Each instructor appeared before one of his own sections in the ordinary instructor prestige condition for face-to-face presentation. He also did the same to another one of his own sections for the TV presentation. He appeared before two other sections face to face, once as a departmental and once as a national expert. For these two prestige conditions over TV, he appeared on camera once with two viewing rooms utilized. Since the instructor in charge of the sections made the announcements, one viewing room could receive the experimental instructor as a departmental expert and the other viewing room could receive the instructor as a national expert.

On the day before the section was to receive the experimental message, dittoed announcements were passed out to students in that section. This announcement carried the name of the guest lecturer, the appropriate prestige label and introduction, and the room in which to assemble in the case of the TV sections. When these announcements were passed out, the instructor in charge read the announcement aloud. He then put the pertinent information on the blackboard. At the end of the class period, the instructor again read the announcement. Just before the experimental message, the instructor in charge introduced the guest lecturer, again giving the prestige information.

After the introduction, the experimental instructor gave his message. The message was written to take about 30 minutes. Instructors had been rehearsed three times to depress practice effect during the experiment. Variation in time of delivery of message ranged from 27 minutes to 31 for the 18 sessions.

After the message, the instructor in charge handed out the test booklets. The time spent completing the booklets ranged from 9 to 18 minutes. The instructor who gave the message was rated in the test booklets only for the departmental expert and national expert conditions. This page was omitted for the ordinary instructor condition and for the control classes.

Eight weeks after the experimental sessions, all classes involved were tested again. The same test booklets were used. Although we started out with 764 experimental and 76 control subjects, the numbers available for retention testing were 649 experimental and 66 control subjects. To see if any section lost students disproportionately, a chi square test was run with proportion of loss from immediate to delayed posttesting for the total group as the multiplying term to compute expected loss for each section. The obtained chi square value of 2.82 was not significant at 18 degrees of freedom (the two control groups were combined for this analysis, making a total of 19 groups). A chi square value of 28.87 is needed to reach the 5 per cent level of significance.

The experiment started on the third day of the term before students were familiar with their instructors. The experiment took three days to run. One class had to be replaced when technical difficulties arose in one of the TV sessions.

Analysis

A three-way classification analysis of variance was used. Equal numbers in each cell are highly desirable from a computational standpoint. The range of class sizes was such that too much information would be thrown away if we threw away cases to equalize cells. Therefore an approximate means was found to conduct the analysis.

Snedecor and Cox [7] have outlined a method of using expected

----

[7] G. W. Snedecor and Gertrude M. Cox, "Disproportionate Subclass Numbers in Tables of Multiple Classification," *Iowa Agricultural Experiment Station Research Bulletin,* No. 180, 1935.

subclass numbers in cases of unequal numbers in cells of multiple classification. A test of proportionality is applied and if the data make the assumption of proportional subclass numbers tenable, then one works with expected numbers. For the immediate posttest, a chi square computed with the 18 experimental classes produced a value of 2.28 which at 8 degrees of freedom is significant at the .95 level. For the delayed posttest, the obtained chi square value was 2.15 which at 8 degrees of freedom is significant at the .95 level. In both posttests, the assumption of proportional subclass numbers seemed justified.

The three instructors were viewed as a random sample from the pool of instructors available. Thus, the instructor variable could be viewed as three replications of the experimental design in which the main variables were mode and prestige conditions.[8]

In the check to see if students had received the correct prestige introduction, two questions were asked in the test booklets. Only the classes involved in the departmental expert and national expert conditions received these questions. Of the 501 subjects, 488, or 97.4 per cent, correctly identified the name of the instructor. On the question of recall of instructor prestige, 483, or 96.4 per cent, made the correct association. It would seem that the prestige announcements were successfully learned.

RESULTS

Before the three-way analysis of variance was undertaken, a comparison of the control classes with the experimental classes was made. The two classes composing the control group were first tested for differences by the *t* test. In all of the comparisons, no significant differences were found between the two classes making up the control group. The combined control group was then compared with all subjects in the television condition groups and then with the combined face-to-face groups by means of *t* tests. Table 1 gives the results of this analysis.

- - - - - - - - - -

[8] In actually doing the analysis, we first tested the second-order interaction against the within-groups mean square. If the F value obtained was not significant, then the first-order or simple interactions were tested against the within-groups mean square as were the main effects. If the F obtained was significant, then the second-order interaction mean square was used to test the first-order interactions. All nonsignificant interactions were pooled with the second-order interaction mean square along with the degrees of freedom for use as the error term in testing for main effects.

TABLE 1. RESULTS OF TESTS BETWEEN CONTROL GROUP AND TELEVISION GROUP, AND BETWEEN CONTROL GROUP AND FACE-TO-FACE GROUP

Test	Control/TV t (433 df)	Control/Face-to-face t (479 df)
TEACHING BY TELEVISION		
Evaluative	.278	.928
Activity	.422	.413
Potency	.330	.148
Interesting-dull	.250	1.306
Clear-hazy	2.238 [a]	.860
FACE-TO-FACE TEACHING		
Evaluative	.113	.568
Activity	1.296	.716
Potency	.850	.256
Interesting-dull	.308	.250
Clear-hazy	.294	.523
AUTHORITY		
Evaluative	2.139 [a]	2.020 [a]
Activity	2.529 [b]	3.042 [b]
Potency	3.708 [b]	4.066 [b]
POWER POLITICS		
Evaluative	5.588 [b]	6.452 [b]
Activity	.245	.546
Potency	.766	.424
CASTE POWER PYRAMID		
Evaluative	8.045 [b]	7.716 [b]
Activity	4.575 [b]	5.772 [b]
Potency	1.923	.805
OLIGARCHICAL POWER PYRAMID		
Evaluative	3.831 [b]	4.419 [b]
Activity	.309	.822
Potency	2.895 [b]	4.256 [b]
DEMOCRATIC POWER PYRAMID		
Evaluative	3.016 [b]	2.453 [b]
Activity	1.349	1.798
Potency	1.050	.641
INFORMATION GAIN TEST	13.304 [b]	15.358 [b]

[a] Significant beyond the .05 level.
[b] Significant beyond the .01 level.

It can be seen from Table 1 that in 26 comparisons, 11 of the t tests between control and television groups were significant, while 10 of the tests between control and face-to-face groups were significant. All 10 of the significant comparisons between control and face-to-face were significant also between control and television.

One concept, FACE-TO-FACE TEACHING, produced no significant differences. The concept TEACHING BY TELEVISION produced only one significant difference. The concept AUTHORITY produced significant differences in all comparisons. The means involved in those comparisons which produced significant differences are listed in Table 2.

TABLE 2. MEANS OF CONTROL, TELEVISION AND FACE-TO-FACE GROUPS

Test	Control Mean [a]	TV Mean	Face-to-face Mean
TEACHING BY TELEVISION			
Clear-hazy	3.40	2.94	n.s.
AUTHORITY			
Evaluative	2.82	3.07	3.07
Activity	2.67	3.02	3.07
Potency	2.46	3.01	3.06
POWER POLITICS			
Evaluative	4.53	3.75	3.66
CASTE POWER PYRAMID			
Evaluative	4.74	5.85	5.82
Activity	3.97	4.98	4.94
OLIGARCHICAL POWER PYRAMID			
Evaluative	4.13	4.71	4.80
Potency	3.73	3.22	3.06
DEMOCRATIC POWER PYRAMID			
Evaluative	2.08	1.79	1.84
INFORMATION GAIN TEST [b]	5.05	8.88	9.42

[a] All means are based on possible scores from 1 (most favorable) to 7 (least favorable) with neutral at 4.
[b] The information gain test contained 15 items.

For the concept TEACHING BY TELEVISION, the television group thought it to be *clearer* than the control group. For the concept AUTHORITY, both the TV and face-to-face groups were *less favorable* compared with the control group, both thought the concept *less active* and *less strong*. All means are on the favorable, active, and strong side of neutral, however.

Both groups were *less unfavorable* toward the concept POWER POLITICS compared with the controls. For the concept CASTE POWER PYRAMID, the TV and face-to-face groups were *more unfavorable* and thought the concept to be *more passive* in comparison with the controls. The experimental groups were *more un-*

favorable toward the concept OLIGARCHICAL POWER PYRA-
MID but thought the concept to be *stronger* compared to controls.
Both groups were *more favorable* toward the concept DEMO-
CRATIC POWER PYRAMID than the control group. In the learning test, both groups did significantly better than the controls. The
experimental message had a definite effect upon attitudes and
learning, it would seem, from the above results.

Thirty-eight separate analyses of variance were carried out to
seek out the effect of varying experimental conditions. In the following discussion, the word *mode* is used to describe the television
or face-to-face conditions, the word *prestige* is used for the three
expertness levels, and the word *instructors* is used for the experimental lecturers who are identified by the letters A, B, and C.

Concept: TEACHING BY TELEVISION

Of the five analyses carried out, only one produced a significant
main effect. For the scale *interesting-dull*, a significant mode difference was found. Those who received face-to-face instruction
thought TEACHING BY TELEVISION to be more interesting
than those who received television instruction.

In three of the analyses, a significant mode x prestige interaction
was found. In each of the analyses—*activity* scales, *potency* scales,
and the scale *interesting-dull*—the same pattern appeared. For the
face-to-face sections, TEACHING BY TELEVISION was regarded
as more active, more interesting, or stronger as prestige level was
lowered. For the TV groups, the opposite tendency was found—the
concept was judged more active, more interesting, or stronger as
prestige level was raised.

For the scale *interesting-dull*, an additional significant interaction
produced was that of prestige x instructors. Here prestige level was
affected by the three instructors in varied ways. For instructor C,
judgments of the concept became *duller* as his prestige level went
up. For instructors A and B, no clear pattern was established.

Concept: FACE-TO-FACE TEACHING

Of the five analyses for this concept, one significant main effect
was found. On *activity*, the face-to-face group judged the concept
as more active than the television group.

A significant mode x prestige interaction was produced for the
scale *interesting-dull*. The pattern was exactly the same as that

found for this scale on the previous concept. For the TV group, ratings of FACE-TO-FACE TEACHING as interesting went up as prestige level was raised; for the face-to-face group, ratings became less interesting as prestige level went up.

Concept: AUTHORITY

No significant differences were produced in the three analyses conducted.

Concept: POWER POLITICS

In the three analyses for this concept, one significant interaction was found. For the *evaluative* scales, there was a significant prestige x instructors interaction. For instructor A, ratings of POWER POLITICS were closest to the desired position advocated by the message when he was a "normal" instructor, next closest when he was a departmental expert, and furthest when he was a national expert. For instructors B and C, ratings were closest to the desired position when they were departmental experts, next closest when they were "normal" instructors, and furthest when they were national experts.

Concept: CASTE POWER PYRAMID

Only the analysis on *potency* scales produced a significant finding. The face-to-face group rated the concept as significantly stronger than did the TV group.

Concept: OLIGARCHICAL POWER PYRAMID

The *activity* scales analysis produced the only significant effect. Those who received the departmental expert prestige condition rated the concept as most active, followed by the national expert group and then by the "normal" instructor group.

Concept: DEMOCRATIC POWER PYRAMID

Of the three analyses carried out, only the *evaluative* scales analysis produced a significant effect. Here a significant prestige x instructors interaction was found. The pattern was similar to that found for the *interesting-dull* scale for the concept TEACHING BY TELEVISION. For instructor C, the concept was rated most favorably when he was a "normal" instructor and least favorably when he was a national expert. For instructors A and B, the pattern was not clear although there was a tendency for the concept to be rated more favorably as prestige level rose.

Ratings of Experimental Instructors

Six analyses were run. The scales were *evaluative, potency, activity, interesting-dull, clear-hazy,* and *expert-inexpert.* In all six, a significant main effect among instructors was found. Instructor C was the lowest on all analyses while instructor A was highest on four out of the six. In addition, a significant main effect for the prestige condition was found for the *potency* scales and the scale *clear-hazy.* The instructors were rated as stronger or clear as prestige level went up. Interestingly, there was no main effect found for prestige on the scale *expert-inexpert.* The *evaluative* scales analysis also produced a significant prestige x instructors interaction. For instructors B and C, ratings of favorability went up as prestige level went up. The opposite was true for instructor A.

Information Gain Test

Analysis of variance on the 15-item information gain test produced two significant main effects. In the mode difference, face-to-face students did significantly better than TV students. This is a surprising finding in light of many past studies in which there is no significant difference between the two groups. The other main effect is an instructor difference. Here, as one might suspect from the findings in the previous paragraph, instructor A produces the most learning, followed by B and then by C.

Prior Instructional Television Exposure

It was hoped that sufficient numbers of subjects who had taken one or more quarters of the social science course by television would be available in our experimental groups so that each cell of the analysis could be split into groups with prior TV experience and without prior experience. Unfortunately, numbers were too small in each cell to warrant analysis. A total of 109 subjects who had taken social science by TV were included in our study. Of these, 53 were in the TV groups and 50 were in the face-to-face sections. Six were in the control group. It was decided to run *t* tests between previously exposed and not previously exposed subjects for the TV, face-to-face, and control groups.

No significant differences were found for the control group. For the concept TEACHING BY TELEVISION, four of the five comparisons were significant for the TV group. Those who had had a prior course by television rated the concept as better, stronger, more interesting, and clearer than those who had not had a prior course. For the face-to-face group, prior TV subjects rated the concept as significantly stronger. In all of the comparisons for this concept, those with prior TV experience rated teaching by television more favorably than those who had no experience. For the concept FACE-TO-FACE TEACHING, those with no prior experience rated the concept as more potent than those with TV experience for both the face-to-face and TV groups. Taking only direction into account, the persons with no prior TV experience rated this concept more favorably in all of the analyses than did the prior TV group—the opposite from what was seen with the concept TEACHING BY TELEVISION.

Intelligence Scores and Learning

Subjects were divided both in the TV and face-to-face groups into three groupings according to their ACE scores—high, medium, and low. Mean scores were computed on learning items for these groups. The results are presented in Table 3.

TABLE 3. INTELLIGENCE SCORE GROUPINGS

Group	Low	Medium	High
Face-to-face	8.48	9.13	10.43
Television	7.91	8.74	9.99

Inspection of Table 3 shows that as intelligence level goes up, information gain test scores go up. Also, television scores are lower than face-to-face scores (as revealed by the mode difference obtained in the analysis of variance). But there is no reversal such as one would expect for low intelligence score groups based on the Army study cited previously.[9] The correlation between ACE scores and information test scores for the face-to-face group was .33, while the correlation for the TV groups was .30. There is no significant difference between these correlations.

----

[9] Kanner, Runyon, and Desiderato, *Television in Army Training*.

Retention Tests

Analyses of variance were conducted on difference scores found by subtracting the delayed test score from the immediate posttest score.

For the concept TEACHING BY TELEVISION, one significant main effect was found for the scale *clear-hazy*. Those who received instruction by TV changed more toward the *hazy* end of the scale than did the face-to-face subjects. A significant mode x prestige interaction was found for *activity* scales. Change was very small from immediate to delayed posttest for all cells except the "normal" instructor face-to-face condition. This group changed almost a scale point toward the passive pole.

For the concept FACE-TO-FACE TEACHING, a significant mode x prestige interaction was found for the scale *interesting-dull*. Again changes are small except in two cells. The "normal" instructor face-to-face condition produced the largest change toward the dull pole while the national expert TV condition produced a change toward more interesting.

The concept AUTHORITY, which produced no differences on the immediate posttest, produced significant prestige and instructors main effects for *activity* scales and a significant prestige x instructors interaction for *potency* scales. All groups rated the concept as more active, with the national expert producing the largest change and the normal instructor producing the least. Instructor A produced the largest change toward more active with instructor C the least. No clear pattern for the *potency* analysis could be found, although instructor C produced the greatest change toward stronger when he was a normal instructor, instructor B when he was a national expert, and instructor A when he was a departmental expert.

None of the analyses with difference scores for the concept POWER POLITICS was significant. For the concept CASTE POWER PYRAMID, a significant prestige x instructors interaction was found. For instructor A and for instructor C, judgments of the concept became stronger when they were normal instructors. The least change took place when they were departmental experts. For instructor B, greatest change took place when he was a departmental expert.

Main effects on the instructors variable were found for the concept OLIGARCHICAL POWER PYRAMID. For *potency* and *ac-*

tivity scales, instructor A produced the least change from immediate to delayed posttest, while instructor C produced the most toward ratings of less potent and less active. A significant mode effect was found for the *evaluative* scales. Face-to-face groups rated the concept more favorably than did the TV group.

For the concept DEMOCRATIC POWER PYRAMID, a significant prestige x instructors interaction was found for the *evaluative* scales. For instructor A, there was less change to a more unfavorable position as prestige level went up. For instructors B and C no clear patterns were present. On *potency* scales, the significant interaction was mode x instructors. Instructors A and C produced least change toward a less strong rating when they were on TV. Instructor B produced least change when he was face to face.

On *activity* scales, three significant effects were found. In the prestige main effect, the national expert condition produced least change toward a less active rating, followed by the normal instructor and then by the departmental expert condition. In the mode x prestige interaction, both TV and face-to-face conditions produced least change toward less active under the national expert condition. TV produced the greatest change in the departmental expert condition while face-to-face produced its greatest change in the normal instructor condition. In the prestige x instructors interaction, no interpretable pattern could be found.

All five of the analyses rating the experimental instructor produced a prestige main effect. In all of the analyses, there was a greater change toward a more unfavorable position as prestige level went up. In four of the analyses, a significant mode x prestige interaction was produced. In three of these, *evaluative, activity,* and *clear-hazy,* the pattern of interaction was the same. There was less change toward a more unfavorable position for the face-to-face group as prestige level went down. For the TV group, there was less change as prestige level went up. In the fourth analysis, *potency,* for both TV and face-to-face, there was less change as prestige level went down.

DISCUSSION

At the outset of this study, it was stated that the main intent of the experiment was to explore the effect of several variables—mode and prestige—upon attitudes. These attitudes were of three kinds—

toward the concept of teaching by television or by face-to-face, toward course-related concepts, and toward the instructor. Our clearest findings from the study, however, are in the area of information gain.

In contradiction to the overwhelming majority of television studies, we found that the mode of presentation significantly affects learning. Further, we found that television-taught students do significantly less well than conventionally taught students.

Because of the large numbers involved, a difference between the TV and the face-to-face groups of about one-half an item on a 15-item test produced a statistically significant difference. One can question the social significance of such a small difference and can claim that such a difference makes no case for utilizing or not utilizing instructional television. To this sort of argument, one answer is that the half-item difference appeared on a test in which the message was less than a class period long. If a series of such tests are given during the course of a school term, then television students may suffer.

Why did such a finding occur in the absence of such results in a multitude of other studies? Several answers are possible here. One is an answer from the standpoint of probability. It can be argued that a type I error has been committed. Another answer is that the information test used was better constructed, and hence a more sensitive measuring instrument than those used previously. One of the most plausible answers is that TV students did less well because of the use of methods tied to conventional-type teaching in the television situation. It is true that in the zeal to control as many extraneous factors as possible, variation in presentation to adapt the lesson to TV was not done.

We cannot offer a clear-cut answer here. What can be done is replication. In a sense the experiment was a unique one even though ostensibly it was concerned with the same kinds of variables with which other TV research has been involved. As Sir Ronald Fisher once put it, "In order to assert that a natural phenomenon is experimentally demonstrable we need, not an isolated record, but a reliable method of procedure."

What can we say about effect on attitudes? A neat and orderly pattern is hard to find. It is obvious that the experimental message was successful in changing attitudes toward almost all of the concepts presented. A glance at Table 2, in which experimental group *vs.* control group comparisons are made, reveals that the differences lie mainly with those concepts talked about in the message. However, in comparisons among our various conditions, such clear-cut evidence does not emerge.

Particularly for the analyses with the evaluative scales, scales which we think cover the area called attitudes, differential effect is not present as a function of differing experimental conditions. Most of the effect is evinced in the two other dimensions used in the study, activity and potency.

The variable of perceived prestige was introduced to see if we could not get the same kinds of findings with television that Hovland and others have found using written and aural messages. Because we were working within the framework of an ongoing course and were using instructors for this course, we could not vary prestige as much as would have been desirable from an experimental standpoint. We did not have a condition of low prestige or credibility. We assumed also that three degrees of expertness would be recognized by subjects as distinct steps.

The interesting part of the analyses on attitudes is the number of significant interactions which appeared. However, in the immediate posttest, not one instance of a mode-instructor interaction appeared. All of the significant interactions were a function of prestige and mode or prestige and instructor. This absence of a mode-instructor interaction is indirect evidence which would tend to refute the claim of some that there are "television teachers" and "classroom teachers" and that these are not interchangeable.

We have not been able to throw much light on the question of acceptance of television. The concept TEACHING BY TELEVISION produced a significant main effect only for the scale *interesting-dull*. Oddly enough, those who received the lecture in the face-to-face situation rated TV teaching as more interesting in comparison with TV students. The significant mode-prestige interactions in connection with this concept are interesting. In each case—for activity, potency, and the scale *interesting-dull*—face-to-face students gave the highest ratings when they received the lecture from the normal instructor and the lowest ratings when they received the lecture from the national expert. One could interpret this to mean that the prestige announcement had an effect in that if the student were getting a renowned expert there would be no reason for him to rate TV teaching highly. On the other hand, TV students take an opposite pattern in their ratings.

On ratings for experimental instructors, the instructor main effect shows again and again. Two of our instructors were quite close to each other in being rated along various dimensions, but the third instructor was rated the lowest consistently. Some internal cross check on instructor ratings is available in the study in the information gain test. There, not only was a mode difference found but also an instructor difference. The amount learned from each instructor followed the same ordering of instructors as the ratings on the instructors themselves.

The delayed posttest difference scores did not present an interpretable pattern. One of the difficulties in delayed posttesting was that although the experimental message was given only once, the subject matter of the course was such that discussion of some of the points in the experimental message was inevitable during the six weeks which elapsed.

We could not find evidence for a novelty effect. Rather, we found that persons who had been previously exposed were significantly more favorable toward teaching by television than those who were experiencing it for the first time. This is some evidence to support the point of view that exposure creates favorable attitudes. Prior exposure and higher favorability toward television teaching has no effect, however, on differential changes in attitudes toward concepts about the subject matter or on amount learned.

There is no support in our study of low-ability students learning better by television than by face-to-face. Again, we are not doing a replication but a variant of the procedure which Kanner [10] undertook. Our low-ability subjects are low with respect to the university population. They probably are not comparable to the low-ability subject of Kanner's basic trainees. Although several other studies have found no evidence to support Kanner's finding, these too are dealing mainly with college-enrolled samples.

Other Studies of Instructional Television Commissioned by NETRC

1. UNIVERSITY OF WISCONSIN. R. N. Dick, project director: A *Comparison of the Effectiveness of Teaching Reading Skill* [increasing

---

[10] Kanner, Runyon, and Desiderato, *Television in Army Training.*

speed and comprehension] *via Television with That of Conventional Classroom Situations.*

Still in progress.

2. UNIVERSITY OF NEBRASKA. C. O. Neidt and J. L. French, in charge: *Reaction of High School Students to Television Teachers.*

Although these high school students preferred conventional classroom instruction to television-correspondence instruction, it seems not to be because they perceived the characteristics differently in the two situations, but rather because of factors inherent in the two methods of instruction.

3. DENVER PUBLIC SCHOOLS. G. J. Willsea, project director: *A Testing Survey to Determine Learning and Comprehension of the French Language Taught via Television.*

After television instructions, pupils did very well in tests. No control group.

4. RENSSELAER POLYTECHNIC INSTITUTE. J. F. Throop, L. T. Assini, and G. W. Boguslavsky, project directors: *The Effectiveness of Laboratory Instruction in Strength of Materials by Closed Circuit Television.*

On the basis of this study, it was decided that students learned at least as much from television as from the conventional laboratory procedure, and that television had certain other advantages. Therefore, Rensselaer decided to equip a classroom with television and teach the course by that means.

5. INDIANA UNIVERSITY. F. V. Mills, project director: *The Influence of the NET Art Films on Art Appreciation of Some High School Students at the University School, Bloomington, Indiana.*

In progress.

6. MADISON COLLEGE. Crystal Theodore, project director: *A Survey of the Use of Television in Art Education in the Southeastern Arts Association Area.*

Art educators who have used television are enthusiastic over it.

7. UNIVERSITY OF WASHINGTON. M. Ryan, project director: *An Evaluation of the Instructional Value of the Television Series, "Discovery."*

The series was found to be useful and valuable in elementary schools.

8. ST. LOUIS PUBLIC SCHOOLS. E. G. Herminghaus and L. M. Smith, project directors: *A Depth Analysis of Student Attitudes Toward Their Classroom Television Experiences.*

In progress.

In 1956, Kumata compiled an inventory of research on instructional television, which was published and distributed by NETRC. Now he has brought his conclusions up to date, in the light of the research that has appeared in the last three years. He has placed with his review a selected bibliography of the most significant research on instructional television. Dr. Kumata is a member of the staff of the Communications Research Center at Michigan State University.

A DECADE OF
TEACHING BY TELEVISION

by Hideya Kumata

A scant ten years ago, there was one institution of higher learning offering two courses by television. Last year, the number was 117 colleges, universities, and school systems offering 464 courses.[1] Ten years ago, there was one television station licensed to an educational institution. This year 45 are in operation and in addition, 119 institutions are using closed-circuit television for instructional purposes (29).

In Chicago, it is now possible for a person to get the first two years of college by television. If one is an early riser, he can learn physics over a national television network from one of the foremost teachers in the country. The high school student in rural Nebraska or Oklahoma can get courses in mathematics and science by television, courses not offered before in his small school. If he is a medical student, he can get an unobstructed close-up view of surgical techniques through color television.

If he is a busy schoolteacher, he can get in-service training by means of television without leaving his school. If he is a prospective schoolteacher, he can observe classroom procedures by looking at a television screen. When he goes practice teaching, he can get valuable insights into his performance as a teacher by viewing his efforts on videotape immediately after teaching. If he is a student having

----

[1] L. E. McKune, *Telecourses for Credit. Volume 5*, East Lansing, Mich.: Continuing Education Service, Michigan State University, 1958.

difficulty in settling down to school routine, he can tune in at his dormitory to a course in effective study methods. Just before lunch, he can view one of the great minds of the country discussing a vital issue—later, he can raise questions with one of his faculty members in a small discussion group.

All of the above uses and many more have been tried with television. There seems to be sufficient promise for continued imaginative use of the medium. Sheer growth may be a sufficient vote of confidence for the effectiveness of using television for educational purposes. But acceptance is not universal in the educational community. Some point to the glowing promises of educational radio made some 30 years ago and the imaginative uses to which that medium was put. Educational radio is still with us, but those promises have been largely unfulfilled.

Others point to the subsidy base of most of the television efforts. This subsidization by private foundations and more recently by the federal government may have put many into the position of being tempted by availability of funds. The test of acceptance will be that day when these funds are no longer available, when institutions will have to budget their own money to carry on television instruction.

The critical question in acceptance and usage is what effect television has in furthering educational objectives. Quite a sizable body of research literature has now been accumulated on ascertaining effects. A great deal of this literature is unsystematic, to be sure, but it constitutes the base from which arguments on utilizing or rejecting television may proceed.

In 1956, a small booklet was published which attempted to bring together all of the research done on instructional television (75). At that time, the major findings seemed to be these: (1) On subject-matter tests, no significant differences was the overwhelming finding in comparisons of television students with conventionally taught students. (2) On short-term retention tests on subject-matter content, the usual finding was that of no significant difference between TV and conventionally taught students. (3) Acceptance of television by students varied, although there was a tendency toward rejection of TV. (4) Increasing the size of classes, having proctors in the TV room, providing for talk-back facilities did not have any significant effect on amount learned for television students. (5) It was uncertain whether a novelty effect existed or not. (6) Not enough evidence had been obtained to make definite statements about attitude change toward subject-matter content or gain in critical thinking ability, some of the so-called "intangibles" of education. (7) In open-broadcast, adult education courses, acceptance of TV was usually very high. The typical student was a married housewife between 30 and 40 years old with about a year of college education.

We can now re-examine these findings in the light of a number of additional studies. Systematic programs of research have been increasing in the field. In 1956, very few systematic programs of research could be reported. Chief among these were those undertaken by the military (62, 70) and by Pennsylvania State University (22, 23). Now one can point to a number of similar programs. For example, we can cite the group of studies sponsored by the Fund for the Advancement of Education for examination of public school use of television (109), the studies in conducting discussion courses by television (9, 10), the conduct of laboratory work on television (58, 59, 95, 96, 97), open-circuit broadcasts for college credit in the field of adult education (37, 38), large group teaching procedures and television (78, 79), and many others.

LEARNING OF SUBJECT MATTER

The overwhelming majority of studies have been concerned with the problem of information gain. It is apparent that students exposed to television learn some factual items from viewing. The big question has been on the appropriate level of information gain where decision makers can say that TV is worth the time and money. Although some claim that a decision to adopt TV should come only after television teaching shows results markedly superior to conventional teaching, most administrators seem satisfied with findings of equivalent learning. The assumption which is implicit and seldom questioned, however, is that present conventional teaching methods produce the optimum possible in the teaching situation and therefore provide an adequate base for comparison.

Most of the studies report no significant differences when information gain is compared between students taught by TV and students taught under face-to-face conditions. One source reports that of 281 comparisons reported, he found 246 which produced no significant differences between TV and face-to-face.[2] This finding has been reported in a variety of conditions—large and small TV classes (22, 23, 31, 78, 79), TV classes with discussion follow-up (23), TV classes with two-way microphones (10, 75, 112), TV classes of varying lengths (22, 23).

One of the more interesting findings is that of Becker and associates (8), who included a condition in which students read assignments for a class but did not have regular class meetings. The students under this condition produced scores which were not significantly different from the other conditions. It seems students learn in spite of methods!

When differences are found, these seem to be better explained by conditions other than the mere fact of TV transmission. For example, a great many differences favoring TV students have appeared in studies at the elementary and secondary school levels (86, 90, 109, 118). In these studies, TV did not carry the entire load in the class but was used as an augmentation to regular classroom instruction.

Where TV transmission may have a definite effect is in the possible increased attention on the part of students because of the novelty of the situation. This has been investigated in several studies. Macomber and Siegel (79) found that TV students did less well than conventionally taught students in the second semester of a year-long sequence where no difference was found in the first semester. Kumata (74) found that there was no difference in information gain between students who had had a prior course by TV and those who were getting it for the first time. However, he found that students who had previous TV experience were significantly more favorable in their attitudes toward instruction by television. It is quite apparent by the large number of findings of no significant differences in achievement that if a novelty factor is operating, one school term is not enough to ascertain its effects. As the pool of TV-taught students grows, opportunities to check on the novelty factor should become more plentiful than in the past.

Another way to look at findings in television research is to split them into various conditions under which television instruction is received. Two categories suggest themselves—normal classroom reception condition and at-home reception condition. The first we

----

[2] P. D. Holmes, Jr., *Television Research in the Teaching-Learning Process,* New York: NETRC, 1960.

might call a "captive" audience situation and the second a "voluntary" audience. If we look at the studies with this split in mind, we find that most of the studies are on the "captive" audience and by and large this produces findings of no significant differences. Studies of "voluntary" audiences are few but these few suggest that TV students do better than conventionally taught students (32, 37, 38, 77). This does not necessarily mean that somehow at-home conditions are better for learning (although this possibility cannot be ruled out), but that those who voluntarily view TV courses may be more highly motivated. The nature of this voluntary audience differs from captive audiences in some significant ways which will be mentioned later.

The captive audience situation may be split into educational levels. If we look at studies conducted at the grade school, high school, and university levels, we find that TV shows superiority at the lower levels (28, 86, 90, 109, 118). A cursory glance at the conduct of TV teaching at these levels reveals that the lower levels are much more interested in producing a well-rounded total teaching effort in which television plays an important but not necessarily a primary role. This attempt at integration, something very rarely tried at the college level, may account for the appearance of significant differences.

We can also look at the nature of the audiences themselves. One facet which has received attention is that of intelligence level and learning from TV. Kanner (70) first brought this factor up in a study with military basic trainees. There he found that low-ability students learned more from TV than from face-to-face conditions while high-ability students learned more from face-to-face. Later studies (23, 28, 38, 72, 77, 87, 98) have produced mixed results. One explanation lies in comparability of audiences. Kanner's subjects were basic trainees in which low-ability subjects cannot be equated with low-ability subjects used in experiments at the university level. A plausible explanation is offered in the Cincinnati study (28) in which the level of difficulty of subject matter and instructor treatment are cited as possible determining factors. Their argument is that homogeneous ability-level groupings should be used and that TV lessons should be pitched to that level to avoid losing either high- or low-ability students when heterogeneous groupings are used.

RETENTION OF SUBJECT MATTER

The pattern in retention testing is the same as that for immediate information gain tests—no significant differences. The amount of time elapsed between presentation of the course and retention testing has been about 30 to 45 days in most studies, although one case of three years (15) and another of one year (23) are reported. No significant differences were found in the latter two studies. The hypothesis of differential forgetting as a function of mode of presentation is not supported (35, 40, 74, 100).

A study by Kanner (68) with military trainees is an interesting exception. Face-to-face teaching was found to be superior to TV in the immediate posttest situation. In retention tests given a month later, this difference no longer existed. The suggestion is that TV students retained proportionately more of what they had learned than conventionally taught students.

THE QUESTION OF FEEDBACK

It has become clear in recent studies that availability of facilities for TV students to interrupt the TV teacher and ask questions is something which the students desire but does not affect achievement scores. It is also clear that talk-back facilities are very seldom used by students. In all of the studies in which talk-back facilities have been investigated (10, 23, 31, 39, 96, 112), no significant differences have been found in achievement. Almost all report that when such facilities are not present, student evaluation of TV is unfavorable.

The question which can be raised is to what extent sheer opportunity to talk is an adequate substitute for interaction. From the results, assuming that interaction is an important ingredient of learning, opportunity to talk is not a satisfactory substitute. Even when two-way audio-visual facilities are present (104), achievement is not affected. The question of participation becomes moot when open-broadcast facilities are used with numbers of students in the hundreds or thousands. Participation and interaction in the learning process are probably best carried out in discussions held after a TV presentation by a teacher present in the classroom.

ATTITUDES AND ACCEPTANCE

Student attitudes toward teaching by television are largely negative. This statement must be qualified, however, by type of student
involved. Acceptance seems to be enthusiastic by students in elementary schools and by adult students in open-broadcast situations.
High school and university students tend to reject television, with
university students the most negative. In comparison with students
who have not received TV instruction, TV students do give more
favorable responses to TV as a medium of instruction (32, 72, 112).
Confronted with the question of whether they would take another
course by TV, the majority choose the conventional class.

The U-shaped curve of acceptance might be explained in the
following fashion: elementary students are not as yet crystallized
in their notions of what constitutes a formal learning situation. Consequently, their acceptance of television is not mixed with feelings
about what should be "normal." As formal school experience is
gained, a definite expectation is formed as to the nature of formal
education. This leads to rejection of anything which disrupts the
pattern. Thus university students feel TV is not "good" education.
Adult education students, on the other hand, are usually people
who have terminated their formal education. The opportunity TV
presents them to renew learning experiences makes them highly
favorable toward TV.

TV presentations are effective in changing course-related attitudes. However, this change is not significantly different from
changes wrought through conventionally taught classes (8, 10, 22,
23, 75, 76). No boomerang effect is reported—all changes are in the
direction desired, in spite of the fact that student attitudes toward
teaching by television may be extremely negative.

At least two studies have investigated varying the prestige of the
source under TV conditions (44, 74). No significant differences
were found when the presentation was offered as a commercial
network program compared with attribution of the program to the
local educational station with respect to achievement and to amount
of attitude change in the desired direction. Varying the expertness
of the instructor produced no direct influence on course-related attitudes although interactions of prestige with different instructors
were found.

Under certain conditions, students willingly volunteer for additional TV courses (23, 78, 79). One of these is the liking for the instructor. Students prefer certain instructors and will take them whether they are on TV or not. Another condition is size of class. When the face-to-face class is very large, many students choose the television situation. Proximity to the instructor is another factor. If students are seated in the back of the room in conventional classes, or if they see that the probability is great that they will be assigned rear seats, their choice will be for television.

MEASURING THE INTANGIBLES

A general charge raised against instructional television research has been one which has been raised against educational research for a great many years. This is the accusation that information gain tests are not an adequate index of learning. Quite a number of different measures have been tried which attempt to tap this area of "intangibles." Measures of authoritarianism (23), critical thinking ability (37, 78), sociometric choice (32, 77) have been used. In all, although there is a change in the desired direction, there is no difference between this change and that found with conventional classroom groups. Only in the case of sociometric choices is there a significant difference. As one might expect, the conventional classroom situation produces more interaction and liking.

OPEN-BROADCAST AUDIENCES

The Chicago City Junior College project (37, 38) has made the most prolonged study of open-broadcast adult education audiences. The overwhelming majority of credit students have been women in their middle 30's. This corroborates previous findings about the nature of adult education credit students. The Continental Classroom project does not report the typical student although this project is by far the most ambitious ever attempted. Audience estimates for number of viewers were around 300,000 persons daily. Of this number, about 4,500 were enrolled for credit.

The Chicago figures pale beside those of Continental Classroom but are still impressive. In four semesters of TV instruction in which 27 courses were offered, 4,878 different adult students have been enrolled. In addition, another 12,719 students have enrolled not for credit. These adults have accounted for 9,234 credit enrollments and

19,953 noncredit enrollments. On top of this, a sizable eaves-dropping audience exists. All of these students are in addition to the regularly enrolled resident students.

In Chicago as in other locations, the attrition rate for these students during a term is no greater than that experienced normally in a regular class. In follow-up studies done with drop-outs, the reasons have been other than those which might be attributable to television.

WHAT THE RESEARCH SAYS NOW

Compared to the 1956 survey of research, what new information can be added? We have had a great many more findings which report no significant differences. There has been an increase in the number of studies which report significant differences in favor of television. Most of these studies have been done at the elementary or high school level.

The pattern of findings suggests a tentative categorization. The following statements are suggested by the research.

Motivation is a prime factor in ascertaining instructional television effects. Superiority of TV is reported more often in voluntary audience situations than in captive audience situations. This can be interpreted as differences in motivation among the audience rather than the fact of TV transmission.

Subject-matter preparation and integration into a teaching process is a prime factor. Superiority of TV is reported more often in lower educational levels than in higher. This can be interpreted as amount of planning and integration into the educative process rather than the fact of TV transmission.

Intelligence is a prime factor. TV seems to affect intelligence levels differentially but exactly how has not been shown. The findings can be interpreted to mean that the level of difficulty of the message itself and the perceived capability level by the instructor or planner produce different results rather than the fact of TV transmission itself.

The mode of presentation, TV or face-to-face, has no differential effect upon retention of subject matter.

Interaction is a prime factor in learning. However, talk-back facilities or two-way TV is not a substitute for the interaction situation. Presence of such facilities, however, gives students reassurance and a greater willingness to undergo the television experience.

Attitudes toward TV and toward subject matter are a prime factor. However, attitudes toward TV and learning as measured by achievement tests are not related. If they were, the TV student should learn less since he usually has a negative attitude toward the medium. Of prime importance, however, is the return of the student for additional TV courses. If he is negative toward TV, the chances of his taking another course over TV are slight.

Adult education audiences are very important keys to educational television success. The education of adults highly motivated to learn presents a unique opportunity for television. The 300,000 daily viewers of a physics course at 6:30 in the morning attest to the need in this area. When adequate cost figures are available, they may show that adult credit courses such as those offered in Chicago may carry the educational television station.

FUTURE RESEARCH

The recently enacted National Defense Education Act has spurred research activity using the new media. The fruit from this activity may lead to some systematization or codification of instruction by television. Until then, perhaps we will get more demonstration research—demonstrating feasibility to hard-to-convince administrators and policy makers.

List of Selected References on Instructional Television Research

1. Adams, J. C., C. R. Carpenter, and Dorothy R. Smith (eds.) *College Teaching by Television,* Washington, D.C.: American Council on Education, 1958.
2. Allen, M. R., *Quartermaster Training Command Educational Television Study,* Fort Lee, Va.: Quartermaster Training Command, 1954.
3. ———, *Television, Education, and the Armed Forces,* Fort Lee, Va.: Quartermaster Training Command, 1958.
4. Ambrosino, M. J., W. H. Dunstan, and B. F. Haake, *The Schenectady Experiment,* Schenectady, N.Y.: Schenectady Public Schools, 1956.

5. Anderson, G. R., and A. W. VanderMeer, "A Comparative Study of the Effectiveness of Lessons on the Slide Rule Presented via Television and in Person," *The Mathematics Teacher,* 47 (1954), 323–27.
6. Barrow, L. C., Jr., and B. H. Westley, "Comparative Effectiveness of Radio and Television," *Audio-Visual Communication Review,* 7 (1959), 14–23.
7. ———, and B. H. Westley, *Television Effects: A Summary of the Literature and Proposed General Theory,* Madison, Wis.: University of Wisconsin Television Laboratory, Research Bulletin No. 9, 1958.
8. Becker, S. L., C. A. Dallinger, H. H. Crosby, and D. Gold, *Communication Skills: An Experiment in Instructional Methods,* Iowa City: State University of Iowa, 1958.
9. ———, R. Dunlap, and J. C. Gerber, *A Comparison of Three Methods of Teaching Modern Literature,* Iowa City: State University of Iowa, 1957.
10. ———, J. N. Murray, Jr., and H. P. Bechtoldt, *Teaching by the Discussion Method,* Iowa City: State University of Iowa, 1958.
11. Belson, W. A., *Facts and Figures. The Comprehensibility of Two Programmes in the Facts and Figures Series,* London: BBC, 1955.
12. ———, "Learning and Attitude Changes Resulting from Viewing a Television Series 'Bon Voyage,'" *British Journal of Educational Psychology,* 26 (1956), 31–38.
13. Bennett, J. J., *Accounting I by Closed-Circuit Television,* Tuscaloosa, Ala.: University of Alabama, 1958.
14. ———, *Trigonometry by Means of Closed-Circuit Television,* Tuscaloosa, Ala.: University of Alabama, 1958.
15. Benschoter, R. P., and D. C. Charles, "Retention of Classroom and Television Learning," *Journal of Applied Psychology,* 41 (1957), 253–56.
16. Boone, W. F., *Evaluation of the U.S. Naval Academy Educational Television as a Teaching Aid,* Annapolis, Md.: United States Naval Academy, 1954.
17. Brandon, J. R., "The Relative Effectiveness of Lecture, Interview, and Discussion Methods of Presenting Factual Information by Television," *Speech Monographs,* 23 (1956), 118.
18. Broderick, Gertrude G. (ed.), *Proceedings of Conference on Educational Television,* Washington, D.C.: U.S. Department of Health, Education and Welfare, Office of Education, Circular No. 574, 1958.
19. Bundy, E. W., *An Experimental Study of the Relative Effectiveness of Television Presentational Techniques and Conventional Classroom Procedures in Promoting Initial Comprehension of Basic Verb Form Concepts in Elementary Spanish,* Detroit, Mich.: University of Detroit, 1959.
20. CBC, *Television in the Classroom,* Toronto, Canada: CBC, 1954.
21. Capraro, T. C., "A Study of the Effects of Class Size, Supervisory Status, and Two-Way Communication upon Learning and Attitudes of AF-ROTC Cadets in a Closed-Circuit Instructional Television Program," *Dissertation Abstracts,* 17 (1957), 270.

22. Carpenter, C. R., and L. P. Greenhill, *An Investigation of Closed Circuit Television for Teaching University Courses. Instructional Television Research Project Number One,* University Park, Pa.: Pennsylvania State University, 1955.

23. ———, and L. P. Greenhill, *An Investigation of Closed Circuit Television for Teaching University Courses. Instructional Television Research Project Number Two,* University Park, Pa.: Pennsylvania State University, 1958.

24. Carpenter, E., "The New Languages," *Explorations,* No. 7 (1957), 4–21.

25. Carpenter, W. G., Jean E. Fair, J. E. Heald, and Wanda B. Mitchell, "Closed-Circuit Television Is Used at Evanston Township High School," *Bulletin of the National Association of Secondary School Principals,* 1958.

26. Cincinnati Public Schools, *An Experimental Study of the Effectiveness of Television versus Classroom Instruction in Sixth Grade Science in the Cincinnati Public Schools, 1956–57,* Cincinnati, Ohio: Cincinnati Public Schools, 1957.

27. ———, *Report of Three Experiments in the Use of Television in Instruction,* Cincinnati, Ohio: Cincinnati Public Schools, 1959.

28. ———, *A Study of the Effectiveness of Television as a Medium of Instruction in High School Chemistry,* Cincinnati, Ohio: Cincinnati Public Schools, 1956.

29. *Closed Circuit Television Installations in Educational Institutions,* Washington, D.C.: Joint Council on Educational Television, Committee on Television, American Council on Education, 1958.

30. Davies, V., E. Gross, and J. F. Short, Jr., *Experiments in Teaching Effectiveness Applied to Introductory Sociology,* Pullman, Wash.: State College of Washington, 1958.

31. ———, E. Gross, and J. F. Short, Jr., *The Relationship of Teaching Effectiveness to Class Size and Method of Instruction,* Pullman, Wash.: State College of Washington, 1957.

32. Dreher, R. E., and W. H. Beatty, *Instructional Television Research, Project Number One: An Experimental Study of College Instruction Using Broadcast Television,* San Francisco, Calif.: San Francisco State College, 1958.

33. Dunham, F., R. Lowdermilk, and Gertrude G. Broderick, *Television in Education,* Washington, D.C.: U.S. Department of Health, Education and Welfare, Office of Education, Bulletin No. 21, 1957.

34. Dyer-Bennet, J., W. R. Fuller, W. F. Seibert, and M. E. Shanks, "Teaching Calculus by Closed Circuit Television," *American Mathematical Monthly,* 65 (1958), 430–39.

35. Ellery, J. B., *A Pilot Study of the Nature of Aesthetic Experiences Associated with Television and Its Place in Education,* Detroit, Mich.: Wayne State University, 1959.

36. Engelhart, M. D., E. C. Schwachtgen, and Mary M. Nee, "Summary Report on the Instructional Experiment in High School Physics in the Chicago Public Schools," *Audio-Visual Communication Review,* 6 (1958), 157.

37. Erickson, C. G., and H. M. Chausow, *The Chicago City Junior College Experiment in Offering College Courses for Credit via Open Circuit Television. A Report of the First Year of a Three Year Project,* Chicago: Chicago City Junior College, 1958.

38. ———, and H. M. Chausow, *The Chicago City Junior College Experiment in Offering College Courses for Credit via Open Circuit Television. A Report of the Second Year of a Three Year Project,* Chicago: Chicago City Junior College, 1959.

39. *An Evaluation of Closed-Circuit Television for Teaching Junior College Courses,* Los Angeles, Calif.: Los Angeles City School Districts, 1957.

40. *An Evaluation of Closed-Circuit Instructional Television. Report No. 2,* Los Angeles, Calif.: Los Angeles City School Districts, 1958.

41. Evans, R. I., "An Examination of Students' Attitudes Toward Television as a Medium of Instruction in a Psychology Course," *Journal of Applied Psychology,* 40 (1956), 32–34.

42. ———, *An Examination of the Differential Effects on Viewers of Experience in Taking Telecourses on Attitudes Toward Instruction by Television and the Social Psychological Impact of a Controversial Educational Television Program,* Houston, Tex.: University of Houston, 1959.

43. ———, *A Psychological Investigation of a Group of Demographic, Personality, and Behavioral Variables as They Relate to Viewing Educational Television,* Houston, Tex.: University of Houston, 1958.

44. ———, and J. J. Asher, *An Investigation of Some Aspects of the Social Psychological Impact of an Educational Television Program,* Houston, Tex.: University of Houston, 1958.

45. ———, H. B. Roney, and W. J. McAdams, "An Evaluation of the Effectiveness of Instruction and Audience Reaction to Programming on an Educational Television Station," *Journal of Applied Psychology,* 39 (1955), 277–79.

46. *An Experiment in Instructional TV in the Los Angeles Junior Colleges,* Los Angeles, Calif.: Los Angeles City School Districts, 1959.

47. Finn, J. D., "Television and Education: A Review of Research," *Audio-Visual Communication Review,* 1 (1953), 106–26.

48. Frank, J. H., "An Evaluation of Closed Circuit Television for Interceptor Pilot Training," *Dissertation Abstracts,* 15 (1955), 2060–61.

49. Fritschel, A. L., *Teaching General Psychology by Closed-Circuit Instruction,* Macomb, Ill.: Western Illinois State College, 1957.

50. Fritz, M. F., J. E. Humphrey, J. A. Greenlee, and R. L. Madison, *Survey of Television Utilization in Army Training,* Port Washington, L.I., N.Y.: Special Devices Center, Technical Report SDC 530–01–1, 1952.

51. Gordon, O. J., E. C. Nordquist, and K. M. Engar, *Teaching the Use of the Slide Rule via Television,* Salt Lake City, Utah: University of Utah, University Television Report No. 1, 1959.

52. Greenhill, L. P., C. R. Carpenter, and W. S. Ray, "Further Studies of the Use of Television for University Teaching," *Audio-Visual Communication Review,* 4 (1956), 200–215.

53. Hansen, C. F., *Report on an Experiment in Teaching Elementary*

School Music by Television in the Washington Public Schools, Washington, D.C.: Washington Board of Education, 1952.

54. Hard, C. G., and D. P. Watson, "Testing Scientific Terminology on Television," *Science Education,* 39 (1955), 140–41.

55. Hatch, C. V., *Student Attitudes Toward TV as a Medium of Instruction,* Corvallis, Ore.: Oregon State College, 1957.

56. Herminghaus, E. G., *An Investigation of Television Teaching,* St. Louis, Mo.: St. Louis Public Schools, 1957.

57. Hoban, C. F., "Hope and Fulfillment in Educational Television Research," *Audio-Visual Communication Review,* 6 (1958), 165–71.

58. Honig, J. H., *The Utilization of Audio-Visual Aids in the General Chemistry Laboratory Work at Purdue University,* Lafayette, Ind.: Purdue University, 1957.

59. ———, W. F. Seibert, and D. F. Moses, *The Utilization of Audio-Visual Aids in the General Chemistry Laboratory Work at Purdue University,* Lafayette, Ind.: Purdue University, 1958.

60. Husband, R. W., "Television versus Classroom for Learning General Psychology," *American Psychologist,* 9 (1954), 181–83.

61. Hurst, P. M., Jr., *Relative Effectiveness of Verbal Introductions to Kinescope Recordings and Training Films,* Port Washington, L.I., N.Y.: Special Devices Center, Technical Report SDC 269–7–42, 1955.

62. *Instructional Television Research Reports,* Port Washington, L.I., N.Y.: U.S. Naval Training Device Center, NAVEXOS P–1544, NAVTRA-DEVCEN 20–TV–4, 1956.

63. Irwin, J. V., and A. E. Aronson, *Television Teaching, Conventional Lecture versus Highly Visualized Film Presentation,* Madison, Wis.: University of Wisconsin Television Laboratory, Research Bulletin No. 11, 1958.

64. Jackson, R., *Learning from Kinescopes and Films,* Port Washington, L.I., N.Y.: Special Devices Center, Technical Report SDC 20–TV–1, 1952.

65. Joint Council on Educational Television, *Educational Television Today. A Status Report,* Washington, D.C.: Joint Council on Educational Television, 1959.

66. Jorgensen, E. S., Jr., "The Relative Effectiveness of Three Methods of Television Newscasting," *Speech Monographs,* 23 (1956), 120–21.

67. Kanner, J. H., "Future Trends in Television Teaching and Research," *Audio-Visual Communication Review,* 5 (1957), 513–27.

68. ———, S. Katz, and P. B. Goldsmith, *Television in Army Training. Evaluation of "Intensive" Television for Teaching Basic Electricity,* New York: Army Pictorial Center, 1958.

69. ———, W. A. Mindak, and S. Katz, *Television in Army Training. The Application of Television and Kinescope Recordings to Reduce Instructor and Student Training Time and Training Costs,* Washington, D.C.: Department of the Army, Office of the Chief Signal Officer, 1958.

70. ———, R. P. Runyon, and O. Desiderato, *Television in Army Training: Evaluation of Television in Army Basic Training,* Washington, D.C.: Human Resources Research Office, George Washington University, Technical Report No. 14, 1954.

71. Keller, R. J., and O. E. Gould, *Closed Circuit Television in Teacher Education*, Minneapolis, Minn.: College of Education, University of Minnesota, 1957.

72. Klapper, Hope L., *Closed Circuit Television as a Medium of Instruction at New York University, 1956–1957*, New York: New York University, 1958.

73. Kretsinger, E. A., "An Experimental Study of Restiveness in Preschool Educational Television Audiences," *Speech Monographs*, 26 (1959), 72–77.

74. Kumata, H., *Attitude Change and Learning as a Function of Prestige of Instructor and Mode of Presentation*, East Lansing, Mich.: Michigan State University, 1958.

75. ———, *An Inventory of Instructional Television Research*, Ann Arbor, Mich.: ETRC, 1956.

76. ———, *Teaching Advertising by Television*, East Lansing, Mich.: Michigan State University, 1958.

77. Lepore, A. R., and J. D. Wilson, *Project Number Two. An Experimental Study of College Instruction Using Broadcast Television*, San Francisco, Calif.: San Francisco State College, 1958.

78. Macomber, F. G., and L. Siegel, *Experimental Study in Instructional Procedures. Report No. 1*, Oxford, Ohio: Miami University, 1956.

79. ———, and L. Siegel, *Experimental Study in Instructional Procedures. Report No. 2*, Oxford, Ohio: Miami University, 1957.

80. ———, and L. Siegel, "A Study in Large-Group Teaching Procedures," *Educational Record*, July, 1957.

81. Mullin, D. W., "An Experimental Study of Retention in Educational Television," *Speech Monographs*, 24 (1957), 31–38.

82. *The National Program in the Use of Television in the Public Schools. A Report on the First Year, 1957–58*, New York: Fund for the Advancement of Education, 1959.

83. Parsons, T. S., "Comparison of Instruction by Kinescope, Correspondence Study, and Customary Classroom Procedures," *Journal of Educational Psychology*, 48 (1957), 27–40.

84. Pasewark, W. R., *The Effectiveness of Television as a Medium of Learning Typewriting*, unpublished doctoral dissertation, New York University, 1956.

85. Paul, J., and J. C. Ogilvie, "Mass Media and Retention," *Explorations*, No. 4 (1955), 120–23.

86. Pflieger, E. F., *The Television Teaching Project. Report for the Year, 1957–58*, Detroit, Mich.: Detroit Public Schools, 1958.

87. Pollock, T. C., *Closed-Circuit Television as a Medium of Instruction, 1955–56*, New York: New York University, 1956.

88. *Progress Report on Educational Television, New York State Educational Department Experiment—"Instructional Television,"* Albany, N.Y.: New York State Educational Department, 1957.

89. *Report of a Controlled Experiment in Educational Television*, New Haven, Conn.: New Haven State Teachers College, 1956.

90. *Report of the National Experiment of Television Teaching in Large Classes*, Philadelphia: Philadelphia Public Schools, 1958.

91. Rock, R. T., Jr., J. S. Duva, and J. E. Murray, *Training by Television: The Comparative Effectiveness of Instruction by Television, Television Recordings, and Conventional Classroom Procedures*, Port Washington, L.I., N.Y.: Special Devices Center, Technical Report SDC 476–02–2, NAVEXOS P–850–2, undated.

92. ———, J. S. Duva, and J. E. Murray, *Training by Television: A Study in Learning and Retention*, Port Washington, L.I., N.Y.: Special Devices Center, Technical Report SDC 476–02–3, NAVEXOS P–850–3, undated.

93. Sawyer, J. W., and C. M. Woodliff, *A Survey of Policies and Procedures for Selection, Administration, Production, and Evaluation of Formal Adult Instruction for College Credit by Television*, Syracuse, N.Y.: Syracuse University, 1957.

94. Schlaak, O. F., "The Planning, Production, and Evaluation of Two Experimental Series of Classroom Telecasts for Use in the Intermediate Grades in the Columbus, Ohio Area," *Speech Monographs*, 23 (1956), 121–22.

95. Seibert, W. F., *A Brief Report and Evaluation of Closed Circuit Television Instruction in the First Semester Calculus Course*, Lafayette, Ind.: Purdue University, 1957.

96. ———, *A Brief Report and Evaluation of Closed Circuit Television Instruction in Mechanical Engineering*, Lafayette, Ind.: Purdue University, 1957.

97. ———, *A Brief Report and Evaluation of Closed Circuit Television Instruction in Physics*, Lafayette, Ind.: Purdue University, 1957.

98. ———, *An Evaluation of Televised Instruction in College English Composition*, Lafayette, Ind.: Purdue University, 1958.

99. ———, *An Evaluation of Televised Instruction in College Freshman Mathematics*, Lafayette, Ind.: Purdue University, 1958.

100. ———, and J. H. Honig, *A Brief Study of Televised Laboratory Instruction*, Lafayette, Ind.: Purdue University, TVPR Report No. 8, 1959.

101. Siepmann, C. A., *TV and Our School Crisis*, New York: Dodd, Mead, 1958.

102. Skaine, J. C., *A Study Evaluating the Conventional and Televised Lecture Methods as Employed in the Speech I Course at the State University of South Dakota*, Vermillion, S.D.: University of South Dakota, 1958.

103. Stoddard, A. J., *Schools for Tomorrow: An Educator's Blueprint*, New York: Fund for the Advancement of Education, 1957.

104. Stone, O., and J. R. Martin, *Instruction in Graphics by Closed Circuit Television*, Cleveland, Ohio: Case Institute of Technology, Report No. 948–6, 1959.

105. Stromberg, E. L., "College Credit for Television Home Study," *American Psychologist*, 7 (1952), 507–9.

106. Tamminen, A. W., "An Evaluation of Changes in Parents' Attitudes Toward Parent-Child Relationships Occurring During a Televised Program of Parent Panel Discussions," *Dissertation Abstracts,* 17 (1957), 1268–69.

107. Tannenbaum, P. H., *Instruction Through Television: A Comparative Study,* Urbana, Ill.: University of Illinois, 1956.

108. ————, *Instruction Through Television: An Experimental Study,* Urbana, Ill.: University of Illinois, 1956.

109. *Teaching by Television. A Report from the Ford Foundation and the Fund for the Advancement of Education,* New York: Ford Foundation, 1959.

110. *Television Project Report from San Jose State College. Study Report Number 1.* San Jose, Calif.: San Jose State College, 1958.

111. Thomas, K., *Television Research and the Study of Man,* Port Washington, L.I., N.Y.: U.S. Naval Training Device Center, NAVEXOS P–1552, 1956.

112. Throop, J. F., L. T. Assini, and G. W. Boguslavsky, *The Effectiveness of Laboratory Instruction in Strength of Materials by Closed Circuit Television,* Troy, N.Y.: Rensselaer Polytechnic Institute, 1958.

113. *Training by Television,* Washington, D.C.: Department of the Army, Technical Manual TM 11–491, 1959.

114. Tucker, H., R. B. Lewis, Gaither L. Martin, and C. H. Over, "Television Therapy, Effectiveness of Closed Circuit Television as a Medium for Therapy in Treatment of the Mentally Ill," *AMA Archives of Neurology and Psychiatry,* 70 (1957), 57–69.

115. Ulrich, J. H., "An Experimental Study of the Acquisition of Information from Three Types of Recorded Television Presentations," *Dissertation Abstracts,* 15 (1955), 2346.

116. Vernon, M. D., "Perception and Understanding of Instructional Television Programmes," *British Journal of Psychology,* 44 (1953), 116–26.

117. Warman, H. J., "Telecasting Techniques in Geography," *Journal of Geography,* 55 (1956), 217–26.

118. *Washington County Closed Circuit Educational Television Project, Progress Report,* Hagerstown, Md.: Board of Education, 1959.

119. Williams, D. C., "Mass Media and Learning—an Experiment," *Explorations,* No. 3 (1954), 75–82.

120. Willis, B. C., *Evaluation Report of the Two Week Experiment of Direct Teaching on Television,* Chicago: Chicago Public Schools, 1956.

121. Zorbaugh, H. (issue ed.), "Television and College Teaching," *Journal of Educational Sociology,* 31, No. 9 (1958).

EDUCATIONAL TELEVISION
AND CHILDREN

Trained adults can predict fairly well how interested 11- and 12-year-old children will be in a television program, but appear to do quite poorly in predicting the interest of 4- and 5-year-olds. Neither preschool teachers nor parents of preschool children could predict children's interest reliably. The authors therefore advise anyone producing programs for these age levels to test some pilot programs with children. Samuel L. Becker is Associate Professor and Director of the Division of Television, Radio, and Film at the State University of Iowa. Glenn Joseph Wolfe is an Instructor in Radio and Television at the University of Maryland.

CAN ADULTS PREDICT CHILDREN'S INTEREST IN A TELEVISION PROGRAM?

by Samuel L. Becker and Glenn Joseph Wolfe

One of the standard practices in broadcasting, in educational probably more than in commercial broadcasting, has been the evaluation of children's programs solely on the basis of adult reactions. In some cases these adults have been educators trained in the subject matter of the program, in some cases they have been directors or producers or performers, and in some cases sponsors or employees of an advertising agency. In all of these cases, the adults have based their decisions about the program in whole or in part upon their evaluation of what will interest children. The question examined by this study is how good are these evaluations. More specifically, an answer was sought to the following question: *Are there differences between the manifest responses of children, parents, and educators to an educational television program when measures of children's interest are compared to measures of adult predictions of children's interest?*

This is a question which has importance for the researcher as well as the broadcaster. One of the first problems faced by a researcher when he wants to pretest audience reaction to a television program, radio program, film, or play is the selection of a universe from which to sample. The researcher wants to know what sort of people in the test situation will provide the best responses for predicting the effect of a program when it is broad-cast or shown to its intended audience. These questions are par-ticularly pertinent in educational or children's programs. Basic to these questions is the one considered in this study, whether the type of universe sampled makes a difference.

Another problem faced by those who study the responses of audiences is that of the device to be used for recording responses. Many devices have been employed, yet there has been little, if any, systematic research on the effects of different devices upon re-sults obtained. A second purpose of this study was to answer the question: *What are the differences between the response profile obtained when a respondent notes his reaction to a stimulus con-tinuously by pressing or releasing a push button and when he marks his reaction either positive or negative on a sheet of paper each thirty seconds?*

PROCEDURE

We examined these questions by using kinescopes of two 30-minute educational television programs, one aimed at fifth-grade students, the other aimed at preschool or kindergarten-age young-sters. For each, interest responses of the target audience were com-pared to adult predictions of what these responses would be.

The Program

The program aimed at fifth-grade youngsters was one of a series of science films designed for television presentation to children unable to attend formal classes in a community. The program had a single performer who talked about and demonstrated various scientific experiments. The program aimed at younger children was the pilot program of a proposed series designed to provide preschool experiences which would aid in the adjustment of a view-ing child to a school environment later. This series was projected on the assumption that the majority of American children do not have an opportunity to attend kindergarten. Performers on the program were a teacher and a group of four- or five-year-old chil-dren. The major content of the program included a story read by the teacher, painting and clay modeling, and two active games.

Methods of Recording Reactions

Three basic methods for recording responses were used in this study.

1. *Paper and pencil method.* In this method, each respondent was given a long sheet of paper which was marked off in 60 intervals with INTEREST written periodically across the top and DISINTEREST across the bottom. Each 30 seconds, while the program was in progress, a number was flashed on a small screen beside the motion picture screen on which the program was being viewed. The numbers from 1 through 60 were flashed consecutively. These corresponded to the numbered intervals on the respondent's sheet of paper. He was told to note his response with a check (on top of the sheet for interest, on the bottom for disinterest) in the corresponding place on his answer sheet each time a different number was flashed.[1] Each number was held on the screen for approximately 10 seconds. In earlier tests of this method of securing audience response, we found that 30 seconds was an interval at which adults indicated that they found no difficulty responding. This finding was confirmed in this study for both fifth-grade students and adults.

2. *Push-button method.* In this method, each respondent held a plastic box about half the size of a package of cigarettes. On the

----

[1] An example of the instructions given to subjects responding by the paper and pencil method is the following, which was presented to fifth-grade students. "This morning you are going to see a film on science. This film is used to teach science to children who are shut-ins and can't go to school. It was made to be shown in their homes over their television sets and we want to know if it is interesting to them. That's what we want you to tell us. Do you think this film is interesting? The way we want you to tell us is by putting a check mark on the sheet of paper on your desk every time we flash a number on the screen like this [at this point the number 1 was projected on the screen to familiarize the children with the procedure]. You are to put a check mark on the number 1 on the top line if you are interested, or a check mark on the number 1 on the bottom line if you aren't interested. You must make this check quickly because in 30 seconds we will flash a number 2 on the screen and you will have to decide again whether you are interested or not. Don't be afraid to check the not interested line because we know there are parts of the film that aren't interesting and that's what we're trying to find out. Remember now, we are going to flash a number on the screen every 30 seconds throughout the film and you should check the same number on the page that is on the screen. Check on the top line if you are interested and on the bottom line if you are not interested. Are there any questions?"

box was mounted a push button similar to those used for doorbells. Individuals in all but one group who used this method were told to note disinterest responses by pressing the button and holding it until they wished to change their response to interest. The down position was designated disinterest; the up position was designated interest.[2] Respondents were warned that a momentary push of the button registered only momentary disinterest. Individuals in one group, science teachers predicting the interest of fifth-grade students with the push-button method, were given the reverse instructions. Each was told to hold the button down when he wished to predict interest, to release it to indicate disinterest.

Each response of each individual was recorded by an Esterline-Angus 20-pen recorder on a constantly moving paper graph. This device provided a permanent record of the precise moment at which each respondent pressed his button and the length of time for which he held it down. In addition, while each program was being shown to one of the test audiences, identification marks were made on the moving graph which later permitted the responses of each segment of the program to be located on the graph. This made it possible to identify almost the precise moment in the program at which either an individual or group of individuals changed their response from interest to disinterest or vice versa.

----

[2] An example of the instructions given to subjects responding by the push-button method is the following, which was given to mothers of preschool children. "In a moment you will see a film which was designed for preschool children and children of kindergarten age. It is felt that perhaps a venture of this kind might later serve as a substitute in areas where kindergarten is not available. What we would like you to do this evening is to tell us where you think your child might be interested or disinterested in this film. In effect, we are asking you to put yourself in the place of your own preschool child. On your seat you will find a small push-button mechanism which you will use in registering your responses to the film. Throughout the entire running of the film, you will evaluate the film on the basis of interest and disinterest only. Obviously a mechanism of this nature cannot measure a degree of interest or disinterest; consequently, any time you feel that your child would tend to be either interested or disinterested, please register in that direction. Think of this as being on a continuum. There is no neutral position, therefore any time you think your child would tend in either direction from the mid-point, please register in that direction. The down position of the button has been designated disinterest and the up position interest. Remember, if at any point you feel the child would be disinterested, please push the button and hold it until you feel your child's interest would rise. A momentary push of the button registers only momentary disinterest, therefore the button has to be held down. Any time the button is not held down you are indicating that you feel your child would be interested. Remember, down means disinterest and up means interest. Are there any questions?"

3. *Observation method.* As noted above, one of the programs used in this study was directed at four- and five-year-old children. In order to obtain profiles of interest of these children in the program which could be compared with the prediction profiles of adults, it was necessary to develop some technique for observing and recording their interest which would result in a record similar in kind to those obtained from adults. We believe that the technique devised was both unique and practical for this and other studies of the reactions of young children to television, radio, or film programs.

The preschoolers viewed the program in groups of three or four over a 21-inch television set located in the University Television Center. They were brought to the Center by their mothers, who stayed in the room during the running of the program. The room was furnished with two overstuffed chairs, a couch, coffee table, rugs, and children's stools. Coloring books and modeling clay were placed in conspicuous positions around the room. These were offered as side or competitive activities. These playthings were not called to the attention of the children, but were available for play at any time. The children were allowed to sit anywhere in the room and were told only that they were to see a television show. All of the above was done in an effort to simulate the home viewing situation as much as possible.

In the initial contact interview, mothers were instructed to tell their children nothing more than that they were going to see a television show. They were directed to give the children complete freedom in the viewing situation and were asked not to structure the viewing of their children in any way. If the children were not interested in the program, they were to be given freedom to do anything they desired, even to the point of conversing with the other children in the room. This competition (i.e., clay, coloring, conversation, freedom of movement) was considered a relatively realistic simulation of the conditions under which this program would be viewed if telecast.

Observers were chosen from among graduate students at the University. Each observer was given an instruction sheet two days prior to his scheduled observing period and told to become thoroughly familiar with the instructions prior to the experimental period. In the instructions, he was told that he was to judge only whether the child he was observing was interested or not interested in the television program. He was also told that he would record his observations of interest or disinterest continuously on the push-button device described above. Its operation was also explained. In addition to this, the observer was given a list of criteria which had been used as indexes of interest and disinterest in previous research with children.[3] On the sheet, each observer was told which child he was to observe. Prior to each viewing session, observers and children were introduced. A complete explanation of the observers' presence and function was given the children in an effort to dispel any apprehension which the children might have. The observers were placed in sight of the children on the strength of previous research which has shown that children in this age group are bothered very little by the presence of observers, provided these observers are explained. The observers were seated close to

----

[3] G. D. Stoddard (ed.), *University of Iowa Studies in Child Welfare*, Iowa City: State University of Iowa, 1937, *passim*. The list of criteria provided to aid the observers in recognizing children's interest and lack of interest included the following:

Interest: (1) *smiles;* (2) *bright facial expression,* or lighting up of the face and eyes; (3) *laughs;* (4) *frowns;* (5) *moves nearer television set*—bends body forward toward television set, pulls chair near to it, or walks to it; (6) *repeats*—says words of story or any portion of the show after their appearance on the screen; (7) *discusses*—holds conversation with other children or experimenter about the content; (8) *makes pertinent remark*—makes a statement in any way connected with the content of the story or show, or makes a single reply about the story to another child; (9) *exclaims or chuckles;* (10) *requests more* —states verbally desire for more story, etc.; (11) *bangs feet spontaneously* in rhythm with some aspect of the show or as a matter of excitement; (12) *claps hands spontaneously* in response to or in rhythm with some aspect of the show; (13) *anticipates action*—realizes verbally or looks forward to action and events during the film; (14) *talks*—responds verbally to the film without outside stimuli; (15) *imitates* as suggested by the story—copies action of another child as story or film has suggested the action.

Disinterest: (1) *makes nonpertinent remark*—makes a statement seeming to have no definite connection with content of the story or show; (2) *attempts play with neighbor* by talking, laughing, or touching, or a combination of these directed toward another child; (3) *requests different story or entertainment*—expresses verbally a desire to be elsewhere or to do something else; (4) *eyes not on television set*—this refers to fixation, not momentary glances; (5) *becomes engrossed in side activities*—coloring books, clay, and magazines; (6) *talks with mother* about nonpertinent matters; (7) *leaves viewing area*—begins "exploring" other parts of the room.

The fact that the majority of the items above were listed as interest criteria did not mean that each criterion could exhibit only interest or disinterest (e.g., the frown could conceivably carry both an interest and disinterest reaction). In view of this, it was up to the observer to apply these criteria as he saw fit.

the television set, approximately six to eight feet in front of the children. In this way, they could see each child's facial reactions.

The Sample

There were five groups utilized in this study, none of which was a probability sample of the universe which it represented.

1. The entire fifth-grade population of the State University of Iowa Experimental School present on the day of testing viewed the science program. This included 29 students. In order to make the viewing of and reaction to the program as much an integral part of their regular school work as possible, these students were shown the program in the projection room of their school during the regular meeting time of their science class. This class was randomly divided into one group of 15 and one of 14. While the first group was viewing the film and responding to each section by means of the paper and pencil technique, the second was doing regular work in the science classroom. Following this, the second group viewed the film and responded by the push-button method while the first group returned to the classroom. Some might raise the question of the typicality of students in an experimental school of this type. It was the opinion of the science teacher and the principal of the school that these students are undoubtedly more accustomed than most fifth-grade students to participating in such experiments but that their experience in and knowledge of science and, hence, their reactions to this program were probably typical of fifth graders generally. Each individual in this group was asked to indicate, by his responses, those parts of the program which he found interesting and those parts which did not interest him.

2. The second group consisted of 35 elementary science teachers who were attending a science teachers' workshop on the University campus. All but three or four had previous teaching experience in the field of science. The others were just entering the teaching profession. Twenty of these subjects responded to the science program by means of the push-button method noted above; 15 responded by means of the paper and pencil method. Each individual in this group was asked to indicate, with his overt responses, those sections of the program which he felt would be interesting to *fifth-grade students* and those sections which he felt would not be.

3. The third group was made up of 20 professionals in childhood

education. There was no desire for a random sample of professionals when this group was selected. We wanted the most experienced and knowledgeable group of experts in preschool education which we could obtain. For this reason, we selected 20 staff members, 10 males and 10 females from the Child Welfare Research Station at the State University of Iowa. We asked them to evaluate the kindergarten program "in terms of its communication with children at this age [preschool and kindergarten]." We asked each to indicate, by means of the push-button device, those sections of the program in which these children would tend to be interested and those sections in which they would tend to be disinterested.

4. The fourth group tested consisted of 34 mothers of three- to five-year-old children. These mothers were selected by a canvas of the married student housing areas of the State University of Iowa. The mothers included in the final sample were the ones contacted who agreed to participate for a small fee and who had children between the ages of three and five. The result is that this sample is "atypical" of the universe of young mothers in that all were wives of college students or instructors, that they tended to be slightly above average in education, and that they lived in a somewhat unique community, a college married student housing area. Instead of asking each mother to evaluate the kindergarten program in terms of general preschool or kindergarten-age children, each was asked to evaluate it in terms of her own child. That is to say, each was asked to indicate those parts which she believed would interest her child and those parts which she believed would not. Eighteen of the mothers in this group made their predictions with the push-button device, 16 used the paper and pencil technique.

5. The final group was made up of 20 four- to five-year-old children. They, of course, viewed the kindergarten program. The method used to obtain a record of their interest profiles was described above under "observation method."

Treatment of Data

Since the paper and pencil responses were made each 30 seconds, the continuous graphs recorded by the push-button method were tabulated by 30-second intervals. In the latter case, there were obviously many 30-second intervals in which a subject changed his response from interest to disinterest or vice versa. In such cases, the response was considered to be "interest" if a subject had indicated interest for the greater portion of the 30 seconds; it was considered to be "disinterest" if a subject had indicated disinterest for the greater portion of the 30 seconds.

The response profile for each adult group was compared to the profile of the children's group whose interest was being predicted. This was done first by superimposing them on a single graph. These graphs were studied alone and in conjunction with the interview and questionnaire results in order to determine the reactions to each aspect of the program and, wherever possible, the reasons for each reaction. In order to obtain a more precise index of the relationship between adult and children's profiles, a Pearson product-moment coefficient of correlation was calculated for each pair of groups. The criterion measure in each case was the number of respondents in each group indicating disinterest at each 30-second interval.

For the science program, the difference between the mean number of disinterest predictions by teachers and the mean number of disinterest reactions by fifth graders was tested with a *t* test.[4] This was done separately for the groups which had responded by the paper and pencil method and for the groups which had responded by the push-button method.

For the kindergarten program, an analysis of variance [5] was used to test the differences in mean number of disinterest responses among all groups. When a significant F ratio was found, differences between individual pairs of means were tested with *t* tests.

RESULTS

The Science Program

The response profiles of the teacher and pupil groups which had responded to the science program by the paper and pencil method are compared in Figure 1; those for the groups which responded by the push-button method are compared in Figure 2. Section-by-section comparisons of student and teacher responses are best seen

----

[4] A. L. Edwards, *Experimental Design in Psychological Research,* New York: Rinehart, 1950, pp. 150–51.

[5] E. F. Lindquist, *Design and Analysis of Experiments in Psychology and Education,* Boston: Houghton Mifflin, 1953, pp. 56–91.

in Figure 1. This graph shows the responses of the two groups which responded with essentially the same instructions. Except for two short time segments, the profiles in Figure 1 can be almost perfectly superimposed, line upon line, especially if the profile of the teachers is moved forward one unit. In other words, it appears that the students tended to respond a bit more quickly than the teachers. To see this, note how, in most cases, the student profile reaches a peak or valley approximately one unit ahead of the teachers. The effect of moving the teacher profile up one interval can easily be demonstrated by comparing the product-moment coefficients of correlation of the two original profiles with the co-

Teachers_____ Children....................

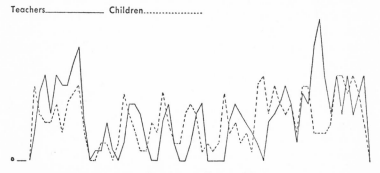

FIGURE 1. SCIENCE PROGRAM. PAPER AND PENCIL METHOD

efficient of correlation of the "corrected" profiles. (In the correlation for the corrected profiles, the number of disinterest reactions for each 30-second interval on the children's profile was matched with the number of disinterest reactions on the *succeeding* interval on the teachers' profile.) In the first case, an r of .295 was obtained, which was only slightly above the level needed for significance.[6] In the corrected case, an r of .492 was obtained. Even though we have one less degree of freedom in this latter case, we obviously have a much closer relationship.

When these paper and pencil groups were compared on the basis of number of disinterest responses made, it was found that the mean numbers of responses were almost equal for the two groups, 17.67 for the students, 18.73 for the teachers. These differ-

----
[6] With 58 degrees of freedom, an r of .255 is needed for significance at the 5 per cent level of confidence.

ences produced a *t* ratio of less than unity. Thus, there was no significant difference between students and teachers on this variable.

Evidence from the postviewing interviews and from a comparison of the profiles in Figure 1 with the profiles in Figure 2 indicates that the two apparent disagreements between the youngsters and teachers, seen in the latter third of Figure 1, may be spurious. The response profile of the push-button group of students was more comparable to the teacher profile at these points. The postviewing comments of students and teachers concerning these parts of the program were also in agreement.

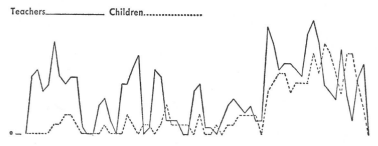

Teachers_____ Children....................

FIGURE 2. SCIENCE PROGRAM. PUSH-BUTTON METHOD

Figure 2 shows the teacher and student group profiles obtained for the science program by means of the push-button device. It is obvious that quite different profiles were obtained, except for the final 11 minutes. During the first two-thirds of the program, the students made far fewer disinterest responses. For the total program, the mean number of negative responses made by these youngsters was 9.93. The mean number made by this group of teachers was 17.90. These means were significantly different, $t = 2.16$ with 32 degrees of freedom. It is important to note here that the student and teacher groups, even though responding by the push-button method, were responding to quite different instructions. The teachers were pushing their response buttons when predicting *interest;* the students were pushing to indicate *disinterest.* Thus, a peak on the teacher profile means that the teacher respondents were doing nothing, having released their response buttons. A peak on the student profile, on the other hand, means that the students were making an overt response; they were pressing their response buttons. In other words, it was more work for the students to make a negative response than for the teachers to do so. Thus, looking at Figure 2 alone, one cannot conclude whether the lack of similarity between the response profiles was caused by differences between teacher predictions and student feelings about the program or whether it was caused by the difference in the mode of response. Figure 1 would make the latter seem a more reasonable assumption. A further indication of the tenability of this assumption is the correlation of .439 which was found between the points on these profiles in Figure 2. The youngsters tended to respond negatively to the same parts of the program as the teachers; they simply responded far less often. This assumption is also consistent with earlier findings by Becker.[7] In one study, this researcher compared the reactions of matched groups of high school students to two educational television kinescopes. Using the same push-button device used in the present study, one group pushed to indicate interest and the other pushed to indicate disinterest in one film. One week later, the methods of indicating interest and disinterest were reversed for the second film. For both films, significantly higher negative responses were obtained when subjects pressed their buttons for interest and released them for disinterest.

The Kindergarten Program

The response profiles of the children, mothers, and experts in preschool education (hereafter called teachers) are compared in Figures 3, 4, and 5. It appears from these figures that the closest agreement among the three groups is to be found between the mothers who responded by the push-button method and the teachers. However, when the response profiles of these two groups were correlated, an r of only .214 was obtained. This is not significant at the 5 per cent level of confidence. The only profiles for the kindergarten program which correlated significantly were those for the children and the group of mothers responding by means of push buttons. An r of .512 was obtained between these groups.

It also appears from Figures 3 and 4 that both teachers and parents greatly overestimated the interest of children in the program or, perhaps, in this situation defined interest at a different

----
[7] S. L. Becker, "Reaction Profiles: Studies of Methodology," in preparation.

level than the operational definition employed in this study. These differences betwen predictions of disinterest and the obtained measure of disinterest can probably best be seen if the mean num-

FIGURE 3. KINDERGARTEN PROGRAM

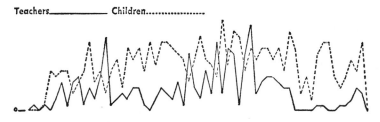

FIGURE 4. KINDERGARTEN PROGRAM

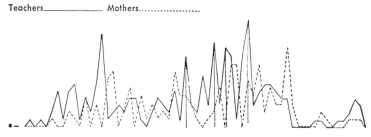

FIGURE 5. KINDERGARTEN PROGRAM. PUSH-BUTTON METHOD

ber of disinterest reactions for the individuals in each group are compared (keeping in mind that a disinterest reaction is a 30-second interval in which disinterest was noted for at least half of the 30 seconds).

As we would expect from the data shown in Table 1, an analysis of variance indicated that these means differed significantly. The F ratio obtained was 14.62. When a t test was run between the children's group and each of the other groups on this criterion, t's of 4.19, 5.03, and 2.84 were obtained for the teachers, push-button mothers, and paper and pencil mothers respectively, indicating that each group of adults averaged significantly fewer disinterest predictions than the amount of disinterest observed in the children appeared to warrant.

TABLE 1

Group	Mean Number of Disinterest Reactions
Teachers (push-button respondents)	10.75
Mothers (push-button respondents)	7.56
Mothers (paper and pencil respondents)	12.88
Children	24.65

It is interesting to note that the group whose profile correlated best with the profile of the children most overestimated the interest which children would have in this program.

An examination of the graphs simultaneously with a transcript of the program showed the major sections at which the adult groups failed to predict what would happen to children's interest. The profiles of none of the adult groups indicated a recognition on the part of these groups that the story read by the teacher, with a few visuals, would fail to hold the interest of the children for 11 minutes. In general, the adults also failed to predict the drop in interest that occurred during discussions and introductions to the games and crafts sections.

Differences Between Response Methods

We had three instances in this study in which two samples drawn from the same population responded to the same program by means of different methods. Two groups of mothers responded to the kindergarten program in different ways, two groups of science teachers responded to the science program by different methods, and two groups of fifth-grade students responded to the science program by different methods. These pairs of response profiles are shown in Figures 6, 7, and 8.

Push-button_____ Paper and Pencil...................

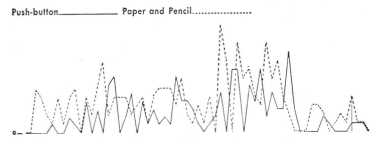

FIGURE 6. KINDERGARTEN PROGRAM. MOTHERS

Push-button_____ Paper and Pencil...................

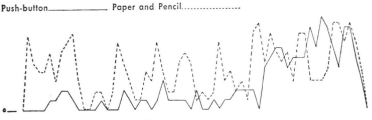

FIGURE 7. SCIENCE PROGRAM. CHILDREN

Push-button_____ Paper and Pencil...................

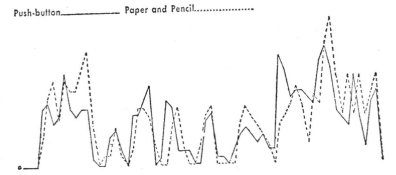

FIGURE 8. SCIENCE PROGRAM. TEACHERS

In Figure 6 we can see that the mothers who indicated disinterest by pressing a button appeared more hesitant to begin disinterest predictions. The mean number of disinterest responses for the entire program was only 7.56 for these machine respondents compared to a mean of 12.88 for the paper and pencil parents. This difference was significant at the 5 per cent level of confidence. The same was true of the fifth-grade students who responded by these methods to the science film. The push-button respondents began indicating disinterest later (this can be seen in Figure 7) and they averaged only 9.93 negative responses compared to 17.67 for the paper and pencil respondents. A t of 2.37 was found for this difference, significant at the 5 per cent level of confidence. However, the science teachers who responded by the push-button method, but *who pressed for interest rather than disinterest,* had neither this lag in beginning to respond nor a significant difference in mean number of disinterest responses, 17.90 compared to 18.73 for the paper and pencil teachers. The t ratio for this difference was less than unity. The profiles for these teachers are shown in Figure 8. It might seem a reasonable hypothesis that respondents will not hesitate to take an overt action if it is to indicate interest but that they will hesitate to take an overt action to indicate disinterest. The problem does not arise with the paper and pencil method because overt responses are forced.

Obtaining Interest Profiles of Young Children to Television Programs

Despite one major limitation, which could probably be overcome, the method used in this study for obtaining continuous profiles of the interest of young children in a stimulus appears to have great promise. Observers had little trouble in following the instructions. As previous research had indicated, the children did not appear to be affected by the presence of observers. The major limitation was that the viewing situation was unique for the children; they did not know all of the other children in their group of three or four and most were not accustomed to having their mothers view television with them. For these reasons, they were probably hesitant to completely "let go." Much of the disinterest registered was probably a result of the children being interested in each other and each other's reaction. However, by using the same children at various times to view programs, and making them secure enough to eliminate the need for their mothers' presence, it is our opinion that a highly valid index of interest can be obtained. It might also prove fruitful to obtain profiles of children viewing television programs individually, as they do in many homes.

One of the important by-products of this study was an account of the way in which youngsters in this age group view television. Only 1 of the 20 children watched the program almost continuously.

He seemed to be an extremely shy boy and he sat with his mother throughout the program. The majority of the children, after the first four or five minutes, seemed to view in a pattern. If they exhibited disinterest by not looking at the screen, they would still glance at the screen periodically in what seemed to be an attempt to satisfy their curiosity rather than a sign of genuine interest. In these cases, they would seldom keep their eyes on the screen for more than 30 seconds. This periodic "checking" was done with amazing regularity and consistency by almost all of the children. If the child was playing with the side activities which had been provided (coloring books, clay, magazines), he would look up at the screen only once each two or three minutes and he would then tend to watch the screen for less than 30 seconds. On the other hand, those children who were, in effect, entertaining themselves rather than using the activities supplied would look up at the screen more often and would stay with the program for longer periods of time, as though in an effort to find something which was more interesting than what they were doing. The majority of these children who were not using the clay or coloring books entertained themselves by watching the activities of other children, by talking to their mothers, by mumbling to themselves, or by typical dreamlike activity such as drawing imaginary pictures on the arm of a chair and just generally gazing around the room. Only one boy paid almost no attention to the program. His mother indicated later that most of the activities which were supplied in the viewing room were not allowed in his home; consequently, he was having a wonderful time with the clay and colors. It appeared that this competition was simply too strong in his case.

Certain types of visual and aural stimuli did cause the children to watch the screen for longer periods of time. A close-up of a child on the screen, a new visual, or an extreme change of angle would tend to hold attention for longer periods than 30 seconds. The major factors, however, were *noise* and *rhythm*. The children's attention was invariably attracted to the screen and held by a sudden increase in the audio level or any sort of rhythmic speaking or game. For example, there was one very rhythmic poem which the teacher read. This was a consistent attention getter. These sounds did not necessarily hold the attention for a long span of time but they did bring the children's eyes back to the screen. Evidence for this contention concerning noise and rhythm is the profile of interest during the two games at the end of the program. Although one was not extremely rhythmic, it was noisy. The second was both noisy and rhythmic. Even though the teacher lost the children's interest during the introduction of each game, once a game started, attention was regained. At least one reason for this, and probably the major reason, was the increase in audio level and possibly the rhythmic pattern developed.

Interestingly, there was little overt reaction to noise and rhythm other than a very *intent* staring at the screen. These were almost the only places in the program where the viewing children seemed oblivious to their surroundings (their mothers, the other children, the playthings, the room in general). In only one case was a child observed making any sort of rhythmic movement, and this was during the theme music at the opening of the program. Here, the audio and video were very closely coordinated, a swinging pendulum, a ticking clock, and music with a clock effect. The boy duplicated the movement of the pendulum with his head. It might have been a lack of motivation or a slight shyness, due to the strange environment, which kept the children from participating in the games. One mother said later that, after seeing the program the preceding semester, she had taught her daughter one of the games. Still, the child did not participate in the game when she saw the program.

As for gross movement, only one child left the immediate viewing area during the program. That is to say, he left the area in front of the couch and chairs. He walked toward the back of the room but quickly returned without prompting from his mother.

CONCLUSIONS

1. It would appear from the results of this study that the predictions of trained adults concerning the interests of older youngsters (in this case, 11- and 12-year-olds) to various portions of an educational television program will be a fair indication of the youngsters' reactions. In the case of programs aimed at younger children, though (in this case, 4- and 5-year-olds), a different situation seems to exist. Neither educators trained for preschool or kindergarten work nor mothers of preschool children seem able to predict, with any high degree of reliability, the interest reactions of youngsters. We would hypothesize on the basis of the limited evidence in this study that the ability of adults to predict the in-

terest of children to television programs decreases with the decreasing age of the children. This, obviously, has important implications for the producers of children's programs. If one is concerned with interest in, as well as learning from, a children's program, pilot programs should probably be tested on a sample of the target audience as well as on a sample of "experts" before being accepted for production or distribution.

2. On the basis of this study, there appears to be little difference between push-button response profiles and paper and pencil response profiles if subjects using the first method are pushing a button for interest and releasing to indicate disinterest. However, if respondents are asked to push to indicate disinterest and release for interest, two major differences will be found. During the early section of the program, the push-button respondents will be hesitant to indicate disinterest and, even more clearly, there will be far fewer indications of disinterest throughout the program.

On the basis of these results and our experience with these methods of obtaining response profiles, it is our opinion that the paper and pencil method is advantageous for most research purposes. It is cheaper in initial capital outlay, it is easier to set up, easier to tabulate in the manner done for this study, and, as shown above, results in a maximum response.

Children from age 3 to age 16 give about one-sixth of all their waking hours to television. What television means to them, when they begin to use it, what programs they like, and what part television plays in their lives, are some of the topics treated briefly in the following paper. It represents an advance look at some of the results of a large study of children's use of television conducted during the last two years in the United States and Canada by Wilbur Schramm, Jack Lyle, and Edwin B. Parker, of the Institute for Communication Research at Stanford University.

A NOTE ON
CHILDREN'S USE OF TELEVISION

by Wilbur Schramm

This is an advance look at a bit of the data from an extensive study of children and television. The study, financed in part by NETRC, included large samples of children from the first six and the eighth, tenth, and twelfth grades in San Francisco, and the entire first, sixth, and tenth grades in five smaller communities in the United States and in two matched Canadian communities, one of which did not yet have television. It also included 188 interviews with entire families, many of which had very young children; a number of questionnaires filled out by parents; and talks with teachers. The study is now in the stage of analysis and will be published as a book. The figures reported here necessarily reflect earlier parts of the study, but so far as is known are in agreement with later findings. The conclusions must be considered tentative.

WHEN DOES TELEVISION VIEWING BEGIN?

More than one-third of all children in television communities are watching the picture tube by the time they are three. Four out of five are television viewers by the time they come to school. Almost all of them are regular television viewers before they begin to read the newspaper. In the preschool years only books, read to them, are serious competitors of television for their mass communication time. Table 1 shows the ages at which they typically begin to use the different media.

TABLE 1. PERCENTAGE OF CHILDREN WHO HAVE BEGUN TO USE GIVEN MEDIA BY A GIVEN AGE (N = 382 San Francisco children)

Age	TV	Radio	Maga-zines	Comic Books	Movies	Books Read to Them	They Read	Newspapers Read to Them	They Read
2	14%	11%	3%	1%	1%	38%	0%	0%	0%
3	37	20	11	6	8	58	0	0	0
4	65	27	20	17	21	72	2	4	0
5	82	40	33	35	39	74	9	9	0
6	91	47	41	50	60	75	40	12	9
7	94	53	53	61	70	75	73	12	44
8	95	62	59	68	76	75	86	12	59
9	96	65	62	70	77	75	89	12	71

HOW MUCH DO CHILDREN VIEW TELEVISION?

The amount of time children spend on television varies not only with age but in response to many other conditions—for example, competing recreations in the community, the norms that prevail in a child's family and peer group, and the satisfactoriness of a child's group relations. When television is new in a community, there is a temporary increase in viewing time. Children in relatively isolated towns seem to spend more time on television than do children in cities. There is also some reason to think that, other things being equal, amount of viewing increases somewhat with the amount of television available. But in general a child in the early elementary grades seems to view a little over two hours a day. Viewing time rises to a peak of a little over three hours in the early teens, and gradually declines throughout high school. Table 2 shows the pattern.

TABLE 2. ESTIMATED HOURS OF TELEVISION VIEWING, BY GRADE (N = 1,740 San Francisco children)

Grade	M Weekday F		M Sunday F	
2	2.2	2.1	2.5	2.8
4	2.2	2.2	2.1	2.6
6	2.5	2.6	2.3	2.6
8	3.2	3.2	3.6	3.2
10	2.8	2.5	3.5	3.4
12	2.5	2.1	2.8	3.1

This means that, from the child's third year of life until some time near the end of high school, television comes near to filling one-sixth of all the child's waking hours. It absorbs from one-half to three-fourths of all media time. It is the one universal mass medium among children, as Table 3 illustrates.

TABLE 3. PERCENTAGE OF CHILDREN MAKING "FAIRLY REGULAR" USE OF MEDIA, BY GRADE (N = 848 San Francisco children)

Percentage Who Used	Grade			
	1	2	3	4
TV	95%	96%	93%	97%
Radio	45	53	62	63
Movies	41	60	77	83
Comic books	47	55	76	60
Magazines	21	29	42	39
Books (outside school)	66	74	70	71
Newspapers	47	62	68	84

But even this does not really show how dominant television is in a child's media behavior. Diaries kept by fifth and sixth graders enabled us to compile a record of the percentage of children who would be using each of the media on an average day during the diary week. These results are shown in Table 4.

TABLE 4. PERCENTAGE OF CHILDREN USING MEDIA ON ANY GIVEN DAY (N = 508 San Francisco children)

Grade	Percentage Who Used						
	TV	Radio	Movies	Comics	Magazines	Books	Newspapers
Fifth grade	74%	25%	3%	5%	5%	23%	19%
Sixth grade	74	32	3	8	6	17	22

In other words, three-quarters of all these children were likely to be looking at television on *any given day*—nearly three times as many as for any other medium. In the diaries of fifth graders, television filled an average of about 145 minutes a day. This compares to 40 minutes for reading, 80 for radio (during which time they were usually doing something else), 88 for homework (during which they were often listening to radio), and 18 for movies (which means an average of a little less than one movie per child per week, the time being distributed over seven days). Free play time, as distinguished from media time, was 182 minutes per average day.

WHAT DOES TELEVISION MEAN TO CHILDREN?

Television is extraordinarily prestigeful and popular with children. Perhaps Table 5 will best illustrate the position it occupies in the early school years. This table was based on interviews with entire families. The children in these families ranged from 2 to 14 years. The question was put to these families, for them to discuss among themselves: Who in the family would most miss each of the media if they had to do without media for a month? Notice that

TABLE 5. WHO IN THE FAMILY WOULD MISS EACH OF THESE MEDIA MOST, IF THEY HAD TO DO WITHOUT MASS MEDIA? (N = 188 mothers, 188 fathers, 449 children)

Who Would Most Miss	TV	Radio	Newspapers	Movies
All equally	16%	7%	8%	3%
Children more	22	2	1	11
Only the children	16	3	0	12
Parents more	2	5	22	1
One parent	20	54	59	11
One child	16	13	1	18
Nobody	5	14	6	43
Can't decide	3	3	3	1

whereas one parent (the mother) would be overwhelmingly most likely to miss radio, one parent (the father) would be overwhelmingly most likely to miss the newspaper, and *nobody* in 43 per cent of the families would be likely to miss the movies, television would clearly be most missed by children and most missed generally in the family.

However, the importance of television fades rapidly during the teen years. This may be for the reason that the child in those years is meeting more intellectually challenging communications, or that social competition is more demanding, or that there is less time for television. Table 6 gives a good picture of the situation, and it will be seen that television declines in importance, while radio (chiefly for popular music) and newspapers gain.

Of nostalgic interest to some readers may be Table 7, which

reports what media the children in a community with *no* television say they would miss most, as compared to a similar community which has television.

TABLE 6. MEDIUM THAT WOULD BE MISSED MOST BY EIGHTH, TENTH, AND TWELFTH GRADERS (N = 650) [a]

Medium	Boys			Girls		
	Eighth	Tenth	Twelfth	Eighth	Tenth	Twelfth
Books	6%	5%	5%	7%	6%	13%
Magazines	4	2	2	0	1	2
Newspapers	5	11	20	4	3	11
Comic books	3	1	0	2	1	0
Television	71	58	33	61	45	38
Radio	4	17	32	22	39	33
Movies	3	5	4	3	3	4

[a] No response from about 3 per cent of the children.

TABLE 7. MEDIUM THAT WOULD BE MISSED MOST BY SIXTH AND TENTH GRADERS IN TWO COMMUNITIES, ONE WITHOUT TELEVISION [a]

Medium	Percentage Who Would Miss It Most	
	In Community Without	In Community With
Books	14%	14%
Newspapers	5	10
Comic books	7	1
Television	3	47
Radio	54	26
Movies	17	2
N =	(209)	(358)

[a] Source—Stanford study of children in two Canadian towns.

It is interesting to see that, even in a town where television has not yet penetrated, 3 per cent of the children list television as the medium they would miss most. These are children who have experienced television during visits to other cities, or in previous locations. A more important meaning of the table, however, is what it says about the media television replaces. Television makes no difference in the importance of books, and actually seems to contribute to the felt importance of newspapers. But it cuts radio's apparent importance in two, and almost completely eliminates movies and comic books as "most missed" experiences. It must be, therefore, that television is replacing the kinds of need satisfactions the child would otherwise have found chiefly in radio, movies, and comics.

WHAT PROGRAMS DO THEY LIKE?

As children go through the elementary grades they pass rapidly from the stage of "children's" programs to the programs of violence and excitement. "Disneyland" and "Zorro" dominate the first six years; westerns and crime programs the second six. Our best estimate is that about three-fourths of all children's viewing, during the twelve school years, is of programs which have adults as the majority of their viewers. Boys seem to hold on to childish programs longer than girls, but boys' and girls' tastes draw closer together in the high school years. Table 8 indicates the programs said by San Francisco School children, in 1958 and 1959, to be their favorites.

HOW IMPORTANT IS EDUCATIONAL TELEVISION TO THEM?

Children's use of educational television is not heavy; on the other hand, it is not so small as to be negligible. Although a direct comparison is not now possible, it seems probable that children make somewhat less use of ETV than do their parents. The best figures we have been able to obtain on children's viewing of ETV come from San Francisco and from a small town which is within the primary coverage area of another educational television station. The San Francisco figures, which were slightly but not significantly higher, are presented in Table 9.

In the early school years, there is a very high correlation in the use of educational television within a family. This is illustrated by Table 10.

As the child grows toward the teens, the influence of the peer group becomes more important with respect to his television behavior. Teenagers appear to feel the contrast between television as entertainment and television as education, described in this volume by Messrs. Geiger and Sokol, more intensely than do their parents. Their lives are already full of educational experiences; they are, therefore, attracted more to experiences that promise a relaxa-

TABLE 8. FAVORITE PROGRAMS OF SAN FRANCISCO CHILDREN

First	Second	Third	Fourth	Fifth	Sixth
Disneyland	Disneyland	Disneyland	Disneyland	Disneyland	Zorro
"Cartoons"	Zorro	Zorro	Zorro	Zorro	Disneyland
Popeye	Popeye	"Cartoons"	"Cartoons"	Maverick	Amer. Bandstand
Zorro	"Cartoons"	Popeye	Popeye	Leave It to Beaver	Father Knows Best
Mickey Mouse Club	Lassie	Mickey Mouse Club	Cheyenne	Danny Thomas	Maverick
Lassie	Mickey Mouse Club	Lassie	Lassie	Cheyenne	Topper
Capt. Fortune	Rin Tin Tin	Leave It to Beaver	Rin Tin Tin	Father Knows Best	Cheyenne
"Westerns"	Cheyenne	Circus Boy	Mickey Mouse Club	Real McCoys	Leave It to Beaver
Rin Tin Tin	Leave It to Beaver	Amos and Andy	Real McCoys	Fury	Real McCoys
Leave It to Beaver	"Westerns"	Cheyenne	Danny Thomas	Sea Hunt	"Science Fiction"

Eighth		Tenth		Twelfth	
Boys	Girls	Boys	Girls	Boys	Girls
Maverick	Amer. Bandstand	77 Sunset Strip	77 Sunset Strip	Peter Gunn	Peter Gunn
77 Sunset Strip	77 Sunset Strip	Maverick	Amer. Bandstand	Maverick	77 Sunset Strip
Sea Hunt	Maverick	Peter Gunn	Father Knows Best	77 Sunset Strip	Maverick
Rifleman	Father Knows Best	Amer. Bandstand	Maverick	Rifleman	Amer. Bandstand
Disneyland	Danny Thomas	Sea Hunt	Danny Thomas	Amer. Bandstand	Alfred Hitchcock
Peter Gunn	Peter Gunn	Rifleman	Peter Gunn	Gunsmoke	Father Knows Best
Amer. Bandstand	Ozzie and Harriet	Red Skelton	Wanted Dead or Alive	Bob Cummings	Steve Allen
Gunsmoke	Donna Reed	Father Knows Best	Donna Reed	Naked City	Real McCoys
Father Knows Best	Perry Mason	Leave It to Beaver	Leave It to Beaver	Father Knows Best	Danny Thomas
Steve Allen	Real McCoys	Steve Allen	Gunsmoke	Science Fiction Theater	Loretta Young
"Science Fiction"		Gunsmoke			

TABLE 9. VIEWING OF A COMMUNITY EDUCATIONAL STATION BY GRADE AND SEX

Frequency	Eighth Boys	Eighth Girls	Tenth Boys	Tenth Girls	Twelfth Boys	Twelfth Girls
Practically every day	2%	1%	1%	3%	1%	4%
At least several times a week	10	10	6	7	5	7
At least one day a week	20	15	12	10	18	9
At least occasionally	38	34	27	28	41	36
Not at all	62	66	73	72	59	64
N =	(114)	(105)	(85)	(116)	(123)	(109)

TABLE 10. CHILDREN'S VIEWING OF COMMUNITY EDUCATIONAL TELEVISION BY FAMILY VIEWING (N = 185 mothers, 182 fathers, 442 children)

Child Views ETV	Father Views ETV One Hour or More per Week	Less than One Hour	Not at All
One hour or more	46%	16%	15%
Less than one hour	38	73	4
Not at all	16	10	81

Child Views ETV	Mother Views ETV One Hour or More per Week	Less than One Hour	Not at All
One hour or more	48	11	14
Less than one hour	26	74	0
Not at all	26	15	86

Younger Child Views ETV	Older Child Views ETV One Hour or More per Week	Less than One Hour	Not at All
One hour or more	74	5	4
Less than one hour	13	87	4
Not at all	13	4	92

tion from school work than to experiences that promise more of the same. Among children in the late elementary and early secondary grades, there tends to be a norm which is expressed by the saying, "Educational television is for the squares!" Or, "Who wants to go to school when school is out?" How much use a teenager makes of educational television is therefore dependent on a number of forces contrary to that childish norm: the extent to which educational television is related to school assignments, how strongly the norms for self-betterment and information-seeking impinge on the child, the child's intelligence level, and so forth. It is a reasonable assumption, however, that the use the child is taught to make of serious television in the elementary school years will largely determine the extent to which he continues to use it through the teens; and if that chance is lost, then the full usefulness of educational television will not become apparent to him, if at all, until he is through school and on his own.

WHAT PART DOES TELEVISION PLAY IN THE LIFE OF A CHILD?

This seems a better way to ask the familiar question: What effect does television have on children? In one sense, television doesn't have an effect on children. It is a great passive source of experiences, a supermarket of gratifications to which the child goes for what he wants. It is a rewarder of drives, a reinforcer of responses, a teacher of facts and skills; and if what television offers is important, more important is the set of needs and expectations which the child brings to television.

What we are really concerned with, then, is the dynamics of the relationship between child and television. We know enough about it now to know that it is not a simple relationship. The simple and perhaps most often heard statements are half-truths at most: that brighter children see less (or more) television; television builds (or reduces) aggression; television is good (or bad) for children; and so on. The dynamics are much more complicated than that, and predictions based on any such simple statements are likely to go wrong. Let us set forth some tentative notions as to how these dynamics work.

At least four sets of forces and relationships enter prominently into the dynamics of a child with television. These are the class norms within which he functions, his family and peer group relationships, and his intelligence.

In general, two sets of social norms seem important here. One of these is the striving, achieving, active, information-seeking, self-bettering norm which has been associated in our history with

upward mobility, and is typical of the American middle class, especially the upper-middle. The other is the passive, live-in-the-
present, entertainment-seeking norm which is often thought of as
associated with the lower class. It may seem anachronistic to introduce the concept of class norms at the very time when most of
America seems to have moved, income-wise and status-wise, into
the middle class. But be assured that these norms are still very
active with children, even though the idea of social class may never
enter their minds. The one set of norms will make them more likely
to try to live in the present, to seek immediate gratification; other
things being equal, it will lead them to make more use of general
television. The other set of norms teaches them to defer gratification
in favor of later and greater achievement; other things being equal,
it leads them to more use of *educational* television, more use of
serious print, and less general television.

But other things are seldom equal, and two things that are often
most unequal among children are their parent and peer group relationships. In the early years, when parental influence is very
strong, a child is likely to act, either from example or precept,
on the pattern of social norms which his parents have internalized.
If they are middle-class norms, he will be more likely to experience
educational television, the more serious and informative commercial
programs, and some of the more serious parts of print. If they are
lower-class norms, he is likely to see more general television than
his friend who lives by the other norms, but he is less likely to
see educational television or "Omnibus." Along toward the teens,
however, comes a time when peer group norms become very important, and sometimes clash with parental norms. This is often
a period of chaos for the child, and his television behavior, like
some of his other behavior, is likely to be erratic.

Whether the child's family and peer group relationships are satisfying to him often makes a great difference in his television behavior. Let a child's group relationships be insufficient to his needs,
let him feel isolated or rejected or misunderstood, and he invariably
runs away to a substitute source of satisfaction. In this day, he often
runs to television. If he has grown up under lower-class norms, this
may not make a great difference in the amount of television he
sees, because the amount is already high; but it may have something
to do with how much fantasy he sees. If he has grown up under
middle-class norms, and has unsatisfactory group relations, then

he is likely to increase greatly the time he spends on television. He retreats into fantasy. One of the most common types of television addicts seems to be the child who is driven by unsatisfactory group relations to view large amounts of television fantasy, finds himself doing a great deal of what his norms tell him he shouldn't be doing, and thereby builds up the pattern of addiction.

A child who retreats from poor group relations into television usually demonstrates a high level of antisocial aggression. But it can hardly be said that he derives this from the violence of television. Rather, it originates in the abrasions on his social life, and feeds on television. Television is a great feeding trough for all kinds of appetites. An appetite for public-affairs information and fine arts can get at least some satisfaction from general television, although admittedly such an appetite cannot be so easily satisfied as an appetite for escape or thrill play or fantasy. Television is a great teacher of many skills. If a child goes to it wanting to learn how to hold a baseball bat or how to behave like a good public official, he can learn something about that; on the other hand, if he wants to know how to commit a burglary or kill a man, that, too, can be learned from television.

What a child is, before he goes to television, what relations he can build up within his family and his peer group, what needs he takes to television, are therefore the chief ingredients of television's effect on him. But not wholly. For there is an interaction. He brings a need to television, and television reinforces certain responses in him. Over the space of years, therefore, the selective reinforcement he gets from 15 to 25 hours of television a week must have something to do with what he knows and what he does.

For this reason, what is available on television becomes important—especially important in relation to the fourth variable we mentioned above—the child's intelligence. A child with high intellectual ability is better able to absorb the serious and informative programs. If he once tries them, he is more likely to get a reward from his action, and to come back for more. With the very intelligent child, we sometimes get the fairly rare but important pattern of deviance in which the child has less than satisfactory group relations because he has *higher* aspirations than his parents or his peers. In this case, of course, the child is less likely to retreat into the wastes of television fantasy at least until he has tried to find the intellectual challenge of which he feels the need. If he doesn't readily find it, then he may fall all the harder into the whodunits and the soap and saddle plays.

In this latter kind of case, we feel that there may have been a waste of intellect and talent. But it has seemed to us also as we have worked with the data that perhaps the question should be asked more generally: Does television offer all the challenge it might? For if one-sixth of a child's waking hours are going to be devoted to a medium that is an unequaled teacher of facts and skills, then surely that medium must have some influence on his developing picture of environment.

It may well be, therefore, that what *isn't* on television is more worthy of our attention than what is. If there is a great deal of fantasy and violence on television, that is less important than it would be if there turns out to be *little else* on television. If a child can learn to commit a crime on television, that seems to be less important than whether a child has developed a need of that skill; and if he has developed such a need, he could doubtless satisfy it elsewhere also. But if there is insufficient opportunity on television to challenge a bright child, and to satisfy the kind of norms that encourage the seeking of information on serious problems and the gratifications of fine arts—in other words if television seems to be heading toward a dull sameness of escape and fantasy material, then we are indeed in danger of wasting some valuable time of our children at a time in the history of the nation when we can ill afford to waste it.

We find, for example, that with a slow teenager a great deal of television does not necessarily mean that the state of his information is below that of his peers. In the case of a bright teenager who watches a great deal of television, however, the level of his knowledge is almost certain to be below that of an equally intelligent child of the same age who sees *less* television. He is apparently being diverted from experiences that are more rewarding intellectually. Even in the case of elementary school students, those who see a large amount of television are likely to know more of the popular arts, and those who see little television are likely to know more of the fine arts and public affairs. This has seemed to us a matter over which the parent, the school, and the television industry all might have some concern.

The Stanford Study of Children and Television

This study, financed in part by NETRC, extended through 1958 and 1959, and into 1960. Wilbur Schramm was chief investigator, assisted by Jack Lyle and Edwin B. Parker. The three will share authorship of the book which reports the findings.

The study began with the first six grades of the San Francisco school system. A large sample was obtained from each grade by making a random choice of classrooms within a sample of schools selected by school officials to represent the social and racial diversity of San Francisco. These students were given tests and questionnaires, asked to keep diaries for a week, and some of them were interviewed especially to ascertain their newspaper reading and other facts. Questionnaires were sent to parents of the first four grades. Besides these, 188 interviews were conducted with whole families, in order to find out something about family relationships and communication patterns.

Tests and questionnaires were administered also to samples of the eighth, tenth, and twelfth grades in San Francisco, the samples being drawn in the same way as for the first six grades.

The study was then extended to the entire first, sixth, and tenth grades in the communities of Longmont, Durango, Steamboat Springs, and Grand Junction, Colorado, and Dillon, Montana. It was further extended to Quesnel, British Columbia, which does not yet have television, and Langley, British Columbia, which does. Special studies were conducted in a large city and a metropolitan suburb.

The design was thus intended to make possible, in addition to the analysis of individual and group patterns, a comparison of children's behavior and characteristics between a community that has television and one that does not, between a large city and smaller one, between Canadian and United States communities, and between communities in relative degrees of isolation and with different amounts of mass media available and different numbers of years with television.

Another Study of Children and Television Commissioned by NETRC

UNIVERSITY OF ILLINOIS. D. W. Smythe, project director: *Toward More Effective Educational TV: A Pilot Study of the Effects of Commercial TV on Verbal Behavior of Pre-school Children.*

Children who had not yet learned to read became able to associate visual with auditory symbols on a commercial children's program. Improvement in reading readiness, however, was not significantly greater than that of a control group.

PROPOSED THEORY FOR THE EFFECT
OF EDUCATIONAL TELEVISION

The author of this paper proposes a "miniature" theory to account for the effect of educational television, and so far as possible tests the theory against existing experimental studies. His theory is based on the concept that audio-visual communication has to face two different kinds of interference—one which distracts attention from the message, another which masks or conceals the message. The program maker must combat these two enemies by introducing qualities which this paper calls potency *and* comprehensibility. *Mr. Barrow, then a study director for the University of Wisconsin Television Laboratory, is now an Assistant Professor in the Communications Research Center at Michigan State University.*

PROPOSED THEORY FOR THE EFFECT OF EDUCATIONAL TELEVISION

by Lionel C. Barrow, Jr.

BASIC DEFINITIONS

When attempting to transmit a message, a communicator has to deal with, minimize, and/or overcome two types of interference.

Type I interference distracts attention from the message. Type II interference masks the message.

Type I interference "competes," type II "conceals." Both lower the probability that the message will be received as sent and/or acted upon with efficiency. Both can arise from stimuli external or internal to the communications system established between the communicator and the receiver. "Noise" as defined by Shannon and Weaver (1949) would be an example of external interference. The inability of the receiver to perceive the message because it is below threshold is an example of internal interference.

To overcome type I interference (internal, external), a communicator must regulate what we have called the relative potency (Po) of the message. To overcome type II interference, he must regulate the relative comprehensibility (Co) of his message. The effectiveness of his message is a function of these two factors.

Relative potency we define as the degree to which a message is able to attract and hold the attention of a receiver. Relative comprehensibility is the degree to which a message is understandable to a receiver. Po, then, equals the actual attention attracted to the message divided by the maximum attention possible; and Co equals the total number of symbols, relationships, concepts, etc., understood by the receiver divided by the total number presented.

Up to this point we have not stated what is meant by "effect." This was left vague because it was hoped that the literature search would turn up enough experiments to warrant deriving both learning and attitude change hypotheses. This, however, was not the case. Out of the 41 television and sound motion picture experiments reviewed and summarized for this report, only two measured changes in attitude. (Several other experimenters measured attitude *toward the communication* by administering a paper and pencil test after the manipulation or by having the subjects manipulate a program analyzer.) Since the goal of this study was to base a theory primarily on empirical evidence, two studies seemed too few to yield any meaningful generalizations. The derivations therefore are confined to learning, or "information gain," with the hope that at some later date hypotheses concerning attitude change may also be derived from the same concepts.

Learning (or information gain) is defined as the difference between a subject's actual response or performance on an information test following receipt of a communication and his response or performance on an equivalent test before receipt of the communication.

Hypothesis 1: With relative comprehensibility held constant, the effectiveness of a communication will increase within limits as relative potency increases.

On the surface it would appear that only one of the studies in Table 1 supports the hypothesis. However, these studies were not designed to test this hypothesis; they were "engineering" studies designed to handle very specific problems. For the most part, the experimenters measured only their independent and dependent variables and thereby assumed that any other variables were having a random effect. Only the experimenters who measured "interest" made any attempt at measuring an indicator of an intervening variable. Our objections to this concept and the methods of operationalizing it have already been stated.

Table 1. Studies Related to Hypothesis 1 [a]

Experimenter	Variable	Results [b]
"Interest"		
Brandon (1955)	Interest	Correlation small (.218).
Jorgensen (1955)	Interest	Correlation negative (−.145) and nonsignificant.
Vernon (1953)	Interest	Positive correlation with learning of simple facts, negative one with learning generalizations and cause-effect relationships.
VanderMeer (1952)	Liking of film	Correlation positive but not high.
"Pleasantness"		
VanderMeer (1953)	Singing commercial. vs. lecture	No significant difference.
McIntyre (1954)	Comedy vs. comedy replaced by titles vs. comedy replaced by blank film	No significant difference between comedy and blank film versions; titles significantly better than both.
Brandon (1955)	Lecture vs. interview vs. discussion	No significant differences.
Jorgensen (1955)	Newscaster alone vs. with stills vs. with motion pictures	No significant differences.
Identification Symbols		
Zuckerman (1949)	Personal reference	Third person imperative and second person (implied) equal and best. First person less effective (but not significantly). Third person passive least effective and significantly below top two.
Nelson & Vander-Meer (1955)	Personalization vs. repetitiousness vs. visual emphasis	No significant differences.
Pleasant x Identification		
Allen (1952)	Very interesting vs. dull	Very interesting version resulted in greater learning.[c]
Blain (1956)	Expository vs. personalized dramatic	No significant difference.
Fletcher (1955)	Reduction of motivational material	Cutting out motivational material did not affect learning.

[a] These studies and others are discussed at length in other chapters of Mr. Barrow's report, not reprinted here.
[b] Results refer only to effect upon or correlation with information gain.
[c] Tends to support hypothesis.

RELATIVE COMPREHENSIBILITY (CO)

Hypothesis 2: With relative potency held constant, the effectiveness of a communication will increase as relative comprehensibility increases.

None of the studies reviewed provides a direct test of any of the following hypotheses or of the above one. Some inferences are possible, however, since usually relative potency elements were held more or less constant while relative comprehensibility elements were being varied. Thus, according to the above hypothesis, learning becomes a function of relative comprehensibility and we may utilize the results reported as an indication of the value of our hypotheses about relative comprehensibility.

Hypothesis 2a: Other things equal, relative comprehensibility is a nonlinear function of the number of relevant cues in the message.

In general, the studies in Table 2 tend to support Hypothesis 2a.

TABLE 2. SUMMARY OF STUDIES RELATED TO HYPOTHESIS 2a

Experimenter	Variable	Results [a]
McIntyre (1954)	Titles added	Significant increase.[b]
Hart et al. (1947)	Participation questions added	Increase significant but small.[b]
Hart et al. (1947)	Motivation questions added	Scores higher but not significant.
Kurtz et al. (1950)	Statements added	Increasing number of statements led to increase in scores.[b]
Kurtz et al. (1950)	Questions added	Better than no questions.[b]
Northrop (1952)	Outlining added	Inconsistent results.
Jaspen (1950a)	"Errors" sequence added	Increased scores.[b]
Jaspen (1950a & b)	"How-It-Works" sequences added	Differences inconsistent, not significant.
Kimble & Wulff (1953)	Guiding responses added	Significant increase.[b]
Lumsdaine et al. (1951)	Animated inserts added	Significant increase.[b]

Table 2. (concluded)

Experimenter	Variable	Results
Miller et al. (1952)	Review added	Only "massed" review version significantly better than no review. No significant difference between no review and two "spaced" review versions.

Comparing the Effect of Different Numbers of Cues

Experimenter	Variable	Results
Kurtz et al. (1950)	Persistent vs. medium questions	Confounded by variation in subjects.
Kurtz et al. (1950)	Persistent vs. medium statements	Same as above.
Kopstein et al. (1952)	Three examples vs. six examples	Significant increase with increase in number of examples.[b]
Northrop (1952)	Titles vs. titles with subheadings	Mean test scores increased with increase in cues for two films, decreased for third.[b]

Deleting Cues

Experimenter	Variable	Results
Fletcher (1955)	Full script vs. two reduced scripts	Deleting as much as 24 per cent of the material did not affect learning.
Lathrop & Norford (1949)	Film introductions vs. none	No significant difference.
Lathrop & Norford (1949)	Film summaries vs. none	No significant difference.
Mercer (1952)	Optical effects: all vs. some vs. none	No significant differences.

[a] Refer to effect upon learning.
[b] Tends to support hypothesis.

However, several of them, particularly the "deleting cues" subset, seem to indicate the need for a refinement of the hypothesis.

Kopstein et al. (1952), in addition to using examples in the films, also gave additional examples following the films. The additional examples "made a significant improvement" but "the 'rate' of improvement diminished as the number of examples increased," they said, "suggesting a 'saturation point,' depending on the difficulty of the material, after which further examples would fail to produce more gain."

Northrop (1952) concluded from his study that "making the organizational outline of an instructional film more prominent may be expected to increase learning significantly if the subject matter is not in itself highly organized. Adding such material to films already well organized may even reduce learning somewhat, presumably by disrupting the continuity of the film. In those cases where prominent outlining is helpful, it is not significantly better to add more than an outline giving the main points covered by the film."

Several of the studies seem to indicate that there is an optimal point beyond which adding cues will not increase the effectiveness of the message. Just what this point is for a given type of material transmitted by one or both of the audio-visual channels will have to be determined empirically.

It was stated earlier that to increase the relative comprehensibility of his message, a communicator must overcome and/or minimize type II (masking) interference. We discussed two possible sources of type II interference: (1) differences in semantic level between the code used by the communicator and the code the receivers can understand; (2) the ambiguity or lack of a clear structure in the message. We have also been implying the existence of a third possible source which we now identify as (3) external stimuli which conceal or distort the meaning of the message.

Hypothesis 2b: Other things equal, relative comprehensibility increases as the difference between the semantic level of the receiver and the semantic level of the message decreases.

TABLE 3. STUDIES RELATED TO HYPOTHESIS 2b

Experimenter	Variable	Results [a]
Allen (1952)	Reading ease: fifth- vs. seventh-grade materials	Fifth-grade commentaries significantly better for sixth-grade students than seventh-grade commentaries.[b]
Moldstad (1955)	Listenability difficulty: fifth-, seventh-, and eleventh-grade materials	No significant difference with seventh graders.
Blain (1956)	Listenability difficulty: fifth- vs. eighth-grade materials	No significant difference for fifth and eighth graders.
Jaspen (1950a & b)	Technical names vs. common names	Inconsistent or nonsignificant results.

[a] Refer only to effect upon learning.
[b] Tends to support hypothesis.

Elsewhere we tentatively defined differences in semantic level as the difference between the code (words, sentence patterns, etc.) used in the message and the code the individual receiver is capable of understanding. Students of readability ordinarily assume that reading ease is facilitated when the semantic level of the message is at or below the semantic level of the receiver. This proposition, however, states that it is the discrepancy between the two semantic levels that makes the difference—when the message is "too hard" for the reader, in which case he will find it too demanding, or "too easy," in which case he will find it not worth the effort.

Only Allen's findings tend to confirm Hypothesis 2b. The findings of Moldstad and Blain do not support the hypothesis.

Molstad suggests that the reason for the contradictory findings might be that in some films the visual elements do most of the "teaching" and the commentary merely supplements. In other films, he says, the relative importance of the two elements may be reversed. Another possible explanation may lie in the way in which the experimenters operationalized the concept. No attempt was made by any of them to obtain an independent measure of the ability of their subjects to comprehend the different commentaries. It was apparently assumed that an above-grade-level commentary would be "difficult" for the subjects while an at- or below-grade-level commentary would be relatively "easy." It is quite possible that none of the commentaries was "difficult" for the subjects to comprehend, in which case the hypothesis has clearly not been tested.

A true test of the hypothesis would involve (1) establishing what words, sentence patterns, etc., the subjects can comprehend easily, and (2) preparing the commentaries at and/or at varying distances above and below this empirically established level. In none of the studies cited in this section was the first step taken. It is suggested that Wilson Taylor's Cloze Procedure (1953) might provide a good method of obtaining the independent measure of the relative comprehensibility of different commentaries.

Po × Co

To this point we have discussed the effects obtained when we manipulated one set of independent variables (viz., the Po set) while holding the other set (viz., Co) relatively constant. However, it is not always possible or even desirable to do this. Both sets can vary at the same time. It is also quite possible that a given independent variable, as operationalized, will be a complex variable with both Po and Co components instead of a simple variable. The problem then becomes one of separating the component parts, where possible, and of measuring their individual and/or combined effects.

Four groups of studies were reviewed elsewhere in which the independent variables were highly complex and were clearly designed to affect both the relative potency and the relative comprehensibility of the communication. These studies were grouped under the following headings: *density* or rate of transmission, the number of phonemes, words, sentences, facts, concepts, scenes, etc., transmitted per unit of time; *audience participation*—an overt act performed by the subjects during the transmission of a message, such as writing down answers to questions flashed on the screen or assembling the parts of a weapon, etc., as the assembly is demonstrated in the film; *realism*—the degree of similarity between the communication and the "reality" it represents; *serial order effects*—the retroactive effect that repeatedly presenting a list of items in serial (constant) order has upon the recall of items in different positions in the list and the tendency to associate items serially when the lists are presented in serial order several times.

Density

Johnson (1955) defines "attention span" as the number of units a person can hold in his consciousness at one time. He says that this number is fairly stable and small (about six or seven units) for a given individual. Johnson also points out that the attention span of the same individual differs with different material according to (1) his familiarity with it and (2) its connectedness; that is, an individual has a larger attention span for (1) material with which he is familiar than for material with which he is not familiar and for (2) material that is meaningful and related or structured than for material that is nonmeaningful—such as nonsense syllables—or relatively unstructured.

The effect that increasing or decreasing the density of a message has, then, appears to depend not only upon the relationship between (1) the rate of encoding and the receiver's attention span or maximal decoding rate, but also upon the relationships between (2) the semantic level of the message and of the receiver, and (3) the structure of the message and the receiver's perception of that structure.

The density of a message can be increased in three ways: (1) decreasing the time used to transmit a constant number of words, facts, etc.; (2) increasing the number of units transmitted in a constant time; (3) combining 1 and 2. If the first were the only method used, the problems involved in measuring the effect of density would be considerably reduced. The message itself would be constant and only the rate of transmission would be changed. However, the other methods occur more often and they both involve changing the message itself.

The added units could consist of (1) entirely new and nonredundant material, (2) redundant material in the form of (a) repetitions and/or explanations of existing facts and (b) summaries and/or other cues to the structure of the message.

Repetitions, etc., can affect semantic-level differences. Summaries, etc., can affect perception of structure. But if either is affected, the attention span is also affected. If the effect is large enough to cause a significant change in the attention span, then, obviously, the attention span for the second or subsequent messages is not equivalent to the attention span for the original message. In this case we would no longer be merely comparing the effect of changing the rate of transmission but would also have to consider the changes in attention span.

Let us, however, assume that the attention spans for our different messages are equivalent and that the messages differ significantly only in rate of transmission.

Hypothesis 3: Other things equal, relative comprehensibility is a nonlinear function of the discrepancy between the density of the message and the attention span of the receiver.

Hypothesis 3a: Other things equal, when the density of a message is increased by adding new, nonredundant material, relative comprehensibility will remain relatively constant so long as the density level is equal to or less than the span of attention.

Hypothesis 3b: Other things equal, when the density of a message is increased by adding redundant material, relative comprehensibility will increase as the density level approaches the span of attention.

Hypothesis 3c: Other things equal, relative comprehensibility will decrease when the density level exceeds the span of attention.

TABLE 4. STUDIES RELATED TO HYPOTHESIS 3

Experimenter	Independent Variable (audio density)	Results [a]
Hard & Watson (1955)	Terms per unit time	No significant difference.
Jaspen (1950a)	High vs. meduim vs. low number of words per unit time	No significant differences.
Jaspen (1950b)	High vs. medium vs. low vs. very low number of words per unit time	Significant difference (.01) between medium and very low but not between medium and high or medium and low. Relationship seems curvilinear.[b]
Zuckerman (1949)	None vs. low vs. medium vs. high number and type of words per unit time	Medium level significantly better than all others. Low and high about equal. All three significantly better than none (no sound) version.[b]
Rimland et al. (1955)	High vs. medium vs. low number of words per unit time	Medium level probably more effective than either the high or low.[b]
Vincent et al. (1949)	Facts and time both varied	Differences inconsistent; only a few significant.
Jaspen (1950a)	Fast vs. slow rate of development	Slow version superior in three comparisons and significantly so in one of the three (.01).
Ash & Jaspen (1953)	Fast vs. slow	Slow film better over all comparable conditions.

[a] Refer only to effect upon learning.
[b] Tends to support hypothesis.

Four of the six studies designed to test the effect of variations in the density of the sound track seem to support Hypothesis 3. One of the other two, Hard and Watson (1955), has methodological shortcomings. Jaspen repeated his study, refined his methodology, and came up with the predicted results.

Only in the Vincent et al. study did the additional information consist primarily of new facts. The findings tend to confirm Hypothesis 3a. The authors concluded: "The data suggest that as more and more information is presented interferences are set up that result in less efficient learning of any particular parts. . . . It seems clear that packing more and more information yields only very slight increments in total measured learning."

In the visual experiments, the authors made only two-point comparisons, making it impossible to check for a nonlinear relationship. The results of both experiments, however, seem to be in the opposite direction from that predicted by Hypothesis 3. One immediate explanation is that the "fast" films may have exceeded the attention span of many of the subjects. A second and related explanation will be discussed shortly when we take up "audience participation."

Actually none of the studies cited in this section tested Hypothesis 3 directly since no measurements of the related audience characteristics—attention span and comprehension—were made. Only if these measures are taken independently of the dependent variable —learning—can these hypotheses be fully tested.

Other questions that future experiments must answer are: What is the better measurement of sound track density—phonemes, words, facts, or what? How much of an effect does redundancy and familiarity with the content have upon attention span?

Experiments designed to answer the above questions might help dissolve the vagueness criticism leveled at the concept of density by Miller (1957).

Hypothesis 4: Other things equal, Po and Co will increase as overt audience participation increases.

Only one of the studies in Table 5 seems to support Hypothesis 4. However, further examination indicates that audience participation is more effective under certain conditions. One of these conditions appears to be (1) that the study situation must be fairly similar to, if not the same as, the eventual testing situation.

Kale *et al.* had students practice pronouncing the Russian cognates to English words. However, the test they gave was not a pronunciation test but a written test. Kale *et al.* comment: "It is quite possible that the results, particularly with respect to the contribution of . . . student participation (in the form of speaking the words) might have been quite different had the criterion involved pronouncing the words."

The second condition appears to be even more important: (2) that the visual density of the message must be sufficiently low to permit the subjects to participate without interfering with their observation of the communication.

The "inconsistencies" in Jaspen's study are only inconsistent in terms of the effect of participation per se. When the combined effect of both participation and density are considered, the results are relatively clear-cut.

Jaspen also varied the visual density of his film versions as well as the participation conditions. Low density with participation produced significantly better scores than low density without participation. On the other hand, high density without participation was better than high density with participation. In addition, low density with participation was more effective than high density with participation. Roshal and Rimland *et al.* both explained the failure of participation to make a difference in their experiments by saying that their films developed at too fast a rate (had too high a visual density). The above three studies all lead to the following hypothesis.

TABLE 5. STUDIES RELATED TO HYPOTHESIS 4

Experimenter	Independent Variable	Results [a]
Roshal (1949)	Audience participation *vs.* none (task: knot tying)	Inconsistent differences.
Jaspen (1950b)	Same as above (task: assembly of breech block)	Inconsistent differences due to interaction with rate of development.
Rimland *et al.* (1955)	Intervening *vs.* concurrent participation *vs.* none (task: knot tying)	No significant differences.
Kale *et al.* (1955)	Audience participation *vs.* none (verbal learning task)	Prompting subjects to pronounce Russian words inhibited learning.
Hart *et al.* (1947)	Audience participation *vs.* none (verbal learning task)	Significant differences in favor of participation.[b]
Kurtz *et al.* (1950)	No questions *vs.* "medium" questions *vs.* "persistent" questions	Inconsistent results.

[a] Refer to effect upon learning.
[b] Tends to support hypothesis.

Hypothesis 5: To maintain high Po and/or Co, density must be decreased as audience participation increases.

Jaspen's study tends to confirm Hypothesis 5.

Realism

Several studies have been reviewed under the heading "realism." Realism is here tentatively defined as the degree to which all relevant sense data about an event are conveyed in a communication— and its fidelity to the event. In terms of the receiver, the more sense modalities the message involves, the greater the realism. In terms of the message, the more dimensions or channels involved, the greater the realism. But realism also involves fidelity. For instance, continuous motion is more "real" than a still picture sequence. Thus, other things equal, television or motion picture with full sound has greater realism than TV or film with sound dubbed in, the latter has greater realism than silent film, silent film has greater realism than still photography, etc.

Miller (1957) relates "realism" to the S-R principle of stimulus generalization, "often referred to as *transfer* of *training*"; he says: "A corollary of this principle is that it is desirable to teach students in situations that are as similar as possible to the ones in which they will be expected to use their habits. The greater the similarity, the less is lost by stimulus-generalization. From this point of view it would be desirable to make training films as realistic as possible." A possible hypothesis, then, is the following.

Hypothesis 6: Other things equal, increasing realism will increase learning effectiveness by increasing both relative comprehensibility and relative potency (within limits).

As can be seen from Table 6, only four of the studies clearly support the hypothesis that greater realism leads to greater effectiveness—when effect is taken to mean information gain. Two studies favored the less realistic method (Roshal's study of hands and Fullerton's) while the others either produced inconsistent or nonsignificant differences. Miller (1957) explains this contrary finding in terms of a conflict between realism and relevant cue. He says:

It can be seen that the various means of directing attention toward the relevant cues or of abstraction will almost inevitably involve departures from strict realism and come into conflict with the principle of stimulus-generalization. The relative importance of these two contradictory principles will depend on the particular conditions of learning. For example, in one situation finding the relevant cue may be the most important factor, so that a cartoon which focuses attention on that cue will be superior to live photography, but in another type of situation realism may be the most important factor so that live photography will be superior.

TABLE 6. SUMMARY OF STUDIES RELATED TO REALISM HYPOTHESIS

Experimenter	Independent Variable	Results [a]
Instructional Film Research (1954)	Realistic scenes vs. substitutes	No significant difference.
Roshal (1949)	Hands vs. no hands	No hands version produced higher scores.
Roshal (1949)	Camera angle: 0 vs. 180 degrees	More realistic (0 degrees) angle significantly more effective.[b]
Rimland et al. (1955)	Camera angle	Same as Roshal's.[b]
Cogswell (1952)	Three dimensions vs. two dimensions	No significant difference.
VanderMeer (1952)	Color vs. black and white	Inconsistent results; some comparisons favor black and white.
Fullerton (1956)	Color vs. black and white	Black and white significantly superior.
Vestal (1952)	Animated vs. direct photography	No significant over-all difference.
Kay (1952)	Cartoon vs. "educational" presentation	No significant difference.
Vernon (1953)	Motion vs. no motion	Negative correlation between motion and the learning of generalizations.
Roshal (1949)	Motion vs. no motion	Motion significantly more effective.[b]
Instructional Film Research (1954)	Motion vs. no motion	Small but significant difference in favor of motion.[b]
Kale et al. (1955)	Motion vs. no motion	No significant difference.

[a] Refer to effect upon learning.
[b] Tends to support hypothesis.

Roshal (1949) supports Miller's contention. He states that the "hands" version of his films produced lower scores because the hands got in the way.

The hands version of his films on knot tying produced lower scores, he said, because "the inclusion of the hands obscured some of the line, and presented a more crowded perceptual field." In other words, the added bit of realism—hands—interfered with the relevant cue—how the knot was being tied. VanderMeer (1952), with reference to his color film study, said: "The films used were selected because they appeared to make effective use of color for emphasis or because color was intrinsic to much of the subject matter being taught. However, it is possible that in these films color was not a crucial cue for learning. Apparently other cues present in the film such as shape, contrast, texture and the information in the commentary provided equally important cues for learning and color added little."

VanderMeer also reported several instances in which the added bit of realism—color—interfered with learning, particularly in his film on snakes which change color. Here the added realism (color) appears to have emphasized a false cue (color in relation to species) at the expense of other relevant cues.

Thus far, we have been emphasizing the effect of realism upon relative comprehensibility (Co). It also can have an obvious effect upon relative potency (Po). Other things equal, the more realistic production should have a higher attention-gaining and maintaining potential than a less realistic production.

Are extra attention-gaining devices actually necessary in the "captive audience" situation where external interference is minimal? The data above suggest that they are not, which leads us to the following hypotheses.

Hypothesis 6a: Relative potency increases with realism in proportion to the relevance of the "realistic" elements.

Hypothesis 6b: Relative potency increases with realism in proportion to the degree of external interference present in the receiving situation.

Hypothesis 6c: Relative potency increases with realism in inverse proportion to the degree of existing motivation to attend.

SUMMARY

A limited and tentative theory of the effectiveness of television and other audio-visual communications has been presented on the basis of a review of the relevant empirical and theoretical literature. The theory states that communication effectiveness depends upon coping with interferences which distract attention and interferences which mask messages. The communicator copes with the former by maximizing the *relative potency* of the message and with the latter by maximizing the *relative comprehensibility* of the message. Relative potency is the degree to which a message is capable of attracting and holding attention; relative comprehensibility is the degree to which a message is understandable to the receiver. These concepts are treated as interdependent; however, relative potency is understood to be a necessary condition for relative comprehensibility (some degree of attention is necessary to any degree of understanding), whereas relative comprehensibility is not assumed to be a necessary condition for relative potency.

A number of implications of these basic relationships and some of their interactions are spelled out in a series of hypotheses which are in turn related to existing findings.

Much work remains to be done in the way of clarifying the meaning of the concepts and testing the suggested hypotheses. It is hoped, however, that this provisional theory will stimulate experiments that will lead either to its acceptance, rejection, or modification—and in the process to a better understanding of the process and effects of mass communication.

Bibliography

Allen, W., "Readability of Instructional Film Commentary," *Journal of Applied Psychology*, 36 (1952), 164–68.

Ash, P., and N. Jaspen, *The Effects and Interactions of Rate of Development, Repetition, Participation and Room Illumination on Learning from a Rear Projected Film*, Port Washington, L.I., N.Y.: Special Devices Center, Technical Report SDC 269–7–39, 1953.

Blain, B. B., *Effects of Film Narration Type and of Listenability Level on Learning of Factual Information*, unpublished doctoral dissertation, Indiana University, 1956.

Brandon, J. E., *The Relative Effectiveness of the Lecture, Interview and Discussion Methods of Presenting Factual Information on Television*, unpublished doctoral dissertation, University of Wisconsin, 1955.

Cogswell, J. F., *Effects of a Stereoscopic Sound Motion Picture on the Learning of a Perceptual-Motor Task*, Port Washington, L.I., N.Y.: Special Devices Center, Human Engineering Report SDC 269–7–32, 1952.

Fletcher, R. M., *Profile Analysis and Its Effect on Learning When Used to Shorten Recorded Film Commentaries*, Port Washington, L.I., N.Y.: Special Devices Center, Technical Report SDC 269–7–55, 1955.

Fullerton, Billie J., *The Comparative Effect of Color and Black and White Guidance Films Employed With and Without "Anticipatory" Remarks upon Acquisition and Retention of Factual Information*, unpublished doctoral dissertation, University of Oklahoma, 1956; abstracted in *Dissertation Abstracts*, 16 (1956), 1413–14.

Hard, C. G., and D. P. Watson, "Testing Scientific Terminology on Television," *Science Education*, 39 (1955), 140–41.

Hart, G., J. W. Whiting, R. S. Handsell, and A. A. Lumsdaine, "Do 'Motivation' and 'Participation' Questions Increase Learning?," *Educational Screen*, 26 (1947), 256–59, 274, 283.

Instructional Film Research Program, *Evaluation of the Film: Military Police Support in Emergencies (Riot Control) TF 19–1701*, Port Washington, L.I., N.Y.: Special Devices Center, Technical Report SDC 269–7–51, 1954.

Jaspen, N., *Effects on Training of Experimental Film Variables, Nomenclature, Errors. "How-It-Works," Repetition*, Port Washington, L.I., N.Y.: Special Devices Center, Technical Report SDC 269–7–17, 1950.

———, *Effects on Training of Experimental Film Variables, Study II: Verbalization, "How-It-Works," Nomenclature. Audience Participation and Succinct Treatment*, Port Washington, L.I., N.Y.: Special Devices Center, Technical Report SDC 269–7–11, 1950.

Johnson, D. M., *The Psychology of Thought and Judgment*, New York: Harper and Brothers, 1955.

Jorgensen, E. S., Jr., *The Relative Effectiveness of Three Methods of Television Newscasting*, unpublished doctoral dissertation, University of Wisconsin, 1955; abstracted in *Dissertation Abstracts*, 16 (1956), 814.

Kale, S. V., J. M. Grosslight, and C. J. McIntyre, *Exploratory Studies in the Use of Pictures and Sound for Teaching Foreign Language Vocabulary*, Port Washington, L.I., N.Y.: Special Devices Center, Technical Report SDC 269–7–53, 1955.

Kay, Lillian W., *A Comparison of "Educational" and Cartoon Film Treatment of the Concept of Productivity*, Washington, D.C.: Brookings Institution, 1952; from an abstract by E. Faison, *Audio-Visual Communication Review*, 1 (1953), 220–21.

Kimble, G. A., and J. J. Wulff, *The Effects of "Response Guidance" on the Value of Audience Participation in Training Film Instruction*, Washington, D.C.: Human Factors Operations Research Laboratories, Bolling Air Force Base, Report No. 35; from an abstract by E. Faison, *Audio-Visual Communication Review*, 1 (1953), 292–93.

Kopstein, F. F., R. L. Sulzer, and A. A. Lumsdaine, *The Value of Using Multiple Examples in Training Film Instructions*, Washington, D.C.: Human Resources Research Laboratories, Bolling Air Force Base, Report No. 25, 1952; from an abstract by E. Faison, *Audio-Visual Communication Review*, 1 (1953), 63–64.

Kurtz, A. K., Jeanette Walter, and H. Brenner, *The Effects of Inverted Questions and Statements on Film Learning*, Port Washington, L.I., N.Y.: Special Devices Center, Technical Report SDC 269–7–16, 1950.

Lathrop, C. W., and C. A. Norford, *Contributions of Film Introductions and Film Summaries to Learning from Instructional Films*, Port Washington, L.I., N.Y.: Special Devices Center, Technical Report SDC 269–7–8, 1949.

Lumsdaine, A. A., R. L. Sulzer, and F. F. Kopstein, *The Influence of Simple Animation Techniques on the Value of a Training Film*, Washington, D.C.: Human Resources Research Laboratories, Bolling Air Force Base, Report No. 24, 1951; from an abstract by E. Faison, *Audio-Visual Communication Review,* 1 (1953), 140–41.

McIntyre, C. J., *Training Film Evaluation: FB 254—Cold Weather Uniforms,* Port Washington, L.I., N.Y.: Special Devices Center, Technical Report SDC 269–7–51, 1954; abstracted by L. Twyford, *Audio-Visual Communication Review,* 4 (1956), 159–60.

Mercer, J., *Optical Effects and Film Literacy,* unpublished doctoral dissertation, University of Nebraska, 1952.

Miller, J., A. V. Levine, and J. H. Kanner, *A Study of the Effects of Different Types of Review and of Structuring Sub-titles on the Amount Learned from a Training Film,* Washington, D.C.: Human Resources Research Laboratories, Bolling Air Force Base, Memo Report No. 17, 1952; from an abstract by E. Faison, *Audio-Visual Communication Review,* 1 (1953), 140.

Miller, N. E., *et al.,* "Graphic Communication and the Crisis in Education," *Audio-Visual Communication Review,* 5 (1957), special edition.

Molstad, J., "Readability Formulas and Film Grade-Placement," *Audio-Visual Communication Review,* 3 (1955), 99–108.

Nelson, H. E., and A. W. VanderMeer, *The Relative Effectiveness of Differing Commentaries in an Animated Film on Elementary Meteorology,* Port Washington, L.I., N.Y.: Special Devices Center, Technical Report SDC 269–7–43, 1955.

Northrop, D. S., *Effects on Learning of the Prominence of the Organizational Outlines in Instructional Films,* Port Washington, L.I., N.Y.: Special Devices Center, Technical Report SDC 269–7–33, 1952.

Rimland, B., C. J. McIntyre, and H. D. Sterk, *Effectiveness of Several Methods of Repetition of Films,* Port Washington, L.I., N.Y.: Special Devices Center, Technical Report SDC 269–7–45, 1955.

Roshal, S. M., *Effects of Learner Representation in Film-Mediated Perceptual-Motor Learning,* Port Washington, L.I., N.Y.: Special Devices Center, Technical Report SDC 269–7–5, 1949.

Shannon, C. E., and W. Weaver, *The Mathematical Theory of Communication,* Urbana, Ill.: University of Illinois Press, 1949.

Taylor, W. L., "Cloze Procedure; a New Tool for Measuring Readability," *Journalism Quarterly,* 30 (1953), 415–33.

VanderMeer, A. W., *Relative Effectiveness of Color and Black and White in Instructional Films,* Port Washington, L.I., N.Y.: Special Devices Center, Human Engineering Report SDC 269–7–28, 1952.

———, *Training Film Evaluation: Comparison Between Two Films on Personal Hygiene TF 8–155 and TF 8–1665,* Port Washington, L.I., N.Y.: Special Devices Center, Technical Report SDC 269–7–50, 1953.

Vernon, M. D., "Perception and Understanding of Instructional Television Programmes," *British Journal of Psychology,* 44 (1953), 116–26.

Vestal, D. A., *The Relative Effectiveness in the Teaching of High School Physics of Two Photographic Techniques Utilized by the Sound Motion Picture,* unpublished doctoral dissertation, University of Nebraska, 1952.

Vincent, W. S., P. Ash, and L. P. Greenhill, *Relationship of Length and Fact Frequency to Effectiveness of Instructional Motion Pictures (Rapid Mass Learning)*, Port Washington, L.I., N.Y.: Special Devices Center, Technical Report SDC 269–7–7, 1949.

Zuckerman, J. V., *Commentary Variations: Level of Verbalization, Personal Reference and Relations in Instructional Films on Perceptual Motor Tasks*, Port Washington, L.I., N.Y.: Special Devices Center, Technical Report SDC 269–7–4, 1949.

Among Other Studies Commissioned by NETRC

1. MICHIGAN STATE UNIVERSITY. I. R. Merrill, project director: *Political Persuasion by Television—Partisan and Public Affairs Broadcasts in a General Election.*

Found, among other things, that viewers of educational television were much more likely than nonviewers to be *issue*-oriented, as opposed to candidate-oriented.

2. SEATTLE PUBLIC SCHOOLS. D. Nylen, project director: *Communication in a Large School System and the Use of Telecasts.*

Contribution of educational television to improved morale not entirely clear, but appears that well-prepared telecasts can be useful, especially in carrying communications on special problems from superintendent and board members.

3. STATE UNIVERSITY OF IOWA. E. B. Kurtz, project director: *Pioneering in Educational Television; a Documentary Presentation.*

To record a chapter of educational television history.

4. WAYNE STATE UNIVERSITY. J. B. Ellery, project director: *A Pilot Study of the Nature of Aesthetic Experiences Associated with Television and Its Place in Education.*

"The obtained results indicate that audience reaction is amenable to objective analysis and evaluation through the instrumentation which has been developed for this purpose."

5. UNIVERSITY OF MIAMI. G. C. Fisher, project director: *A Search for Non-Subject-Matter Test Items for Use in the Evaluation of Educational Television Research.*

Sixty-seven items, out of a total of 215 from four psychological tests, were shown to change from beginning to end of college courses in introductory psychology. The tests measured critical thinking ability, supervisory judgment, values, and certain attitudes.

6. UNIVERSITY OF OREGON. E. A. Kretsinger, project director: *An Experimental Study of Restiveness in Preschool Educational Television Audiences.*

Tests of bodily movement as negative correlate of interest in program.